# *THE EXTRAORDINARY MR POE*

ENDPAPERS Illustration by W. Heath Robinson to *The Raven*, from a 1900 edition of Poe's poems.

FRONTISPIECE Edgar Allan Poe, from a *carte-de-visite* daguerreotype.

# THE EXTRAORDINARY MR POE

*A Biography of Edgar Allan Poe by*
*Wolf Mankowitz*



Weidenfeld and Nicolson
London

Designed by Gill Mouqué
for George Weidenfeld and Nicolson Ltd,
11 St John's Hill London SW11

House editor Esther Jagger

ISBN 0 297 77446 8

Printed in Great Britain by
Butler & Tanner Ltd, Frome and London

Colour separations by Radstock Reproductions

# Contents

CHAPTER ONE 1796–1811 *6*

*The Humane Heart*

CHAPTER TWO 1811–1827 *18*

*The Merchant of Richmond – Refreshing Chillness – Helen Found and Lost – Honour, Elmira and Learning – Not One Cent in the World*

CHAPTER THREE 1827–1831 *44*

*Private Perry – Muddy and Sis – Interlude in Richmond – Cadet Poe*

CHAPTER FOUR 1831–1835 *76*

*The Soul's Terror – The Mystery of Mary Devereaux – A Prize of Gold – Death and Dreams*

CHAPTER FIVE 1835–1842 *102*

*Marriage in Secret – Marriage in Richmond – Grotesques and Gents – A Magazine of My Own*

CHAPTER SIX 1842–1846 *138*

*The Coming of the Red Death – Sensation in Washington – The Flight of the Raven – The Raven Triumphant – The Second Frances – The Wars of the Literati*

CHAPTER SEVEN 1846–1849 *198*

*Appointment in Fordham – The After-Dream – Helen (and Annie) Revisited – So Much to Say – Lenore Found – Appointment in Baltimore*

BIBLIOGRAPHY *243*

ACKNOWLEDGMENTS *244*

INDEX *245*

# CHAPTER ONE
# 1796–1811

## *The Humane Heart*

On 3 January 1796 the Massachusetts *Mercury* noted that the *Outram* had shipped into Boston, its passenger list including a number of emigrating actors from England, among them one Charley Tubbs. With Mr Tubbs was a Mrs Arnold and her eight-year-old daughter, Elizabeth. Mrs Arnold had been playing the Covent Garden Theatre for several years since the death of her actor-husband, but Elizabeth, though destined for the theatre, had not yet appeared on stage. This she soon remedied at a concert in Portland, Maine, where, with Mr Tubbs, an excellent pianoforte accompanist, she had a successful début. Soon afterwards Mr Tubbs made an honest woman of Mrs Arnold and together all three travelled their own acting company, recruiting support from local amateurs. By the time she was ten, Elizabeth was noted by an excitable critic as 'the beautiful Miss Arnold, whose powers as an actress command attention'. So the future mother of Edgar Poe was launched early upon a promising career.

Elizabeth continued to play such suitable roles as Cupid and A Nymph until Mr Tubbs (described by one manager as 'a vermin'), brought his small troupe into the Charleston Comedians, with whom Elizabeth won her first important role in *The Market Lass*. The production was poorly received except for the performances of Elizabeth and her mother; with which final dim testimony Mr and Mrs Tubbs disappear like forgotten performances into the flies of long-decayed theatres, leaving Elizabeth Arnold alone, an actress at twelve in her own right.

In 1802 Miss Arnold was given a benefit performance in Baltimore. It was possibly on this occasion that she was first seen by David Poe, who was about twenty-five and a law student. He was the son of a petty gentleman of Scottish-Irish Protestant origins who rose from chandlering to the post of assistant quartermaster of the Continental Forces after which, out of etiquette, he was styled 'General'. Whether David Poe had courted Elizabeth in 1802 is unknown, but in July of that year she married Mr Charles Hopkins, a comedian who specialized in playing Tony Lumpkin. The Hopkinses were with the Virginia Players in October 1805 when he died, leaving

PREVIOUS PAGES *Boston Harbour from Constitution Wharf*, painted by Robert Salmon – Elizabeth Arnold's first sight of America when she emigrated there in 1796.

An emigrant ship about to leave for America. Conditions on board were usually dreadful, and few emigrants ever saw again the relatives they left behind at home.

Elizabeth to play on alone once again. But not quite, because now David Poe had joined the Virginia Players, having given up law the year before to pursue the Thespian Muse and Elizabeth. Though persistent in love, he was of a retiring, shy disposition, delicate and tubercular, and awkwardness and self-consciousness made him an unlikely actor. Nevertheless, his first notice was not entirely bad:

Of the Young Gentleman, it would be hazardous to take an opinion from his performance this evening. For some time he was overwhelmed with the fears incident on such occasions to an excess that almost deprived him of speech . . . Though he could not, even to the last, divest himself of his fears, we thought he disclosed powers well fitted to the stage. His voice seems to be clear, melodious and variable; what its compass may be can only be shown when he acts unrestrained by timidity. His enunciation seemed to be very distinct and articulate and his face and person are much in his favor. His size is of that pitch well fitted for general action if his talents should be suited to sock and buskin.

This then was the nervous but very persistent acting novice whom Elizabeth married soon after Mr Hopkins died. To pursue his goals the 'Young Gentleman' with the melodious voice was already developing a dependency on drink. It did for him what it has done for many other shy and awkward young men, giving him the temerity to propose to a beautiful widowed actress and the courage to walk on and

# Theatre Royal, Covent Garden,

This present SATURDAY, June 13, 1795,

Will be presented the Comic Opera of

# The Maid of the Mill.

Lord Ainsworth by Mr DAVIES,
Sir Harry Sycamore by Mr POWEL,
Ralph by Mr MUNDEN,
Mervin by Mr TOWNSEND,
Fairfield by Mr RICHARDSON,
Farmer Giles by Mr HAYMES,
Fanny by Mrs MARTYR,
Theodosia by Mrs ARNOLD,
Lady Sycamore by Mrs DAVENPORT,
Patty by Mrs MOUNTAIN.

To which will be added the Farce of

# Two Strings to Your Bow.

Lazarillo by Mr MUNDEN,
Borachio by Mr DAVENPORT,
Octavio by Mr DAVIES,
Ferdinand by Mr MACREADY,
Don Pedro by Mr POWEL,
Don Sancho by Mr THOMPSON,
Drunken Porter by Mr FARLEY,
Waiters, Meff. CROSS and LEDGER,
Leonora by Mifs Stuart, Maid by Mifs Leferve,
Donna Clara by Mifs HOPKINS.

No Money to be Returned.

---

On Monday (by Particular Defire) the new Comedy of *the Deferted Daughter*, with the new Mufical Farce of *the Poor Sailor, or, Little Bob and Little Ben*, and *the Tythe Pig*.
Tuefday *the Woodman*, and *Harlequin & Fauftus*, for the Benefit of Meff. TOWNSEND and FOLLETT.
And on Wednefday the Theatre will CLOSE for this SEASON, with the Comedy of *the Sufpicious Hufband*,

ABOVE A typical benefit playbill of the period.

OPPOSITE A 1795 playbill advertising *The Maid of the Mill* at the Theatre Royal, Covent Garden, with Mrs Arnold – Poe's grandmother – in the part of Theodosia.

FOLLOWING PAGES Baltimore in the early nineteenth century was still a relatively small sea port, close to the countryside.

play with bravado small parts in life. For no matter how pretty he might be or how well sustained by Dutch courage, David Poe remained one of Nature's Laertes, an Allan-a-Dale with a small, charming voice. Mrs Poe, however, continued to appear in leading roles – Ophelia, Cordelia, Juliet or Ariel – as well as delighting the audiences as her husband's partner in the Polish minuet. Though David was an adequate clog dancer, and could reel, hornpipe and Scottish fling, he was never very effective solo. Elizabeth Poe was, unarguably, the star of the Company. Yet even with her working continuously and him when he was required, it was a poor enough living the Poes made. In 1807 when their first son, William Henry Leonard, was born, so bad were things that within three weeks Mrs Poe was back on the stage.

The Poes struggled on, their personal and financial situation deteriorating under the pressure of work and hard times, until two years later when they were playing the Federal Theatre in Boston. Mrs Poe, her condition somewhat concealed by her high-waisted empire gown, was clearly pregnant again, and on 19 January 1809 her second son, Edgar, was born. Again Mrs Poe, the breadwinner of the family, was back at work within three weeks. But David did not respond to the responsibilities of fatherhood, and in April 1809 the Boston theatre gave a benefit in aid of Mrs Poe who had played Ophelia so movingly only two nights previously. The Poes' marriage was foundering under its many pressures, and within a few months the sudden disappearance of David Poe from the records suggests that he was finally upstaged out of Elizabeth's life and had absconded for good. But David was not to drink to his freedom for long. A newspaper clipping of unknown source records his death from consumption in Norfolk, Virginia, on 19 October 1810. At twenty-one months Edgar was fatherless, and his mother confronted the bleak prospects of being an actress alone in the world with her talents, her infant children and her failing health.

Poe's childhood was haunted by the spectre of the 'Red Death' as he was to dramatize it later, for Mrs Poe also had tuberculosis, which was accelerated by her pregnancies. Ill-health had forced her to leave her older son in Baltimore with his Poe grandparents, so that soon after his father's disappearance Edgar had his mother totally to himself, until December 1810 that is, when Mrs Poe was delivered of a daughter, Rosalie. It was an unpromising background for a childhood, but nevertheless for Edgar one infinitely rich, in the company of a mercurial, brilliantly painted, exquisitely ethereal mother. Of course there was a demanding audience, and a pack of theatre-managers and gentlemen admirers to contend with. But he knew that the enchanting Mrs Poe loved only him. He remembered her later as her miniature showed her, and as Beverly Tucker of the *Southern Literary Messenger* described her: 'The childish figure, the great, wide-open mysterious eyes, the abundant curling hair confined in the quaint bonnet of a hundred years ago and shadowing the brow in raven masses, the high waist and attenuated arms clasped in an Empire robe of faint, flowered design, the tiny but rounded neck and shoulders, the head proudly erect. It is the face of an elf, a sprite, an Undine....'

The mysterious, elfin Elizabeth Poe, her health failing rapidly, continued to tour the Southern circuit with her two young children. At Charleston she appeared in her own benefit, the bills describing her condition and begging the public to assist an unfortunate artiste whom it had loved and applauded. In August 1811 Elizabeth rented a cheap room in Richmond, Virginia, from a milliner, Mrs Phillips, who sold perfumes and cosmetics to the ladies of the town. The room overlooked the yard of the Indian Queen Tavern where the other members of the Company lodged. There Elizabeth, 'the sole support of herself and several children', her disease public knowledge, failed fast, and was often unable to go on stage. The children were left more and more to Mrs Phillips and while they played around the shop the fashionable ladies of Richmond, sorry for their mother, cossetted them. It became quite the thing to call on the unfortunate, lovely Mrs Poe and her pretty babes, and one Samuel Mordecai, a sardonic member of the Richmond plantation society, wrote to his sister Rachel: 'A singular fashion prevails here this season – it is – charity. Mrs Poe who you know is a very handsome woman, happens to be very sick, and (having quarreled and parted with her husband) is destitute. The most fashionable place of resort, now is – her chamber. And the skill of cooks and nurses is exerted to procure her delicacies.'

One of the ladies in attendance was a Mrs Mackenzie who was much concerned for the deserted actress and her children, and recommended them to her childless friend, Mrs Frances Kelling Allan, wife of a wealthy Scottish merchant, John Allan. It was an introduction scored with the deep runes of destiny in the heavy style of a contemporary romance. As Edgar's mother waned with the year, so the angelic vision of the protective Mrs Allan grew stronger.

Mr Placide, manager of the Charleston Players, was very helpful to Mrs Poe, but absences could not go on being covered, and certainly could not be paid for. Mrs

Miniature of Elizabeth Arnold Poe.

St John's church in Richmond, Virginia. Elizabeth Arnold Poe was buried there in 1811, leaving Edgar and Rosalie Poe orphans.

Phillips was kind about the rent, Mrs Mackenzie sent food and clothes, and Mrs Allan was there in the background. But Elizabeth Poe lay dying in a small, damp room which still smelt of the recent flood when the James River had broken its banks. Malarial mosquitoes whined through the thick air, settling on the walls, the two broken chairs and the wretched bed on which Mrs Poe sighed, cheeks flushed and eyes brilliant. Her faded, soiled and tattered costumes, her props and relics, hung about the room, and close to her always was a small chest containing a few letters and the shabby clothes of her infants. No doctor visited her as she lay listening to her baby crying and to Edgar playing in the shop below. When Edgar was in the room, however, he doubtless saw only a bright-faced fairy-lady whose magical wings hung motionless, waiting to transform her into a scintillating Ariel. To the observant child the final stages of tuberculosis would not look very different from the excited flush of his actress-mother after a successful performance. The consumptive cough, held back by a lacy white handkerchief which occasionally lifted a small, red rose from the lips, would not have sounded like the mutterings of approaching death. Mrs Poe coughed on while kind Mr Placide arranged more benefit performances and advertised them in the Richmond newspapers:

TO THE HUMANE HEART

On this night, Mrs Poe, lingering on the bed of disease and surrounded by her children, asks your assistance; and asks it perhaps for the last time. The generosity of a Richmond audience can need no other appeal. For particulars, see the Bills of the day.

It was indeed the last appeal. On 8 December 1811 Elizabeth, aged twenty-four, died of pneumonia, and as our subject is Edgar Poe we must dwell upon this, the first death he knew, for it contained images which were to haunt his life and works.

Poe was a month short of three years old, extremely observant and immensely impressionable, when Elizabeth died. The small fairy-like figure of his mother wearing her best gown, her face white as wax after the hectic colour of her last days, illuminated by candles, an ultimate dream-lady deep in her mysterious sleep, remained one of the most haunting images of Poe's childhood. One can imagine the child's puzzlement. He had seen his mother die beautifully on the stage often. Was this another performance? Would the ethereal but eternal Elizabeth Arnold Poe rise again soon? Of course she would, for no child understands or accepts the finality of a parent's death. And Elizabeth, peaceful as pure marble, free at last of her racking cough and frightening haemorrhages, was even more beautiful in the guttering candlelight. Thus love and death came together in the childish experience of Edgar Poe, never to separate. Behind the women in Poe's life and those he created in his stories glows always Elizabeth Poe's pale beauty idealized; and the terrible sickness which infused it became the thrilling and dangerous, but romantic and essential, companion of love.

# CHAPTER TWO
# 1811–1827

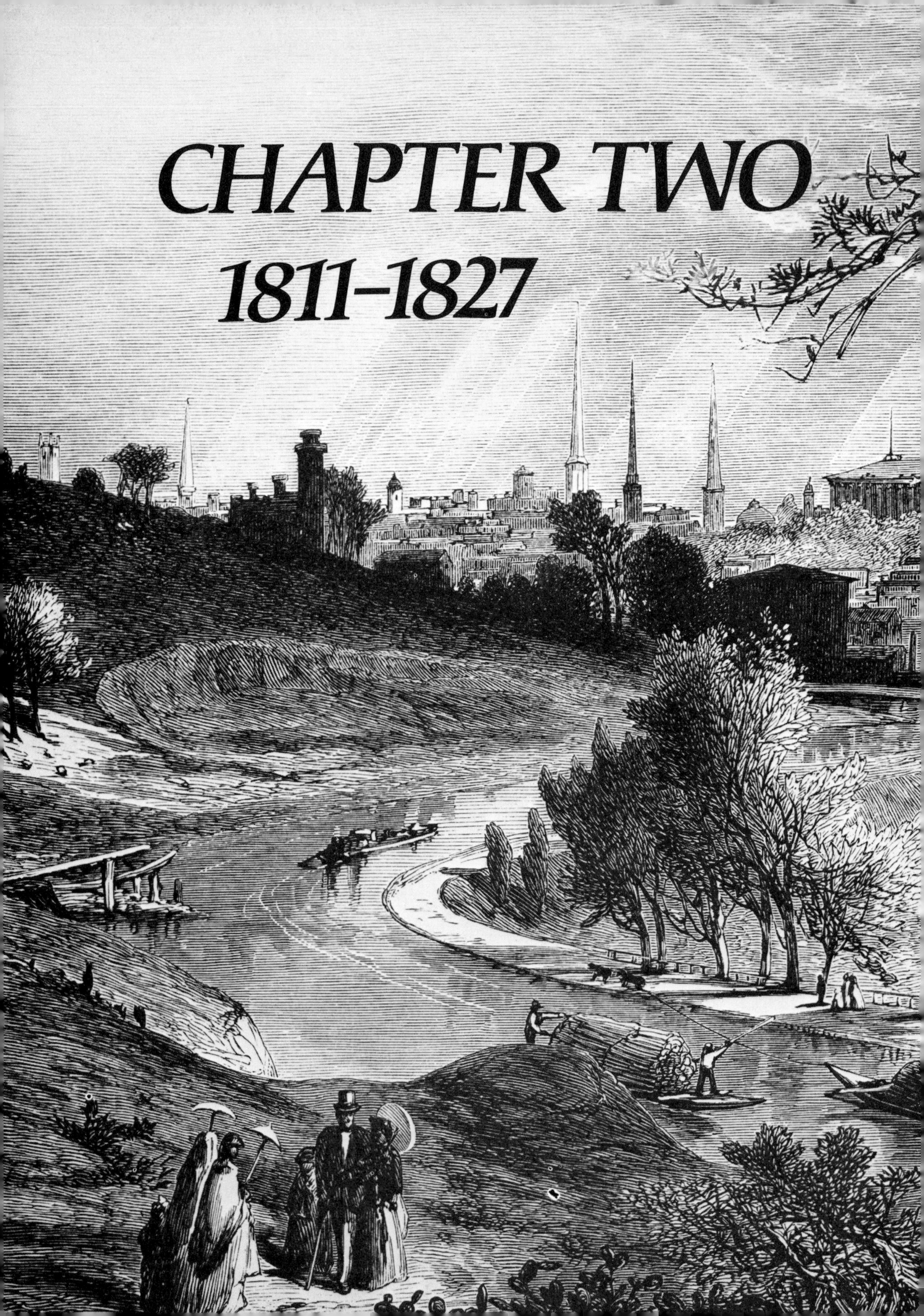

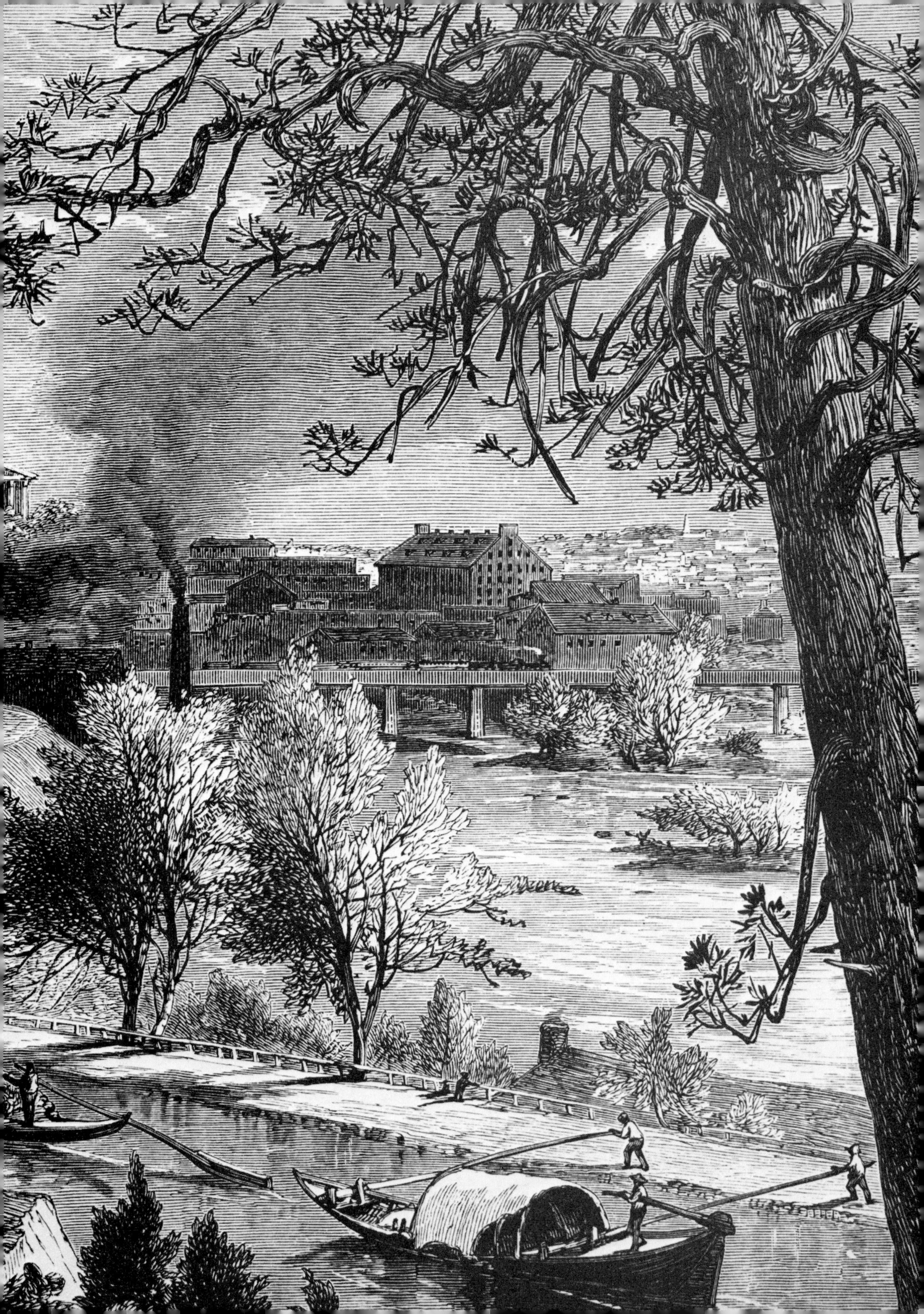

## *The Merchant of Richmond*

On the morning of 9 December 1811 Edgar Poe, not yet three years old, was taken to the home of John Allan, who had yielded to pressure from his childless wife, Frances. Rosalie Poe, just a year old, was taken by Mrs Mackenzie. The children bore their inheritance with them: for Rosalie, an empty jewel box; for Edgar, the miniature of his mother, and a little painting she had made of the port of Boston with a message on the back to Edgar to love the place of his birth where his mother had found her best and most sympathetic friends. There was also a pocket-book with locks of his father's hair and her own, and a bundle of letters, since lost, about which speculation has never ceased.

The family house of John Allan, the Scottish merchant of Richmond, was at the corner of 14th Street and Tobacco Alley. It was a spacious, three-storey brick building in the Georgian style with some twelve rooms, to Edgar a palatial setting after the mean lodgings he had shared with his actor-parents. John Allan was in partnership with a former fellow-clerk, Charles Ellis. They were carriers and shippers, mainly of tobacco, but the newly formed firm of Ellis and Allan was well-connected through the uncles of the partners, both of whom were considerable merchants, and their contacts enabled them to deal in everything from wheat and hay, through wines and coffee, to horses, pigs and, of course, slaves, which the firm both sold and hired out. However the future might prosper John Allan, his assets were no small matter to be lightly bestowed upon the head of an orphan. Furthermore, though Frances was childless she was only twenty-five, and he was a healthy thirty-one, so that they might well produce children at any time. While he was prepared to entertain his wife's fancy for a little one about the house, he had no intention of making a son of this pretty progeny of 'poor devils of actors'. No doubt, too, there had been talk around Mrs Poe since the 'disappearance' of her husband, and if there were tales told about Rosalie's legitimacy Allan would certainly have heard of them. Even if there were no such rumours, he was hardly the man to overlook scandalous possibilities, for he had two illegitimate children in Richmond. This then was the hearty,

PREVIOUS PAGES View of Richmond, Virginia, from an area of the town called Hollywood, with the James River and its canal in the foreground.

Miniatures of Edgar Poe's foster-parents, John Allan and his first wife, Frances. While John Allan was authoritarian, Frances adored and spoilt Edgar.

powerful, worldly man of ambition to whom Edgar was brought in the last days of 1811. The auspices for their relationship were poor from the start.

If John Allan's inclinations were to dispose of Edgar as soon as was decent, his wife was equally determined to keep the child by any means possible. The matter is of the greatest importance in understanding the catastrophic effects of the relationship with Allan on Poe's future life. Allan felt that he had never willingly adopted Edgar; but Edgar wrote to his guardian in 1830 from West Point that, unwillingly or not, his foster-father had followed his own desire, or that of his wife, in adopting him, despite the expressed wishes of 'General' David Poe. Poe argued that his grandfather was in good circumstances at the time the Allans had induced the Poe family, with promises of adoption and liberal education, to leave Edgar with them. Poe further reasoned that because Allan supported his wife in taking over the child Edgar's life and affairs, Allan was committed to greater financial responsibilities than he ever subsequently acknowledged.

Certainly if Poe had never fallen out with Allan then the horrifying poverty which dogged and crippled him from student days until death might have been easily and quite inexpensively eradicated. But perhaps even to consider such a possibility is pointless, for it often seems that Poe was as determined to make a bad father-figure out of John Allan as Allan was set upon making a degenerate, prodigal son out of Edgar. The relationship between the two was of that fateful cut which makes tragic consequences inevitable.

Slaves were just one of the commodities that the firm of Ellis and Allan dealt in, along with coffee, wines, livestock and feedingstuffs. This early nineteenth-century engraving shows a mixed auction of estates, paintings and slaves in the Southern states.

As evidence of Mrs Allan's determination to keep Edgar there is a sad letter from Eliza Poe, his aunt:

Tis the Aunt of Edgar that addresses Mrs Allen [sic] for the second time, impressed with the idea that a letter if received could not remain unacknowledged so long as from the month of July, she is induced to write again in order to inquire in her family's as well as in her own name after the health of the child of her Brother, as well as that of his adopted Parents. I cannot suppose my dear Mrs Allen that a heart possessed of such original humanity as yours must without doubt be, could so long keep in suspense, the anxious inquiries made through the medium of my letter by the Grand Parents of the Orphan of an unfortunate son, surely ere this allowing that you did not wish to commence a correspondence with one who is utterly unknown to you had you received it Mr Allen would have written to my Father or Brother if it had been only to let them know how he was, but I am confident that you never received it. . . .

Mrs Allan was aided by the public feeling occasioned by a fire at the Richmond theatre two weeks after Mrs Poe was buried, in which seventy-three lives were lost. The tragedy made ungenerous actions by local merchants unpopular in Richmond, so that regardless of John Allan's feelings Edgar remained safe in the loving care of a black mammy, Frances – his new 'Ma', and his Aunt Nancy Valentine, Frances' sister, all of whom doted on the charming child.

Mrs Allan dressed Edgar in a black velvet suit which matched the dark curls surrounding his bright eyes, and produced him to recite, or, mounted on the table, to pledge her guests in watered wine. He was also an attractive accoutrement at church, and when visiting friends could be relied upon to enchant and amuse. But the charming, pious and affectionate life with 'Ma' was bedevilled by Mr Allan. Affectionate and charming he was not; pious neither, holding to rationalist opinions in religious matters. Allan was the first atheist Edgar heard pronounce on the subject, and in later life it was the only opinion he shared with his foster-father. Poe remained convinced that the world lacked a protective deity. But Mr Allan did firmly believe in corporal punishment, whipping Edgar whenever he misbehaved, no doubt to harden him against the soft influences of his wife and sister-in-law. For their part they could only protect Edgar from his godless father's wrath by encouraging him in the little tricks and cunning devices to which the weak resort when confusing the powerful. The wheedling tone which characterizes much of Edgar Poe's later correspondence with John Allan derives from these early devices for avoiding paternal correction and punishment. When Poe left kindergarten Allan sent him to the school for boys which housed his illegitimate son, Edwin Collier. There Edgar first heard stories about his foster-father which inflamed his antagonism and encouraged his protectiveness towards 'Ma'. We see Poe's image of John Allan developing as an authoritarian, god-defying, vengeful figure, immensely potent both financially and sexually, dwarfing all Edgar's resources other than those in his brain.

Through John Allan's association with the sea Poe met skippers and merchants whose tales fed his imagination. Through his black mammy and the house-slaves quartered on the Allan estate he was also familiar with Negro songs and folklore. Powerful Negro feelings of the indestructible dead who walked by moonlight must have supported Edgar's sense that there were more things in heaven and earth than were dreamt of in John Allan's philosophy. Edward Valentine, a great friend of Edgar's in his childhood, recorded an occasion when he took the six-year-old on his horse for a ride. Edgar surprised the local farmers in the rural post office by reading newspapers aloud. On their return they passed a graveyard and the child was seized with terror. 'They will run after us and drag me down!' he screamed. Marie Bonaparte, in her brilliant psychoanalytic interpretation of Poe and his works, writes of this incident: 'This convulsive terror of death is worth noting, for the first big repression of this precocious child's instinctual urges would then, doubtless, have been taking place, under the increasing pressure of his upbringing.' The convulsive terror was never to leave Edgar Poe. It was to become the spirit of his genius and the curse of any joy he might ever have had from it.

## *Refreshing Chillness*

John Allan decided to visit Scotland. The Peace of Ghent had ended the Napoleonic Wars and by 1815 the seas were free and the Allans prepared to depart. The merchant had good business reasons for the trip. American tobacco had been hard hit by the interruption of trade between England and America and he was owed a great deal of money for deliveries made prior to the war. He wanted to collect and to rebuild his English connection. The English were short of tobacco and prices were very high, but these would soon drop, so time was of the essence if he wanted to profit from the situation.

After a voyage of thirty-six days Allan and his family reached Liverpool on 18 July, 1815, and continued to Irvine in Scotland where most of the Allan relations lived. There Edgar was sent to school, but when the Allan entourage travelled on to Glasgow and Edinburgh Edgar accompanied them, though John Allan would have preferred to leave him behind.

By October the Allans had reached London and John had his way. A miserable Edgar left the adoring women of the house, to go back to the bleak school at Irvine. There, at the age of seven, Poe experienced the first of those 'fugues', the flights from immediate reality, which were to become his characteristic response to unhappiness or unbearable pressure. At Irvine discipline was hard, corporal punishment much indulged, and religious services endless. A typical writing exercise was the copying of epitaphs from the local churchyard. Apart from endless reading and walks in Lord Kilmarnock's park, where the ghost of a lady was sometimes seen, Edgar found few pleasures in his exile from the women to whose loving attention he was already addicted. Withdrawn, he grew ill and rebellious, planning to escape from the school

OPPOSITE ABOVE An engraving of Edinburgh – the Old Town from Princes Street – dated 1814.

OPPOSITE BELOW When John and Frances moved south from Scotland to London, Edgar returned to school in Irvine. A nineteenth-century photograph of the school.

and go to London or America. Finally his protests were successful and he was sent to the Allans in London, there to be entered as a day-boy in a dame school. But to be at school and learning even the little the inept Misses Dubourg could teach him was no imposition for Edgar. He was back in the bosom of his dear 'Ma', and, even though she was ill with some mysterious malady, he felt loved and protected by her presence.

As Mrs Allan's illness became worse, Edgar began to blame the dominant and irresistible John Allan for his beloved's condition, and though she improved after a visit in 1817 to a spa, Edgar's dislike of Allan grew. The antipathy was mutual and Edgar was sent as a boarder to the Manor House School in Stoke Newington, 'a misty village of old England', under the Rev. Mr Bransby. Later Poe wrote of the ancient village: 'I feel the refreshing chillness of its deeply-shadowed avenues, inhale the fragrance of its thousand shrubberies, and thrill anew with undefinable delight, at the deep hollow note of the church-bell, breaking, each hour, with sullen and sudden roar, upon the stillness of the dusky atmosphere in which the fretted Gothic steeple lay imbedded and asleep.' Romantic, medieval and gothic qualities were already dear to Edgar Poe when he entered Manor House.

In Poe's great *doppelgänger* story, *William Wilson*, there is a much heightened description of Manor House. All the qualities of the school are extended to somewhat gothic proportions, including the jolly Rev. Bransby himself who is aged, hardened, and elevated to doctor. It is as if Poe wanted the figure of authority to be harsh; certainly John Bransby in later years was quite put out by the unfair portrait, observing of 'Allan' (as Poe was known at school) that his parents spoilt him with too much pocket money, and that the boy was 'intelligent, wayward and wilful'. In this judgment Poe himself would seem to concur. 'The ardour, the enthusiasm, and the imperiousness of my disposition, soon rendered me a marked character among my school-mates, gave me an ascendancy over all not greatly older than myself.' No wonder that Poe was soon complaining of 'moral isolation'. Imperious intelligence is not a quality which recommends itself very highly to schoolboys or their teachers.

When Poe went home for weekends and holidays Mrs Allan was often absent, her mysterious malady being attended to, so that his sense of isolation was not always warmed away by the presence of his adoring 'Ma'. As Frances' health declined, so John Allan's affairs went badly. For the first time, too, his own health failed him and he developed a dropsy which was almost fatal. There were business troubles back in Richmond, and, depressed by his debts, his own and his wife's sickness, and the

OPPOSITE ABOVE Drawing of the Manor House School, Stoke Newington, where Edgar was a boarder. He later drew on his experiences there when writing *William Wilson*.

OPPOSITE BELOW A portrait believed to be of the Rev. Mr Bransby, who ran the school at Stoke Newington.

One of the bedrooms in the house on 2nd and Franklin Streets, where the Allans stayed with John Allan's partner Ellis during 1820.

failure of the high hopes of five years ago, Allan prepared to return. The English years had shown him little profit after all; but his disaffected, unwilling foster-son Edgar Poe had gained those indelibly European qualities which were, in the future, to make his writings so unlike those of his American contemporaries. Edgar had always felt that his origins gave him a distinction not entirely American. Now the English years added to his sense of aristocratic superiority. The 'moral isolation' which he had felt as a schoolboy was, like the taste for the 'refreshing chillness' of the gothic, to remain with him for life.

## *Helen Found and Lost*

The Allans were back in Richmond by mid-1820. Their house being rented, they stayed with Allan's partner Ellis on 2nd and Franklin Streets until the autumn, and then moved into a new house on Clay Street. Richmond was drowsy in the sun when Edgar, a strong eleven-year-old, went swimming and sailing with his friend Ebenezer Burling in the James River. Though Edgar was at times solitary and silent, he seems during these renewed Richmond days to have been a boy among the boys of the English and Classical School kept by a fervent Irish patriot and Latinist, Joseph J. Clarke, under whose tuition his erratic educational background in French, Latin, literature and mathematics was filled out.

John Allan's financial problems after his unsuccessful English trip, together with Edgar's growing adolescent moodiness, strained their relationship further. It would seem from Joseph Clarke's evidence that Poe was already interested in poetry. By the age of fourteen he was assuming the traditional romantic postures associated with the poet's image. His first known poetic lines (found by Hervey Allen on a page of accounts) are:

> Last night with many cares and toils oppress'd
> Weary . . . I laid me on a couch to rest –

Another early poem found in an 1822 Ellis and Allan file expresses pained love:

> Oh feast my soul, revenge is sweet
> Louisa, take my scorn; –
> Curs'd was the hour that saw us meet
> The hour when we were born.

Neither posture was likely to appease Poe's irritable foster-father, though Mrs Allan found great satisfaction in the handsome boy's romantic inclinations, and encouraged them.

Poe's sister Rosalie, though pretty and good-natured, was as underdeveloped and backward as Edgar was advanced. She was devoted to her clever and attractive brother, and was happy to act as messenger between him and a number of Richmond girls whose principal importance to him was their suitability (like Louisa) as poetic subjects. Apart from writing agonized expressions of love, Edgar attacked the establishment by disguising himself as a ghost and frightening a card-party, and by raiding a local judge's poultry yard. Even at fourteen Edgar was still not too old to be whipped by John Allan for such pranks. Nevertheless, he would not be put down, and added to his reputation among the pretty girls of Richmond by swimming the James River from Ludlam's Wharf to Warwick – several miles – against a strong current. This feat, his poetic extravagances, his defiance of his foster-father, and his mad pranks added to the somewhat Byronic image Edgar was already assuming in Richmond society. Among the more impressed was a young boy called Robert Stanard, an enthusiastic admirer who brought his hero home one day to see his pigeons, rabbits and superb mother. Towards the animals Poe was indifferent, but Mrs Stanard, with her dark hair and classical gown flowing about her slender figure, struck him dumb. It was as if the fairy had floated out of the deepest recesses of his memory. As he listened to her voice and watched her beauty, his juvenile sweethearts were forgotten and 'Helen' possessed him. Though Mrs Stanard was twice his age Edgar threw himself into the formidable task of winning her love.

Mrs Stanard was available to the platonic courtship of the passionate boy. She listened to his verses, encouraged his talent and allowed him to worship her ecstatically. It was in accordance with the 'predestined' quality of Poe's life that this first great love should soon be lost. His melancholy deepened throughout her illness, and after her death in 1824 he was said to have haunted her grave at night. Certainly he himself claimed to have done so, and whether it was literally true or not, the idea of such a haunting was deep in him. As he wrote in his late teens:

I could not love except where Death
Was mingling his with Beauty's breath.

During this same period of tragic, unfulfillable love, Poe also witnessed the decline of Frances Allan. Her malady was chronic and growing worse, and, in spite of the temporary success of 'treatments', she was beginning to assume the bright-eyed, fairy-like appearance which Poe adored. Adding to her attractive martyrdom was the agony of her discovery about this time of her husband's many infidelities. Now John Allan, the monster authoritarian, could be said to be directly responsible for beloved 'Ma's' decline. And so with the death of Mrs Stanard and the decline of Frances, Poe's ideal woman, Helen, stepped for the first time out of the tomb-like recesses of his mind, and a memorable poem evolved:

TO HELEN

Helen, thy beauty is to me
Like those Nicéan barks of yore,
That gently, o'er a perfumed sea,
The weary, way-worn wanderer bore
To his own native shore.

On desperate seas long wont to roam
Thy hyacinth hair, thy classic face,
Thy Naiad airs have brought me home
To the glory that was Greece,
To the grandeur that was Rome.

Lo! in yon brilliant window-niche
How statue-like I see thee stand,
The agate lamp within thy hand!
Ah, Psyche, from the regions which
Are Holy-Land!

Marie Bonaparte, most incisive of Poe's commentators, wrote of *To Helen*:

Possibly these lines contain a reminiscence of the Elgin marbles, which Edgar may have seen as a child, soon after reaching London. But another, far older, memory undoubtedly

OPPOSITE In 1824 General Lafayette, a hero of the war of 1776, visited Richmond. Poe commanded the guard of honour.

informs the poem. The hyacinth hair, the classic face, the Naiad airs which lead the poet *home*, gleam with the light of that face and form – the mother's – which, though buried deep in the past, were ever to haunt Poe's life and work. Thus, our *wanderer*, while still an adolescent, beginning his life's march, had already, in imagination, retreated *weary and way-worn* to his *native shore* and made that mournful return to the mother who, for him, would always be one who was dying or dead... With reason, he feared both himself and his desires, which were projected on such hideous and nightmarish forms that, on awaking, he would bury his head beneath the blankets in his effort to escape. During these nights of his adolescence, as culminating horror, he would imagine an icy, corpse-like hand being laid on his face.

So in the fifteen-year-old Poe a haunted poet is already apparent; and the tomb from which his ghost arose, frightening and irresistible, was not yet so far away as to be quite out of sight. Poe's Helen walked out of the grave of Elizabeth Poe. It was his mother's chilling hand he loved and feared to feel upon his heart.

## *Honour, Elmira and Learning*

However, 1824 was not an entirely bad year for Edgar Poe. In the autumn the great Lafayette, defender of liberty, friend of George Washington, the apostle of Rousseau and ally of America, visited Richmond, Virginia. To welcome him a volunteer guard corps was formed, an institution long overdue, thought some, not only in view of the need for constant vigilance in defence of liberty, but also in case of Negro uprisings, fear of such being quite as strong as respect for the principles to which Lafayette had dedicated his life. It was some palliative to a poor year for Edgar that he, the grandson of 'General' David Poe over whose grave Lafayette had recently announced 'Here lies a noble heart', should be elected lieutenant of the Richmond Junior Volunteers. When the great French hero arrived in cocked hat and knee-breeches by steamer from Norfolk to meet veterans of the Revolution, the cadet guard of honour was commanded by Lieutenant Edgar Allan Poe.

We may reasonably surmise that this initiation into honourable manliness stiffened Edgar's resistance to John Allan, for certainly after assuming his lieutenancy Poe rebelled more stubbornly against the Allan regime. His foster-father accused him of ingratitude and openly spoke of Rosalie as being only 'half-sister' to Edgar and Henry. The uncompromising slur upon his mother's memory was, for Edgar, tantamount to a declaration of war, and from this point on there was no longer any possibility of a lasting *rapprochement* between Poe and Allan. This was most unfortunate because when William Galt, Allan's rich merchant uncle, died in March 1825, he left $750,000 to Allan, according to Poe. Edgar's antagonism may

With a legacy from a rich uncle, John Allan bought this large and elegant house on Main and 5th Streets, Richmond, in 1825.

have exaggerated the cash figure, but certainly 'old swell-foot' Allan was rich again. Within a few months the gouty tyrant had bought a large house on the south corner of Main and 5th Streets for $14,950. It had beautiful gardens, a superb view, spacious hall, a ballroom, numerous stylish bedrooms, servants' quarters and Edgar's small room at the end of a hall landing beyond a dark turn of the stairs. Here an agate lamp was kept burning, and perhaps when Poe later added the reference to 'the agate lamp within thy hand' in *To Helen* he remembered Frances Allan bringing light to this dark corner by the room which became his kingdom, defended against his intrusion by sullen rebellion against John Allan. Here Edgar was left alone to lie and read upon his couch every book he could get, the rebel Byron being most favoured. On Edgar's desk there was a sad reminder of earlier days and a happier relationship with his foster-father – a brass inkstand with sand-caster, gifts from Allan and clearly much valued by Edgar since he took them with him when he finally left home. It was at this desk that Poe wrote to the greatest of his 'sister-loves', Sarah Elmira Royster, fifteen, with large dark eyes

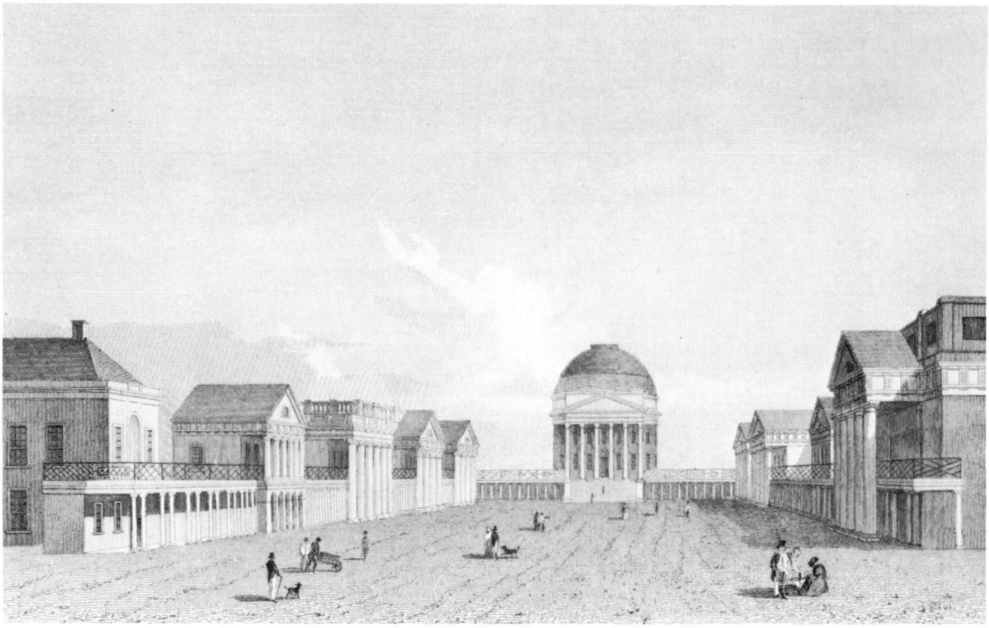

The University of Virginia at Charlottesville – the 'Oxford of the New World' – was founded by Thomas Jefferson. Poe arrived there as an undergraduate in the spring of 1826 and was soon to acquire a reputation as a gambler, a drinker and an excellent story-teller.

and black curls. 'Myra' was the daughter of friendly neighbours and had comforted Edgar while he suffered through Mrs Stanard's last days. The two young people were in love, and Mr Allan and Mr Royster were not very pleased about it. Yet for all the tension known to exist in his home, Edgar, with his Virginian breeding and distinction, was much sought after by the mothers of marriageable daughters. But now that Helen was a ghost Edgar thought only of 'Myra', playing his flute to her piano, and singing duets with her. He sketched her portrait and wrote her poems, and soon the couple were secretly promised to one another.

Displeasing as Edgar was now habitually to John Allan, his foster-father must have felt that his improved fortunes called for some gesture towards the boy. On the other hand, perhaps he no longer felt that he could bear to have Edgar working in his firm as had been his former intention. Whichever was the stronger motivation, the result was a decision to raise Poe for the law, and in March 1825 he was withdrawn from Mr Burke's school and put with private tutors to be schooled for entrance to the University of Virginia. Edgar felt that he was being disposed of cheaply. His poetic ambitions were of no interest to John Allan, no matter how much confidence Frances may still have had in him. Her support was of little value now since her knowledge of her husband's infidelities had deteriorated their relationship beyond the point where she could bring any influence to bear upon him. When Henry Poe, now a sailor, visited Richmond, he and Edgar found they had poetic and literary inclinations in common. As a result Edgar talked of 'running away to sea'. He also complained to Rosalie's foster-parents, the Mackenzies, about Allan, saying that he wished Mrs Mackenzie had adopted him. None of this ingratiated him with the increasingly choleric John Allan, who, when it came to sending Edgar off to college in February 1826, showed his anger in a typically mercantile way.

When Edgar Poe arrived at Thomas Jefferson's 'Oxford of the New World' at Charlottesville, Virginia, the entire fortune provided him by his detested foster-father was $110. This fact speaks Allan's feelings for Edgar more clearly than any of his letters. Edgar's grasp of arithmetic was never very good, but John Allan's was perfect. He knew that an inexperienced boy of seventeen with $110, in a university in which the minimum annual expenses were $350 plus room, bed, blankets and ordinaries at $149 per annum, was assuredly committed to confusion, misery and failure. So that when Allan sent this arrogant, brilliant, stylish young man as a beggar among the wealthiest young men in Virginia, it was a calculated and cruel mortification, unforgettable and unforgivable in any circumstances. For one as delicately balanced as Poe, it produced strains and tensions with which he could not begin to cope rationally. He took up playing cards, for the battle against chance challenged him intellectually and offered hope of meeting his debts. His inevitable losses he paid by selling his clothes, or borrowing, or issuing orders on a tailor. To pay for his servant, for fuel and for laundry, when miserably small allowances failed to arrive from Allan, he continued to borrow. Tradesmen gave him credit because it was understood in the university that although the law declared such student debts invalid, wealthy and indulgent parents invariably settled them. But indulgence was not a signal characteristic of Poe's wealthy foster-father. Within one year Edgar was irretrievably in debt. John Allan, the Scottish merchant, was succeeding in making him into precisely the 'libertine' he wished him to be – prodigal, extravagant, debt-ridden, and, soon, intemperate.

Still, the thought of his fated union with Elmira in a love that would transfigure life into something more approximating to poetry sustained Edgar. He wrote to her frequently, with passion, hope and touching unawareness that Mr Royster had discovered and was intercepting their correspondence. Quite possibly he had been advised by John Allan, who would certainly have let him know that Edgar's prospects were extremely thin. Consequently Mr Royster found a much more suitable and socially acceptable husband for her. At first Elmira held out against her father's wishes, but finally, miserable at Edgar's apparent silence, perplexed at the lack of response to her letters, constantly plagued by her father, she consented to marry a certain well-founded Mr Shelton.

Meanwhile Edgar, for his part, was in the deepest depression at Myra's silence. When eventually he heard that she had broken their 'engagement' and was committed to another, his pride was shattered and his misery complete. Poe had occasionally indulged in the student's drink called 'peach and honey'; now deeply in

Poe's sparsely furnished room at the University of Virginia is still preserved as it would have looked during Poe's brief residence there.

debt, confused and disappointed in love, seventeen and quite without prospects, he drank more seriously for the first time. One of his contemporaries, Thomas Tucker, described Poe's drinking-style:

> He would always seize the tempting glass, generally unmixed with sugar or water – in fact, perfectly straight – and without the least apparent pleasure, swallow the contents, never pausing until the last drop had passed his lips. One glass at a time was all that he could take; but this was sufficient to rouse his whole nervous nature into a state of strongest excitement, which found vent in a continuous flow of wild, fascinating talk that irresistibly enchanted every listener with siren-like power.

Among all the accounts of Poe as a drinker there is none clearer than this. He had no resistance to alcohol and a small quantity put him in 'a state of the strongest excitement'. Since he was of a markedly manic depressive type, this excitement would certainly be followed by depression. If Poe then continued drinking, to lift the depression and sustain the 'flow of wild, fascinating talk', very soon he would have grown violent and irrational in his behaviour. Whether he was also technically an alcoholic or whether his over-reaction to drink was caused by what has been described, somewhat meaninglessly, as 'a brain lesion', has very little bearing upon either his moral character or his genius, both of which were of an extremely high order but disturbed by the extremes of his psychological constitution.

These disturbances were quite undeniable. We cannot take up the position of commentators like William Bittner, who argues that:

> With the aid of Poe's psychological stories critics have proclaimed him necrophilic, dipsomanic, paranoid, impotent, neurotic, oversexed, a habitual taker of drugs, until all that is left in the public eye is an unstable creature sitting gloomily in a dim room, the raven over the door, the bottle on the table, the opium in the pipe, scribbling mad verses – a simple composite of the characters in his stories.

A writer is indeed a 'composite' (though a complex one) of his works, and a study of his life should help the reader to an understanding of why that composite shows certain recurrent images and themes. Poe was an extremely 'unstable creature'. But it is less profitable to moralize about it than to try to understand why it was, and how it affected his work.

## *Not One Cent in the World*

At Charlottesville Poe had done well in French and Latin, moderately in Greek but better in Italian. He won the admiration and envy of his fellows, engaged in military drill, read extensively and intensively and, considering the wildness of student life in Jefferson's anarchic university, was not particularly prankish.

But he got into debt to the tune of some $2,000 and all his good reports did not balance such a figure in John Allan's accounts. The vengeful foster-father fell like a storm on Charlottesville in the autumn of 1826, called down by Edgar's creditors to a meeting. There he doubtless reminded the tradesmen that such debts were not binding and pointed out that though he might be wealthy, he had no vanity to play the Southern gentleman and pay up. He would rather withdraw Edgar from the university and leave them all to whistle for their money. So it was that on 21 December Edgar returned by stagecoach to a Richmond that shivered in the midst of winter but was certainly no colder on its windiest street than was the atmosphere in John Allan's fine house.

Mrs Allan and Aunt Nancy had arranged a Christmas party to cheer up Edgar and soften the blow. Frances knew that, even before her husband's calamitous descent upon Charlottesville, Edgar had constantly considered leaving home. Desperately she asked his friends to come and help her warm his return to Richmond. But the only friend he cared for, Elmira Royster, would not be there and any party without her was merely another mockery of his life. Soon after the party started Edgar left with a friend to drink in a tavern, confirming Allan's complaints against him yet again. So even the attempts at comfort made by his adoring 'Ma' were spurned by him! Was he not indeed an unreformable ingrate 'eating the bread of idleness'?

Secretly Poe sought an alternative to dependence upon Allan. But the trading firms he wrote to for jobs referred to his foster-father, and Allan became further infuriated on finding that Edgar was trying to leave home without his authority. The final break came after dinner on 18 March 1827. Allan produced a letter of Edgar's seeking work, and wondered if he intended ever to pay off his debts. Poe attacked Allan's meanness and reminded him of his moral responsibilities. Allan spoke contemptuously of Edgar's gambling and drinking and asked what he proposed doing with his life. Edgar spoke of his writings. Allan dismissed such 'scribbling' as a mere excuse for idleness. Finally he laid the law down: Edgar must stay under his authority or leave forever. He might care to think it over, bearing in mind that his adored 'Ma' was seriously ill. Proving yet again his chronic 'ingratitude' Poe decided, that very night, to leave the Allan house. His true father, David Poe, had left home in order to pursue a chosen and despised career as an actor; he would follow the Poe family tradition. At breakfast the next morning Edgar told Allan once more what he thought of him, listened to his rage, watched 'Ma' and Aunt Nancy tremble, and finally left the house dramatically with only what he wore.

From the Court House Tavern Poe wrote to Allan listing his grievances, based upon his conviction that his foster-father had taken responsibility for his life when he adopted him, and, having inspired him with ambition, was now cutting off

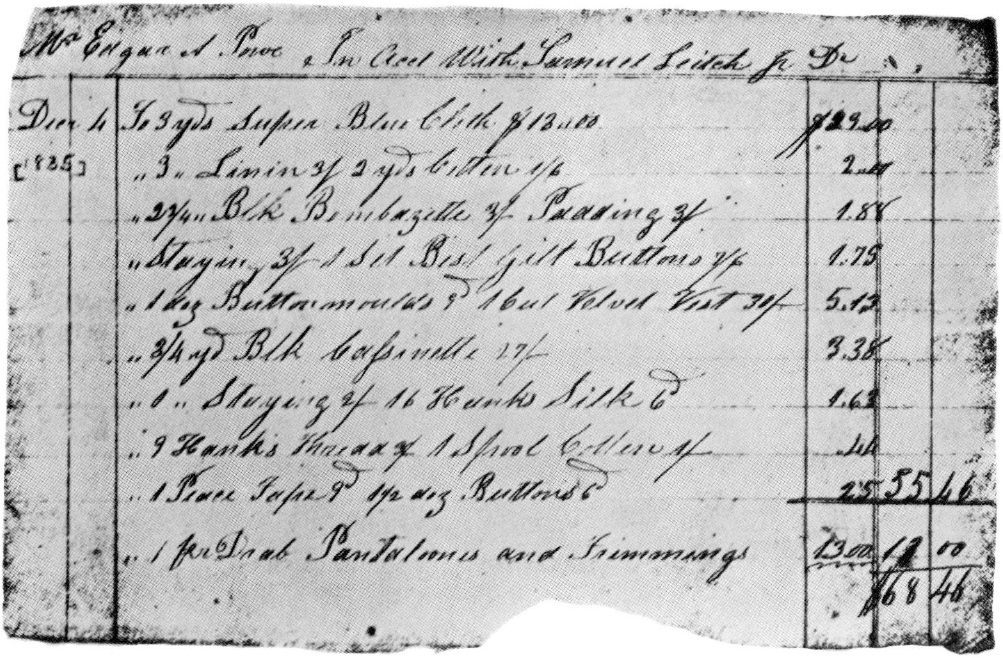

Mr Edgar A Poe In Acct With Samuel Leitch Jr Dr

Dec 4 [1826] To 3 yds Super Blue Cloth $13.00 — $39.00
" 3 " Linen 3/ 2 yds Cotton 1/6 — 2.00
" 2 3/4 " Blk Bombazette 3/ Padding 3/ — 1.88
" Staying 3/ 1 Set Best Gilt Buttons 7/6 — 1.75
" 1 doz Buttonmoulds 3 1 cut Velvet Vest 30/ — 5.13
" 3/4 yd Blk Cassinette 27/ — 3.38
" 1 " Staying 3/ 16 Hanks Silk 6d — 1.63
" 9 Hanks Thread 3/ 1 Spool Cotton 1/ — .44
" 1 Piece Tape 9d 1/2 doz Buttons 6 — .25 55 46
" 1 pr Drab Pantaloons and Trimmings — 13.00 13 00
68 46

John Allan's continued lack of financial support caused his foster-son to accumulate many bad debts while he was at university. This bill, rendered to John Allan by a Charlottesville tailor, is for a suit of clothes he made for Poe to wear home to Richmond for Christmas 1826. In view of John Allan's attitudes to Poe's creditors it is unlikely that the tailor was paid.

all his chances of success. Allan had mortified him, subjected him to the whims of others and the authority of black servants. He asked now only that his trunk of clothes and books be sent to him, and for enough money to pay his fare to some city in the north. There was no reply. Next morning Edgar wrote again, this time begging for his trunk and clothes and a mere $12 for the fare to Boston. If Allan would not give him the money, perhaps he would lend it to him. In a postscript he unnecessarily reminded Allan: 'I have not one cent in the world to provide any food.' To this appeal he received a cold reply, but no money and no trunk.

Poe moved on to the Richmond Tavern, where his dissolute friend Ebenezer Burling was in credit. An Allan house slave named Dab brought some of his things and money from 'Ma' and Aunt Nancy. Edgar gave Dab letters to deliver to a local young lady, and, accompanied by an intoxicated Burling, went on to take passage from Norfolk under the name of Henri Le Rennet.

Though Edgar's destination was Boston (which he reached finally in a coal ship),

the drunken Ebenezer put it out that Poe had left for remote places on romantic missions. In 1841 Poe substantiated the 'legend' begun by Burling and himself, in a memorandum for the Rev. Rufus Griswold who was writing a biographical sketch of his life. 'I ran away from home without a dollar on a quixotic expedition to join the Greeks, then struggling for liberty', wrote Poe, confirming his boyhood Byronism. 'Failed in reaching Greece, but made my way to St Petersburg, in Russia. Got into many difficulties, but was extricated by the kindness of Mr H. Middleton, the American Consul at St P. Came home safe in 1829....' In his *Memoir of the Author*, Griswold added that Mr Middleton saved Edgar 'from penalties incurred in a drunken debauch', but then Poe's self-destructiveness led him to choose for biographer and literary executor someone who actively disapproved of him. The 'legend' was later supported by the stories Poe wrote in autobiographical form; but they, together with his lies, were the entire substance of Edgar's foreign adventures. When Henri Le Rennet left Norfolk it was only to journey to the city where Poe was born and which his mother had recommended to him on the back of an insipid watercolour.

In Boston Poe met a jobbing printer, Calvin Thomas, newly the owner of a printing shop at 70 Washington Street. Thomas was nineteen and Poe persuaded him to print his first book, *Tamerlane and Other Poems*, 'by A Bostonian'. The edition probably consisted of no more than fifty copies, most of which were left with Thomas, for, regardless of his mother's commendation, Boston was not yet ready for Poe. Two copies were sent to reviewers and Poe bought a few himself. The book was in pamphlet form, about forty pages, 6⅜ inches by 4⅛ inches, bound in yellow tea-coloured covers. Only four authentic copies are known to exist, thus putting the first published Poe among the rarest and most valuable of printed books, though in 1827 the young author was starving.

Poe's first published poems reveal a sensitive young man with a strong musical sense, a good deal of technique, and a great inclination towards dreams and melancholy moods. In his preface to the book Poe wrote: 'The greater part of the poems which compose this little volume were written in the year 1821–2, when the author had not completed his fourteenth year. They were of course not intended for publication; why they are now published concerns no one but himself. Of the smaller pieces very little need be said, they perhaps savour too much of egotism; but they were written by one too young to have any knowledge of the world but from his own breast....' *Tamerlane* tells the story of the conquering son of a shepherd,

OPPOSITE *Tamerlane and Other Poems* was the first of Poe's writings to be published – a small edition came out in Boston in 1827 under the nom-de-plume 'A Bostonian'. This illustration to *Tamerlane* is by Edmund Dulac, from an early twentieth-century edition of Poe's poems.

torn between love and ambition. It is addressed to the hero's father:

I was ambitious – have you known
The passion, father? You have not:

The hero achieves his ambition, but at the cost of all else:

O, human love! thou spirit given,
Oh Earth, of all we hope in Heaven! ...
Farewell! for I have won the Earth.

This strongly suggests that Poe hoped by publishing to establish a poetic

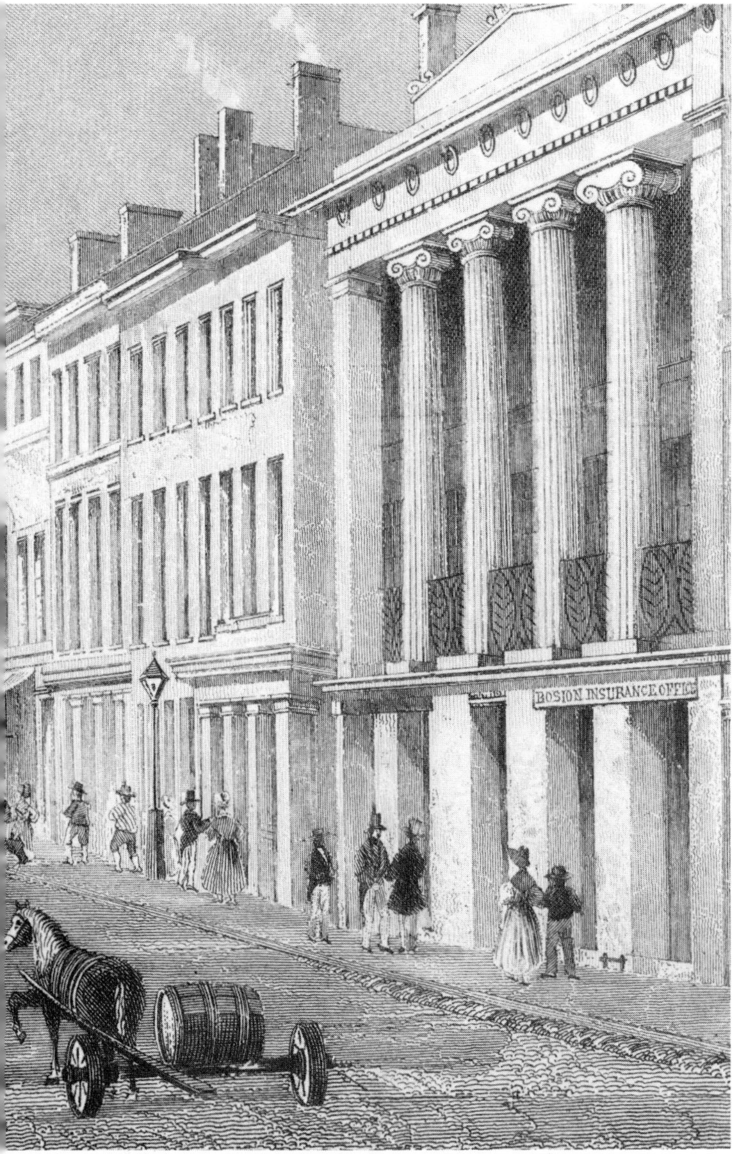


Engraving of State Street, Boston. Poe disappeared to Boston from Richmond after a violent quarrel with John Allan early in 1827.

Samarcand with which to defy the world, especially John Allan and the Roysters. Along with powerful adolescent protest the poems offer funereal imagery, dark, deep lakes, mother-symbolic entrances into the depths of the unconscious and death. Already the young Edgar felt the 'Nevermore' despair to be embodied in his poem, *The Raven*, the conviction that the happiest moments of his life were already over. Were these moments the times with Helen? The dreams with Elmira? Or were they, as Marie Bonaparte suggests, remoter yet, the times when his mother, the dazzling embodiment in her stage finery of past heroines, a beloved, wonderful creature, was ever growing as ethereal as the fatal sylphs about whom he was to weave so many fascinating tales?

# CHAPTER THREE
## 1827–1831

## *Private Perry*

The melancholy mood of *Tamerlane and Other Poems* certainly echoed the poet's experience of Boston. Soon after the book was published Poe, already Henri Le Rennet and A Bostonian, disappeared again, becoming one Edgar A. Perry. This time the alias was assumed for the purpose of enlisting in the United States Army. The eighteen-year-old Poe, desperate for a roof over his head and regular meals, gave his age as twenty-two, born in Boston, a clerk by occupation. The enlistment record further describes him as having grey eyes, brown hair, a fair complexion, and being five feet eight inches in height. The slim young recruit was posted to Battery H of the 1st Artillery stationed in Boston Harbour at Fort Independence. There he was assigned to the quartermaster's department, where he was marked for early promotion by his exemplary conduct and (rare soldier!) total sobriety. Dead sober, then, Poe wrote letters to Mrs Allan dated from St Petersburg, Russia, thus establishing his 'legend' from the security of Fort Independence.

It is possible that Poe's brother Henry knew that St Petersburg stood for Boston. Certainly Poe sent him a copy of *Tamerlane*, because two poems from it were published in a Baltimore paper, *The North American*. But the publication was of no help to Edgar, because Henry signed the poems with his own initials. The unscrupulous brother also published a story called *The Pirate* in which he utilized Edgar's love-affair with Elmira, and possibly this tale also was based upon Edgar's work. Not surprisingly, then, Edgar wrote:

> And, pride, what have I now with thee?
> Another brow may even inherit
> The venom thou has pour'd on me –
> Be still, my spirit!

Byronism and pride, publication and undying love, all had failed him. Even a brother and fellow-writer was no help. No wonder the anonymity of the army was such a blessed relief.

PREVIOUS PAGES The picturesque waterfront at Charleston, South Carolina, as Poe would have known it in the 1830s; from a painting by S. Bernard.

Before the year's end Private Perry was posted to Fort Moultrie, on Sullivan's Island in the mouth of Charleston Harbour, South Carolina. There, in the warm autumn, Poe relaxed into the subtropical setting with few duties to keep him from writing. The deserted island with its sand beetles, and tales of pirates and treasure, generated the material for his great story *The Gold Bug*, but for the present the young soldier was committed to poetry. Against the sounds of the windswept palms and the sea he set himself to the composition of a cosmic poem in which the spirit of Beauty would descend from her star to talk with God. The poem, called *Al Aaraaf*, would also feature a pair of star-crossed lovers who, dead on earth, lived on in space. Based upon a passion he had for astronomy (the Allan house possessed an excellent telescope), *Al Aaraaf* reveals a profound need to escape from earth-bound problems. To some extent the army supplied this need. Clothes, food and the tedious necessity for a little money at regular intervals were taken care of by an impersonal authority considerably more beneficent than the Merchant of Richmond. The army, associated with his benevolent grandfather, symbolized this kind of security to Edgar Poe throughout his life. He was to return to the comforting thought of it again and again. Touchingly, in his last years he always carried with him on his tragic hopeless 'fugues' his warm and protective army greatcoat.

For the time being Poe, securely established as Perry, studied the stars and composed his poem on Sullivan's Island, of which he wrote (in *The Gold Bug*) the following description:

> This island is a very singular one. It consists of little else than the sea sand, and is about three miles long. Its breadth at no point exceeds a quarter of a mile. It is separated from the main land by a scarcely perceptible creek, oozing its way through a wilderness of reeds and slime, a favourite resort of the marsh-hen. The vegetation, as might be supposed, is scant, or at least dwarfish. No trees of any magnitude are to be seen. Near the western extremity, where Fort Moultrie stands, and where are some miserable frame buildings, tenanted, during summer, by the fugitives from Charleston dust and fever, may be found, indeed, the bristly palmetto; but the whole island, with the exception of this western point, and a line of hard, white beach on the seacoast, is covered with dense undergrowth of the sweet myrtle, so much prized by the horticulturalists of England. The shrub here often attains the height of fifteen or twenty feet, and forms an almost impenetrable coppice, burdening the air with its fragrance.

On the island the fugitive Poe did well. His gentlemanly manners and appearance helped, and his education put him well above the average recruit. On 1 May 1828 he was appointed 'artificer', the first stage of promotion. By 1 January 1829 he was regimental sergeant-major at Fortress Monroe, Virginia, surely as rapid a rise through the ranks as may be found in any literary history. With Poe's new rank came greater personal freedom, and he often visited Charleston, not knowing that he had been there before as a child in the arms of his dying mother in 1811

when Elizabeth Poe had played for Mr Placide in *The Wonder*. Yet though Poe's army career was going well, he was restless to leave before his five-year term of was over. Once again he must write to his foster-father, this time to request Mr Allan's permission for his company commander, Lieutenant J. Howard, to agree to his discharge. Howard had developed a great interest in Poe, whose true identity and story he seems to have been told, and was strongly recommending reconciliation with John Allan. Perversely the relentless foster-father replied that he thought the military life a good one for Edgar and that he was satisfied to let him pursue it, certainly until he could return to Richmond in an officer's uniform, for Allan's inheritance of his uncle's fortune had strengthened his social snobbism. Edgar wrote back pointing out that army regulations did not permit promotion from the ranks and that his age precluded West Point. Nevertheless, rapid promotion had given him confidence, and he was no longer a wayward boy, but a man with important work ahead of him. He was convinced of his future greatness and wrote that he felt within him that which would enable him to fulfil all of Allan's ambitions for him; he continued, rashly: 'I have thrown myself on the world like a Norman conqueror on the shores of Britain and, by my avowed assurance of victory, have destroyed the fleet that can alone cover my retreat – I must either conquer or die – succeed or be disgraced.' Edgar had already forgotten that heroic, Byronic postures had no appeal for the Merchant of Richmond. Yet again after days of silence he wrote another letter protesting that Richmond, even the United States, was too narrow a sphere for his talents. He conveyed the feeling that army life in the ranks bored and disgusted him, and the information that various officers, recognizing his abilities, and acknowledging respectfully his relationship with 'General' Poe, were prepared to help him around the formal objections to his going to West Point, if only Allan would give him a little support. Allan's silence remained unbroken.

One may perhaps ask why, at this stage in his life, Poe, successful and secure for the first time, with ample opportunities for writing and a career of some sort clearly before him, insisted upon yet another confrontation with his foster-father. The answer might well be that Poe had a morbid need to suffer and be rejected, that his genius was compounded with the psychology of a compulsive loser. And yet he might still have avoided his own perverseness and have been forced to remain in the army, had not destiny struck another of those cruel blows which she seems to delight in awarding subjects like Edgar. On 28 February 1829 Sergeant-Major Edgar A. Perry was taking the morning roll-call at Fortress Monroe

OPPOSITE The setting of Poe's story *The Gold Bug* was based on the landscape around Fort Moultrie in Charleston harbour, where Poe was stationed. This illustration to *The Gold Bug* is by the Irish artist Harry Clarke, and dated 1919.

while, a few miles away in Richmond, Mrs Frances Allan was dying.

On her deathbed 'Ma' made her husband promise not to abandon Edgar entirely. She also begged not to be buried before her adoptive son saw her for the last time. But Edgar arrived on the evening of 2 March and Frances was already buried. He wrote later, 'If she had not have died while I was away there would have been nothing for me to regret.' The regret over past harsh errors was apparently shared by John Allan. Confused by his loss, he sent a misdated note: 'Mr Ellis, please furnish Edgar A. Poe with a suit of clothes, 3 pairs of socks or threadhose, Macready will make them. Also a pair of suspenders and hat and knife, pair of gloves.' His loss had induced in Allan a touch of out-of-character generosity which lasted long enough for him to agree a compromise with regard to West Point. He would support Poe's application for release from the artillery. On the basis of this assurance Colonel House, Poe's commanding officer, wrote to the general commanding the E. Department, New York, USA, a letter which presented very largely Edgar's own account of his history and present situation:

Fortress Monroe,
March 30th 1829.

General, – I request your permission to discharge from the service Edgar A. Perry, at present the Sergeant-Major of the 1st Reg't of Artillery, on his procuring a substitute.

The said Perry is one of a family of orphans whose unfortunate parents were the victims of the conflagration of the Richmond Theatre in 1809 [*sic*]. The subject of this letter was taken under the protection of a Mr Allan, a gentleman of wealth and respectability, of that city, who, as I understand, adopted his protégé as son and heir; with the intention of giving him a liberal education, he had placed him at the University of Virginia from which, after considerable progress in his studies, in a moment of youthful indiscretion he absconded, and was not heard from by his Patron for several years; in the meantime he became reduced to the necessity of enlisting into the service, and accordingly entered as a soldier in my Regiment, at Fort Independence, in 1827. Since the arrival of his company at this place he has made his situation known to his Patron, at whose request the young man has been permitted to visit him; the result, is an entire reconciliation on the part of Mr. Allan, who reinstates him into his family and favor, and who in a letter I have received from him requests that his son may be discharged on procuring a substitute. An experienced soldier and approved sergeant is ready to take the place of Perry as soon as his discharge can be obtained. The good of the service, therefore, cannot be materially injured by the discharge.

I have the honor to be,

With great respect, your obedient servant,
Jas. House
Col. 1st Art'y.

The normal fee for the substitute was $12 but Edgar, like many young gentlemen with a characteristic disinclination for trade, was frequently overcharged. His substitute cost $75. But Allan had, typically, given Poe precisely the $12 he had said the operation was going to cost, so that Edgar was from the outset some $60 short, which he eventually paid out of $100 sent to him by Allan. Typical of Edgar's unending financial bad luck, his cousin Mosher Poe, who shared a room with him in Baltimore, robbed him of most of the balance. Thus did Poe 'squander' (his foster-father's word) what was to be Allan's last substantial contribution to his life and future and provided the merchant with a reason for terminating his dealings with his foster-son.

For the time being, however, things went well. Edgar Poe was released from Edgar Perry and, in April 1829, left Fortress Monroe for Richmond with testimonials from all his officers recommending his sobriety, conduct, and high intelligence. John Allan later added the following chilling introduction:

Richmond, May 6, 1829

Dr Sir, – The youth who presents this is the same alluded to by Lt. Howard, Capt. Griswold, Col. Worth, our representative and the speaker, the Hon'ble Andrew Stevenson, and my friend Major Jno Campbell.

He left me in consequence of some gambling at the University of Charlottesville, because (I presume) I refused to sanction a rule that the shop-keepers and others had adopted there, making Debts of Honour of all indiscretions. I have much pleasure in asserting that he stood his examination at the close of the year with great credit to himself. His history is short. He is the grandson of Quartermaster-Gen'l Poe of Maryland, whose widow, as I understand, still receives a pension for the services or disability of her husband. Frankly, Sir, do I declare that he is no relation to me whatever; that I have many whom I have taken an active interest to promote theirs; with no other feeling than that every man is my care, if he be in distress; for myself I ask nothing but I do request your kindness to aid this youth in the promotion of his future prospects. And it will afford me great pleasure to reciprocate any kindness you can show him. Pardon my frankness; but I address a soldier.

Your Ob'd't Se'v't,
John Allan

The Hon'ble,
John H. Eaton,
Sec'y of War,
Washington City.

Such was the cold dismissive 'frankness' of Allan's feelings towards Edgar even before the ultimate $100 had been 'squandered'.

With his testimonials and some $40 in his pocket, Poe left Richmond for Washington early in May, hoping to be interviewed by the Secretary of War, but his papers went into the bureaucratic machine and time passed. By mid-May he was in Baltimore where he became acquainted with his old grandmother Mrs David Poe and

ABOVE An early nineteenth-century engraving of Baltimore.

OPPOSITE In 1829 Poe's first attempts to get *Al Aaraaf* published were unsuccessful. This illustration is by W. Heath Robinson, from a 1900 edition of the poems.

others of his family, from whom he learned much about his background, parents and ancestry. All this made him feel more Poe than Allan for the first time in his life, and though (perhaps in a nether tradition of the Poes) his cousin had robbed him, it felt good to be with his own.

If the news that Edgar's substitute was still owed money annoyed John Allan, he was even more infuriated to hear that Edgar, unredeemed by the total failure of *Tamerlane*, was trying to publish *Al Aaraaf*. Would the arrogant boy never learn that indulging genius wasted money? But there was no possibility any more of Allan's fury influencing Edgar. With his poems and an introduction to the publishers Carey, Lea and Carey, he was off to Philadelphia to talk about his second book. As it turned out, the publishers liked the poems but, fearing the risk, requested a guarantee of $100. Edgar, with a persistence to annoy which must be attributed to his imp of perversity rather than to his intelligence, wrote again to John Allan for yet another $100-worth of support for his genius. Allan, livid and appalled, refused the risk,

AL AARAAF

offering only censure on Edgar's thoughtless conduct of his life and affairs.

Meanwhile, there was no news from West Point and nothing to live on. Poe waited until 23 July and then set out on foot for Washington, determined, somehow or other, to get a response from the Secretary of War's office. When he finally did it was the information that there were ten cadets on the roll for entry before him. There was no hope of immediately settling down under the warming greatcoat of military security.

Edgar doggedly walked back to Baltimore. Once again he swallowed his pride and wrote to Allan, saying that he was anxious to return home. He received no reply. Nor did Carey, Lea and Carey write to say they had now corporately recognized the full genius of his poems and would proceed to promote his literary career without guarantee. He wrote to them asking for the return of *Al Aaraaf* and began searching Baltimore for some dark, warm corner in which to wait for the tide of his life to turn.

## *Muddy and Sis*

Poe at twenty had three times lost divine mothers: Elizabeth by consumption; Helen through insanity and perhaps consumption again; and Frances of a 'mysterious malady', almost certainly again compounded with consumption. To none of them had he been able to bid farewell. All three had descended into the earth out of his sight and knowledge, remaining ever-present in his deepest longings and fears. The experience was fraught with love and horror, and to it Poe imparted a beauty which he found irresistible. Later, in *The Philosophy of Composition*, he elevated it to an aesthetic principle:

> Of all melancholy topics, what according to the *universal* understanding of mankind, is the *most* melancholy? Death – was the obvious reply. 'And when,' I said, 'is the most melancholy of topics most poetical?' From what I have already explained at some length, the answer, here also, is obvious – When it most closely allies itself to Beauty; the death, then, of a beautiful woman is, unquestionably, the most poetical topic in the world – and equally is it beyond doubt that the lips best suited for such topic are those of a bereaved lover.

Alongside Poe's desperate passion for beautiful mothers dying of consumption was his equally persistent affection for 'sister-loves', of whom there had been several in his life, with Elmira Royster as their paragon. While death prevented consummation with the older loves, youth and its fickleness intervened between his passion and the second group of recipients. Now, as he searched for a haven, destiny, always willing to award Edgar ambivalent gifts, provided a complex answer to his needs in the establishment of his aunt, Maria Poe Clemm.

Maria Clemm was several years younger than her brother David Poe, Edgar's mysteriously 'lost' father. At twenty-seven she had married a reasonably well-founded Baltimore widower with five children. When he died in 1826 she was left entirely without means of support for herself and her own two children, Mr Clemm's modest fortune going to his first family. Maria Clemm's son, Henry, was eleven, and her daughter, Virginia Eliza, seven, when their twenty-year-old poet cousin came to live with them. Mrs Clemm was about forty, and though she did not have either consumption or a 'mysterious malady', her health was not very good. Nevertheless her temperament was positive, protective, and outgoing. When Edgar came to her, badly in need of a home, she already had her mother ('General' Poe's widow) living with her, together with Edgar's brother Henry, yet she welcomed another Poe, despite the fact that the old lady was paralysed, and Henry was unemployed and a hard drinker, dying of consumption. Mrs Clemm earned trifling sums for household tasks for neighbours, adding to old Mrs Poe's small pension. But hard-pressed as she was, Edgar in her threadbare clothes appealed to her humane heart, and she added him to her family.

In the sad Clemm household the only bright creature was Virginia, a happy, laughing, pretty child with violet eyes who soon came to adore her big cousin Eddy. He called her 'Sis' or 'Sissy', and her complete trust and unpretending natural affection made him protective towards her. Sis seems to have deserved and needed all the protection she could get, for she was Mrs Clemm's only helpmate in looking after her senile mother, her dying nephew, her somewhat difficult son, and now the moody and emotional Edgar. Mrs Clemm sewed and cooked, and Virginia served, cleaned, fetched, carried and distributed her sunshine temperament without reserve. She listened to her old grandmother's reminiscences of the 'general' and the good old days; she put up with the bad temper of her brother when he came home from the stone-cutter's yard where he worked; she cleaned up after the drunken Henry; and she listened to Edgar's accounts of the difficulties of publishing poems with such attention that he often forgot she was a mere child to whom his problems could make no sense whatever. Yet her sympathy was already important to him. After the depressing family had eaten its simple evening meal by the light of a tallow dip, he would help Virginia improve her reading and her arithmetic beside the miserable fire, until retiring to the small attic room he shared with his brother. In that same room Henry was soon to die, but though Edgar was not as physically robust as he had promised to be in his boyhood, his constitution must have been strongly resistant to the dreaded disease. Perhaps his early and extended contact with tuberculosis had immunized him against it.

The year was passing, and no news came from West Point. For the lack of response Mr Allan blamed Edgar, suspecting some subtle deception, and resenting the occasional paltry sums he sent to bind him over until the public charge could take

ABOVE LEFT Poe's cousin and child-bride, Virginia. The original drawing was probably made on her deathbed.

ABOVE RIGHT Virginia's mother, Maria Clemm – 'Muddy'.

over his account. One of Poe's last letters to Allan begs the wealthy merchant for 'a piece of linen, or a half piece . . . I could get it made up *gratis* by Aunt Maria'. Whether the low cost of making up appealed to Allan's meanness is not recorded. Edgar, however, was receiving encouragement from others. Not far from Mrs Clemm's house, on Exeter Street, there lived a Mr Henry Herring who had married Poe's Aunt Eliza, the writer of the sad letter to Frances Allan years before. His compassionate aunt was dead, but Poe's Uncle Herring had numerous literary and journalistic acquaintances in Baltimore whom he managed to interest in Edgar's work. One of these gentlemen, John Neal (who wrote under the name of Jehu O'Cataract), was starting a paper in Portland, Maine, and it was in his *Yankee and Boston Literary Gazette* that Poe received his first good review: 'If E. A. P. of Baltimore – whose lines about 'Heaven' though he professes to regard them as altogether superior to anything in the whole range of American poetry save two or three trifles referred to, are, though nonsense, rather exquisite nonsense – would but do himself justice

OPPOSITE Illustration by Edmund Dulac to *The Raven*.

FOLLOWING PAGES *Cotton Plantation*, painting by Giroux.

might [*sic*] make a beautiful and perhaps a magnificent poem. There is a good deal here to justify such a hope.' Poe was profoundly grateful. 'The very first words of Encouragement I ever remember to have heard', he wrote. In December 1829 a long letter from him containing selections from his forthcoming volume was published in the *Yankee*:

I would give the world to embody one half the ideas afloat in my imagination. I appeal to you as a man who loves the same beauty which I adore – the beauty of the natural blue sky and the sunshiny earth.... I am and I have been from childhood, an idler. It cannot therefore be said that:

> 'I left a calling for this idle trade,
> A duty broke – a father disobeyed.'

For I have no father – nor mother.

It exemplifies clearly Poe's manner of 'puffing' his own work, and elicited from John Neal this advance notice: 'The following passages are from the manuscript works of a young author, about to be published in Baltimore. He is entirely a stranger to us, but with all their faults, if the remainder of *Al Aaraaf* and *Tamerlane* are as good as the body of the extracts here given, to say nothing of the more extraordinary parts, he will deserve to stand high – very high, in the estimation of the shining brother-hood.' It is possible that Poe had a copy of this advance review sent to John Allan. Certainly in mid-December he received from Allan $80, an unusually large contribution for these days, sufficient for Hatch and Dunning of Baltimore to proceed with the printing of his second volume of poems. Two hundred and fifty copies were 'given' to the author, no doubt charged against Allan's investment.

*Al Aaraaf, Tamerlane and Minor Poems* was a thin octavo volume bound in blue board containing seventy-one pages padded out with many fly-leaves on which were printed mottoes from English and Spanish poets. The volume is generally considered to be Poe's first serious contribution to American poetry, embodying in some of its lines that mystical, melancholy, and highly personal use of rhyme which became his mark. He sent a copy to the editor of the *Yankee* with the following eagerly respectful letter:

I thank you, sir, for the kind interest you express for my worldly as well as poetical welfare – a sermon of prosing would have met with much less attention.

You will see that I have made the alterations you suggest... and some other corrections of the same kind – there is much, however, (in metre) to be corrected – for I did not observe it till too late.

OPPOSITE

ABOVE LEFT Version of the Whitman daguerreotype of Poe.

ABOVE RIGHT The Poe house in Philadelphia.

BELOW Engraving of the Richmond theatre fire in 1811.

I wait consciously for your notice of the book. I think the best lines for *sound* are those in *Al Aaraaf* –

All Nature speaks and ev'n ideal things
Flap shadowy sounds from visionary wings.

I am certain that these lines have never been surpassed. –

Of late, eternal Condor years
So shake the very Heaven on high,
With tumult as they thunder by,
I have no time for idle cares,
Through gazing on the unquiet sky.

'It is well to think well of one's self' – so says somebody. You will do me justice, however,

Most truly yours,
Edgar A. Poe.

None of the reviews of the new book was as good as the notice Edgar gave himself, but at least the *Ladies Magazine* compared him with Shelley, and the Baltimore *Minerva and Emerald* praised *Tamerlane*. Edgar A. Poe existed as an American poet and, for a young man not yet twenty-one, consistently opposed in his ambition by the only one who could have helped him, dealing with the problems of daily survival and the politics of ambition entirely without material means, it was an extraordinary achievement. Poe's cousin Neilson wrote to his fiancée: 'Edgar Poe has published a volume of Poems one of which is dedicated to John Neal the great autocrat of critics – Neal has accordingly published Edgar as a poet of great genius etc. . . . – *Our* name will be a great one *yet*.' Even though Neilson was more aware of the techniques of mutual backscratching than he was of his cousin's literary quality, his pride was irrepressible. It was shared by the literary circles of Baltimore, delighted to find an attractive, dashing-looking young poet in their midst, and though Henry Poe may have been somewhat put out by his younger brother's success, the Clemm household basked in the thin warmth that filtered down upon them through the December air.

Mrs Clemm and Virginia loved every moment of Eddy's success and every word of his sometimes obscure but beautiful, sad poetics. Edgar knew that their love for him was unconditional and that here in Mrs Clemm's poor house he would always find a home. She became his 'Muddy', a childish word for 'mother' which also suggests a commitment to the low and menial tasks which were the entire life of this good woman. Muddy is remembered in one of the last poems Poe was to write:

TO MY MOTHER

Because I feel that, in the Heavens above,
The angels, whispering to one another,
Can find, among their burning terms of love,

None so devotional as that of 'Mother',
Therefore by that dear name I long have called you –
You who are more than mother unto me,
And fill my heart of hearts, where Death installed you,
In setting my Virginia's spirit free.
My mother – my own mother, who died early,
Was but the mother of myself; but you
Are mother to the one I loved so dearly,
And thus are dearer than the mother I knew
By that infinity with which my wife
Was dearer to my soul than its soul-life.

But the sonnet of mother-love was still to come; and so was marriage to Virginia, at present a bright child shedding bright tears because success was taking Eddy away from her, for the momentary respectability Poe had won had brought him an invitation to return to John Allan's cold house in Richmond; and Edgar was already too committed an opportunist not to accept.

## *Interlude in Richmond*

When Edgar A. Poe returned to Richmond in the new year 1830, it was as a self-confident young man of the world, with a plentiful supply of his well-received new book of poems for distribution among friends and potential allies. There was something of a triumphal quality in Poe's return. Aunt Nancy was longing for him both on her own part and on that of his recently sadly departed 'Ma'. The black servant Dab, who had always been devoted to him, was waiting to serve him. Even John Allan, though always moody, was more careful in his behaviour and concerned enough to supply Edgar again with new clothes including a fine 'London hat', suited to a successful poet.

The second night after his return Poe met Thomas Bolling, a charming friend from the University of Virginia, at home for the holidays. They met at Sanxey's Book Store where Poe was perhaps checking to see if his new volume of poems was receiving attention. He gave Tom Bolling a copy of *Al Aaraaf* and treated him to a completely apocryphal account of his foreign adventures, covering the time he had spent in the army. Bolling was deeply impressed and his reports of Gaffy's adventures (Poe was known as Gaffy at the university after a character in a lost story of his), helped to support the 'legend' which later was so well reported that it appeared in a Russian encyclopedia which offered a detailed account of Poe's arrest in St Petersburg and his rescue, drunk, from prison in Siberia by an American priest, armed only with a Bible. There is no doubt that in discovering how easily people were hoaxed by a well-founded 'legend' Poe developed some of the story-telling techniques which were later to make many of his tales seem so factual.

Though many in Richmond were suitably impressed by young Poe's new status, not all were by any means, and an unkind review in the Baltimore *Minerva and Emerald* mocking the new poet was quoted extensively. Still, his old friends were reconfirmed in their shaky confidence in Edgar, and his new enemies he would remember for the future, when he would write of the editor of the *Minerva*, 'no man in America has been more shamefully over-estimated.' For the present he used his arrogance to keep the mockers at bay. Among the less admiring was, of course, John Allan. He had returned recently from 'The Springs' where the treatment had done his disorders little good. He had still not recovered from his wife's death and was bothered at having no legitimate heirs or woman to look after his household and inherit his business. On 3 May he quarrelled violently with Poe and all the old issues between them were again raised. Allan reproached Edgar, insulting his family at a time, said Poe, 'when you knew my heart was almost breaking'.

It was an appalling but familiar scene; soon after it Poe wrote to Sergeant 'Bully' Graves of his old company at Fortress Monroe to say that the reason he had not paid his debt to him was because of the impossibility of getting money out of his guardian. The sergeant was only one of several in the regiment to whom Poe owed small sums, and Allan already knew about these debts, for someone from Fortress Monroe had called upon him hoping for some sort of satisfaction for Poe's military 'creditors'. The caller had been received wrathfully, which Poe explained by saying that Mr Allan was 'not often sober' and that his words could therefore be discounted. It was this statement which John Allan subsequently regarded as the most discreditable Edgar had ever made about him. It provided him with the final cause and excuse for totally disinheriting his foster-son.

John Allan was now a highly eligible if ill-tempered widower and was, regardless of his illicit liaisons, feeling lonely. Aunt Nancy was, as Allan had observed, 'as fat and hearty as ever', and apart from being a fine figure of a woman Miss Valentine knew how he liked his food and his home kept. Consequently, it occurred to the merchant that she might very well be a suitable and convenient replacement for Frances. He began to pay Aunt Nancy marked attentions and it is not unreasonable to suggest that she, to some extent, welcomed them. After all, she had lived with the Allans for twenty-five years and life was unlikely to offer her any better alternative to that of being mistress of the Allan establishment. But Edgar was outraged. He knew very well that John Allan was no parfit gentle knight, but a sexual ogre attacking Aunt Nancy with the same brutality that had brought beloved

'Ma' to her grave scarcely a year ago. Edgar's attitude influenced the vacillating spinster and the giant was scotched, which made him no fonder of Edgar than he had been at the worst moments in their history. Now Allan brought all his means to bear upon influential friends, eventually prevailing upon a senator to persuade the War Department to give Edgar, on the threshold of literary success, the earliest possible ticket to West Point. By 31 March the trick had been turned and John Allan wrote, no doubt with same satisfaction:

Sir – as the guardian of Edgar Allan Poe I hereby signify my assent to his signing articles by which he shall bind himself to serve the United States for five years, unless sooner discharged, as stipulated in your official letter appointing him cadet.

Respectfully,
Your obt. – servant.
John Allan

The Hon Sec'y of War,
Washington.

On 12 May John Allan added to Edgar's outfit a pair of blankets from the store and, just to make sure there were no slip-ups, silently accompanied him to the boat for Baltimore. There, as the steamer waited to leave, Allan shook hands firmly with Edgar, leaving him certain that this farewell was meant to be final. In Baltimore

ABOVE John Allan's second wife, Louisa Gabriella Patterson, loathed her husband's adopted son.

Poe spent a little time at the Clemm household basking in the affection of Muddy and Sis, and then travelled on by way of Philadelphia and New York to West Point, arriving in time for the admission examinations in the last week of June. He was somewhat put out by the disciplined, business-like atmosphere of the academy which was obviously going to be a tougher assignment than the artillery. But he passed the examination, took the oath on 1 July, and was, the next day, caught up in the rigid meaninglessness of military training.

Meanwhile, back in Richmond, John Allan visited his friend John Mayo at his splendid Belleville plantation to drown his irritating troubles in Southern hospitality. He was successful. Among the guests was Mrs Mayo's niece, Louisa Gabriella Patterson, a lady of strong character from New York, some thirty years old. She and Allan were drawn to each other from the start and the family approved a match. Shortly afterwards Allan and Miss Patterson were engaged to be married. That marriage finally severed Poe forever from the Allan house, for the new Mrs Allan was in no way to be one of Edgar's divine mothers.

## *Cadet Poe*

Waiting for Edgar at West Point was a letter from John Allan forwarded by brother Henry from Baltimore. It contained $20, and a charge that Edgar had taken from the house some articles which did not belong to him – some books and the brass inkstand, sand-caster and pen-holder which Poe had always regarded as Allan's gifts. Something of the ritualistic dignity of writing was vested in them for Edgar, and, few as the objects were that he kept on his travels, he carried these *lares* with him.

As a cadet Poe would receive $28 a month and rations, and clearly John Allan considered this income finally replaced his financial responsibility. The course was to last four years and Allan wanted no charges upon himself, even though textbooks and personal articles had to be paid for additionally. Poe therefore found himself very quickly in debt again, having to borrow petty sums to buy soap, candles, fuel, writing paper and clothes. Once again Allan was loading the dice against him, degrading him in a singularly painful manner, for Poe was intensely neat and careful in his personal appearance; fresh linen was important to him. But the expense of such style was regarded by Allan as an absurd luxury for a penniless

OPPOSITE ABOVE *View of West Point*, painted by the well-known American artist George Catlin.

OPPOSITE BELOW American soldiers of the 1830s.

charity-boy, and inflating to the arrogance which must be expelled from his character. So Edgar was mortified, as he had been at the University of Virginia, and his social pretensions were ridiculed by his poverty. It was also detrimental to Poe's social status that he had served in the ranks, for the military academy snobs looked down on common soldiering. Further, he identified himself with the Virginians in the academy and, as if all this were not sufficient to irritate his fellow-cadets, he promoted the 'legend' of his Byronic adventures in remote places. Yet if social life at the academy was not amenable, the studies were simulating and the district around the bare, stone, barrack-like buildings attractive. The nearby Catskill mountains had acquired literary virtue through the writings of Washington Irving, and Poe might wander in them if he ever got enough time off from duties, for the academy routine was arduous.

In the morning cadets attended lectures till dinner, then at four in the afternoon they changed into uniform for parades and drills which filled the rest of the day. After supper there was another study period, the call to quarters sounding at 9.00 pm. There were few leaves and holidays and the atmosphere was harsh and severe. Poe later wrote that the decline in his physical condition began at West Point, for in spite of his strong swimming as a boy, he was generally disinclined to physical activities and tired easily, his heart being 'weak'; certainly he had no energy or enthusiasm for the long, boring drill sessions. Physical and social conditions in the officers' academy were harder and more brutal than Sergeant-Major Perry had found them in the artillery, and many of the young cadets were ignorant and boorish. Even though his veteran experience kept the stupid somewhat at bay, Edgar needed the protection of aloofness and arrogance. As a result he was both joked about and feared by the cadets and, as the latter reaction suited him better, he played upon it for all he was worth. When a cadet heard that Edgar's mother was named Arnold and wondered whether Poe was a grandson of Benedict Arnold, he allowed it to be believed that he was. He had encouraged the belief a year before in a letter to Allan, for the notoriety achieved by being related to a famous traitor suited his diabolic inclinations well, and now anything that kept the sillier puppies off was an advantage. Left to himself, he continued those studies of Shelley, Keats, Byron, Wordsworth and Coleridge which were more to his taste than mindless drilling and the tedious sciences. His feelings upon science he published in a sonnet in the *Philadelphia Casket* of October 1830:

> Science! true daughter of Old Time thou art!
> Who alterest all things with thy peering eyes.
> Why preyest thou thus upon the poet's heart,
> Vulture, whose wings are dull realities?
> How should he love thee? or how deem thee wise,

Who wouldst not leave him in his wandering
To seek for treasure in the jewelled skies,
Albeit he soared with an undaunted wing?
Hast thou not dragged Diana from her car,
And driven the Hamadryad from the wood
To seek a shelter in some happier star?
Hast thou not torn the Naiad from her flood,
The Elfin from the green grass, and from me
The summer dream beneath the tamarind tree?

The poem powerfully expresses Poe's rebellion against a world in which materialism is triumphing over poetry, but in the images may also be seen Edgar, the poet, torn from his hamadryad and elfin 'mothers', Elizabeth, Helen and Frances, with Science, symbol of his loathed 'father' Allan, the great vulture preying upon the poet's heart.

In fact during the summer of 1830 John Allan was not much concerning himself with the poet's heart, being deeply involved in a great affair of his own. Miss Patterson had been sharing the beautiful summer with him at his plantation in Goochland; their marriage took place on 5 October in the Patterson house in New York, after which Mr and Mrs Allan returned to Richmond without it occurring to Allan that he might call upon Edgar at the nearby Academy. Poe thought it a typically heartless demonstration by his foster-father, though it is understandable that Allan did not wish to expose his new wife to the adoptive son of his old one; nor would he be eager for her to witness a row. Allan had confessed his indiscretions to Miss Patterson before their marriage, and she had accepted him on condition that he was a changed man. Edgar belonged very firmly in the past and now Allan would insist on keeping him there. So far as the new Mrs Allan was concerned, Edgar Poe was the name of an ill-disposed young man, the scribbler son of penniless actors, upon whom Mr Allan's generosity had been wastefully bestowed over the years. Poe continued writing to 'Dear Pa', hoping somehow to keep a line to Allan's assets alive, but 'Dear Pa' did not write back. As the long winter of 1830–1 settled in, Poe, depressed by both his present and the vision of his future, settled down with two other cadets in room number 28 of the old South Barracks and drank brandy whenever any of them could afford it.

Number 28 quickly gained the name of a 'hard' room whose occupants scorned

FOLLOWING PAGES *In the Catskills*, by F. E. Church. The rugged landscape of the Catskills lay close to West Point, and Poe could wander among the hills and forests in his little free time. The area had acquired literary fame through its association with Washington Irving.

Illustration by W. Heath Robinson to *Lenore*, one of the poems written at West Point.

as much of the academy discipline as they could and wrote rhymes against officers, especially the martinet Lieutenant Locke:

> As for Locke, he is all my eye;
> May the devil right soon for his soul call.

One of Poe's room-mates in number 28 was Cadet T.H. Gibson who, in November 1867, published in *Harper's New Monthly Magazine* a reminiscence of Cadet Poe nearly forty years previously:

The first conversation I had with Poe after we became installed as room-mates was characteristic of the man. A volume of Campbell's Poems was lying upon our table, and he tossed it contemptuously aside with the curt remark: 'Campbell is a plagiarist'; then without waiting for a reply he picked up the book, and turned the leaves over rapidly until he found the passage he was looking for.

'There', he said, 'is a line more often quoted than any other passage of his: "Like angel visits few and far between", and he stole it bodily from Blair's Grave. Not satisfied with the theft he has spoiled it in the effort to disguise it. Blair wrote: "Like angel visits short and far between", Campbell's 'few and far between' is mere tautology.'

The studies of the Academy, Poe utterly ignored....

Gibson's account details visits to Old Benny's, the out-of-bounds groggery near the academy, exchanging four pounds of candles and Poe's 'last blanket' for brandy. He also reports a horrific hoax devised by Poe, using a dead and bloody gander to simulate the cut-off head of one of their officers. Thus Benedict Arnold's grandson, a 'hard' man with the brandy, and a poet with a diabolical sense of humour, was established among the legends of West Point.

Protected by the demonic image, Poe drafted and polished his first great poems. As his days and evenings were filled by routine and the revolt against it, it was at night that he worked. There is in all Poe's work a post-midnight atmosphere, a quality of night-writing which developed at this time when the night was all he owned. In the nights at West Point, *To Helen*, *Irene*, *The Doomed City*, and the first *Lenore* emerged and shone, poems with themes of beautiful dead women and a doomed mortuary atmosphere. They shared Poe's nights with *Israfel*, the arrogant protest:

> In Heaven a spirit doth dwell
> 'Whose heart-strings are a lute;'
> None sing so wildly well
> As the angel Israfel,
> And the giddy stars (so legends tell)
> Ceasing their hymns, attend the spell
>     Of his voice, all mute
>
> If I could dwell
> Where Israfel
>     Hath dwelt, and he where I,
> He might not sing so wildly well
>     A mortal melody,
> While a bolder note than this might swell
>     From my lyre within the sky.

But always beyond the complaining self-confidence was the growing preoccupation embodied in those most telling lines:

> I could not love except where Death
> Was mingling his with Beauty's breath –
> Or Hymen, Time, and Destiny
> Were stalking between her and me.

Here the lost 'sister-love' Elmira's marriage occasioned the reflection. But time and again in the shadows of the candle-lit night his thoughts returned to the epic love of his life. *The Sleeper* remembers his mother as a great love in the setting of a theatrically royal funeral:

My love, she sleeps! Oh, may her sleep,
As it is lasting so be deep!
Soft may the worms about her creep!
Far in the forest, dim and old,
For her may some tall vault unfold:
Some vault that oft hath flung its black
And winged panels fluttering back,
Triumphant, o'er the crested palls
Of her grand family funerals....

Colonel Thayer, the Superintendent of West Point who, like Lieutenant Locke, had been satirized by Poe, saw the young poet's serious work and was sensitive and sympathetic enough to be deeply impressed by it. Once again a military 'father' showed benevolence towards Edgar and an unexpected sympathy for his quite unmilitary writings, in spite of all that the demon of Number 28 had done to mock the academy. No wonder that Poe in the dreadful years to come would return in his dreams to the warmth and security of the army. Now he exploited to the full Colonel Thayer's appreciation and obtained permission for his fellow-cadets to subscribe towards the publication of his poems at seventy-five cents a copy, deductible from their pay. It was a remarkable *coup* in such unpromising circumstances. Poe allowed the cadets to believe that humorous, satirical and scurrilous rhymes about their officers were being collected into a book which would remind them of jolly West Point times. Thus Poe compiled a subscription list guaranteeing an advance sale of several hundred copies and, with its support, approached Elam Bliss, a New York publisher. Mr Bliss visited West Point towards the end of 1830 and concluded arrangements with Poe to publish his third volume, *Poems*. Edgar was not much concerned that his subscribers would, by and large, be somewhat disappointed when they saw the book, for he had the intention of being over the hills and far away by the time his public realized that they had bought a work of genius rather than a collection of schoolboy jokes. But Poe's departure from West Point was not to be what he would have designed for himself.

Now it was that an unfriendly ghost of the past rose up. Sergeant 'Bully' Graves had waited until the end of that year, hoping the money Poe had promised him would arrive. Now he wrote to John Allan firmly demanding that the matter be settled. Graves was the soldier to whom Poe had said that Mr Allan was not often sober. Mr Allan, a reformed and newly-married gentleman, did not want a common soldier showing around a letter from his ungrateful foster-son which pilloried him as a drunk. The second Mrs Allan summed up the affair very concisely when she wrote that: 'Mr Allan sent him the money . . . and banished Poe from his affections.' The banishment was signalled in a letter of invective in which Allan finally and totally disowned Edgar, wishing no further communications from him. Poe replied, reasserting Mr Allan's tendency to drink, reproaching him for his parsimony and its ruinous effects upon his own health and career, for his treatment of his late wife, and his abuse of Edgar's parents and family. He expressed the conviction that his own life would be short, and his future one of indigence and sickness. He had no energy nor health left, he wrote. West Point had exhausted him and he intended to resign. If John Allan did not grant the necessary permission he would thenceforward neglect his studies and duties, subjecting himself to dismissal. John Allan received this letter in January 1831. On it he wrote: 'Can see no good reason to alter my opinion. I do not think the boy has one good quality. He may do or act as he pleases tho' I would have saved him but not on his own terms and conditions since I cannot believe a word he writes. His letter is the most barefaced one-sided statement.'

On 28 January 1831 a court martial tried Cadet E.A.Poe:

CHARGE 1st – Gross Neglect of Duty

Specification 1st – In this, that he, the said Cadet Poe, did absent himself from the following parades and roll calls between the 7th January and 27th January 1831. . . .

Specification 2nd – In this, that he, the said Cadet E.A.Poe, did absent himself from all Academical duties between the 15th and 27th January 1831. . . .

CHARGE 2nd – Disobedience of Orders

Specification 1st – In this, that he, the said Cadet Poe, after having been directed by the officer of the day to attend church on the 23rd of January 1831 did fail to obey such order. . . .

Specification 2nd – In this, that he, the said Cadet Poe, did fail to attend the Academy on the 25th January 1831, after having been directed to do so by the officer of the day.

Poe pleaded guilty to all but the first part of the first charge, putting himself beyond any recommendation for mercy. The 'prisoner' was found guilty on all the charges and specifications and it was recommended that he be dismissed from the service of the United States as from 6 March, in order to provide sufficient sums out of his pay to satisfy his indebtedness to the academy. On that day when, Poe was officially discharged with a balance to his credit of twenty-four cents. But he had already left West Point on 19 February. With his iron-bound trunk of manuscripts and books, the contested inkstand, sand-caster and pen-holder, wearing his threadbare civilian clothes beneath the West Point greatcoat which he was to keep with him for the rest of his life, Edgar Allan Poe, a man of destiny with no destination, took passage on the *Henry Eckford* bound for New York.

# CHAPTER FOUR
# 1831–1835

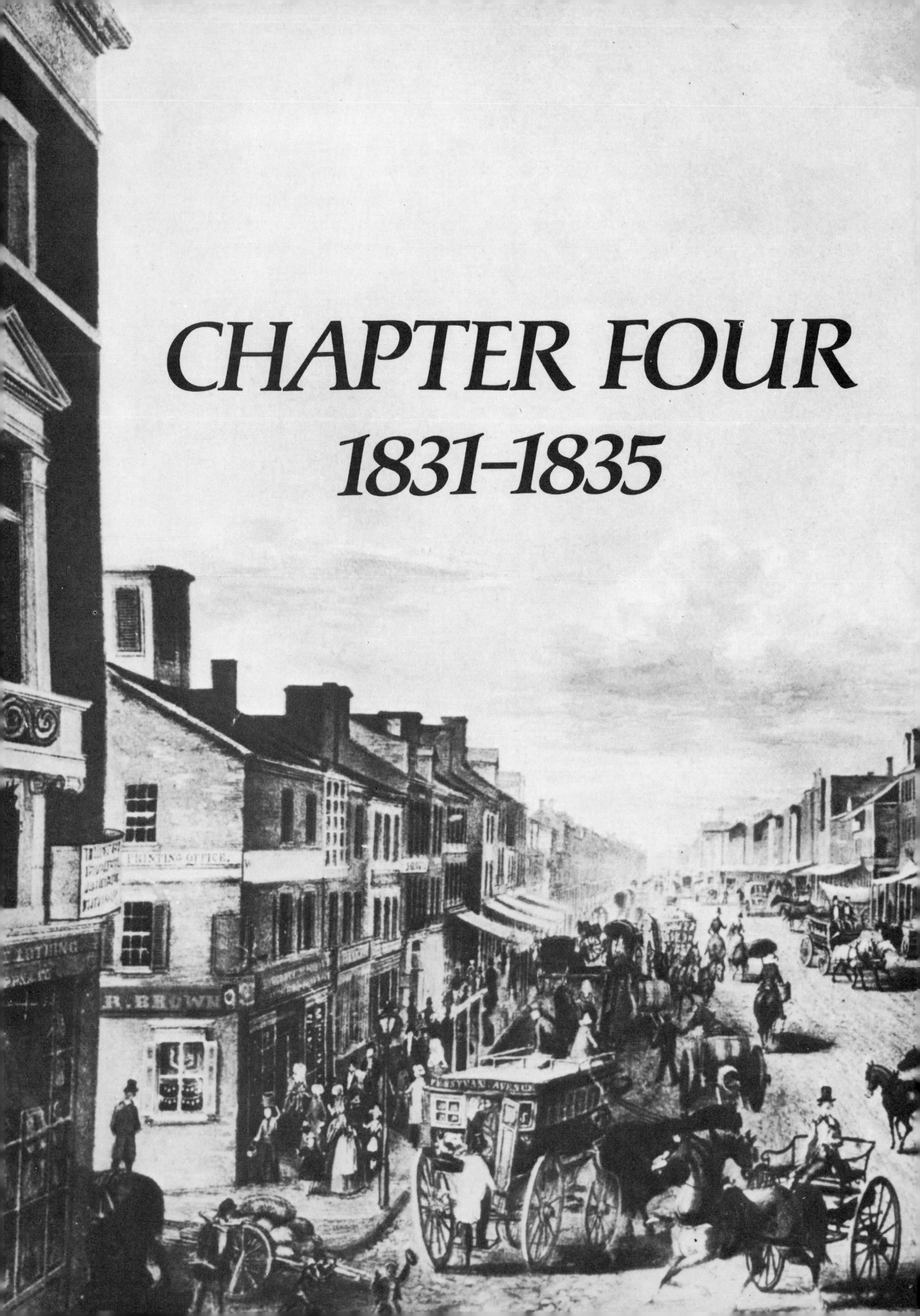

BALTIMORE MUSEUM
&
GALLERY OF
FINE ARTS
ARMSTRONG AND BERRY
BALTIMORE
MUSEUM
and GALLERY of
FINE ARTS.

## *The Soul's Terror*

Poe spent a miserable month in New York. The greatcoat was not warm enough to keep out the intense cold and, exhausted and hungry, in a poor room near Madison Square, he developed a bad chill on the lungs, his ear discharged blood and he had appalling headaches. In despair he forgot both pride and reason and wrote to John Allan describing his condition, writing from 'his death-bed'. Surely a little help during these last hours would be forthcoming? No doubt Edgar exaggerated, but he knew that only an extreme might elicit a response from his hardened foster-father. Apparently it was not enough to move the newly married merchant, but the exercise of hating his unresponsive 'Pa', together with the laudanum which he would have taken for his cold, stimulated Poe, and within a week, no longer despairing, he was in the offices of Elam Bliss correcting the proofs of *Poems*, and composing a preface, 'Letter to Mr B.' – possibly Bliss himself. The 'Letter' is a re-written West Point essay which complains of the difficulties of being an American author, and lifts bodily from Chapter 19 of Coleridge's *Biographia Literaria* the well-known theory which became the credo of those who believed that art was created for art's sake.

A poem in my opinion is opposed to a work of science by having, for its immediate object, pleasure, not truth: to romance, by having for its object an indefinite instead of a definite pleasure, being a poem only so far as this object is attained: romance presenting perceptible images with definite, poetry with indefinite sensations, to which end music is an essential, since the comprehension of sweet sound is our most indefinite conception. Music, when combined with a pleasurable idea, is poetry: music, without the idea, is simply music: the idea, without the music, is prose from its very definiteness.

Poe's lecture years later on *The Poetic Principle* had the same derivation, his aesthetic rationale remaining unchanged throughout his life.

*Poems* was dedicated 'To the U.S. Corps of Cadets', not unreasonably since the Corps had paid for half of the 'second' edition, 500 copies of a duodecimo volume of 124 pages, bound in pale green boards and poorly printed on rag paper. Its publication put Poe into a mood of high optimism. One Peter Pindar Pease, an anti-saloon

PREVIOUS PAGES A busy street scene in Baltimore.

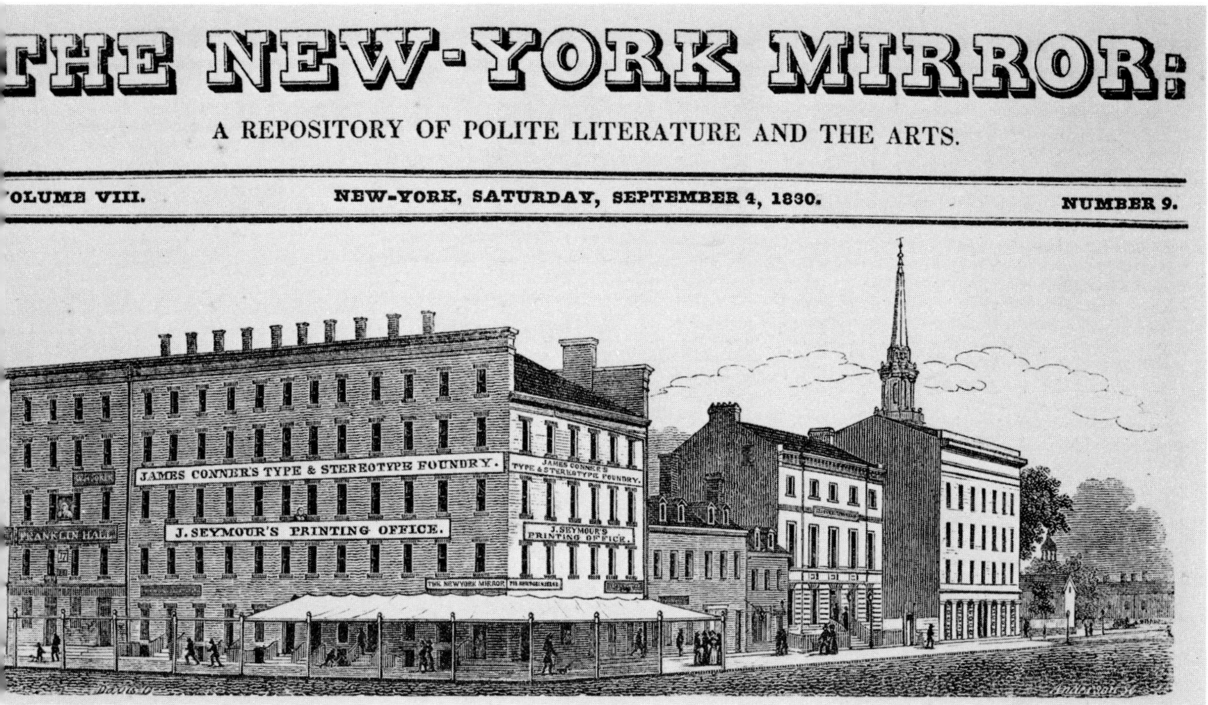


An 1830 *New York Mirror*, showing Ann and Nassau Streets.

man and prohibitionist who doubtless regarded Edgar as a subject for demonstrating the evils of drink, and who had known the poet in Charlottesville and Boston, now met him again in New York, walking under the elms in Madison Square. At dinner Poe enthusiastically proclaimed his good luck, saying he had finally 'struck it hard'. In the same mood of high optimism he had the gall to write to Colonel Thayer requesting a favour and propounding a somewhat lunatic intention more appropriate to the 'legend' than to life:

New York, March 10, 1831

Sir; Having no longer any ties which can bind me to my native country – no projects – nor any friends – I intend by the first opportunity to proceed to Paris with a view of obtaining through the interest of the Marquis de La Fayette an appointment (if possible) in the Polish Army.

In the event of the interference of France in behalf of Poland this may easily be effected – at all events it will be my only feasible plan of procedure.

The object of this letter is respectfully to request that you will give me such assistance as may be in your power in furtherance of my views.

A certificate of 'standing' in my class is all that I have any right to expect. Anything further – a letter to a friend in Paris – or to the Marquis – would be a kindness which I should never forget. Most respectfully,

Yr. obt. s't,
Edgar A. Poe

Col. S. Thayer, Supt. U.S.M.A.

The English poet Samuel Taylor Coleridge, from whom Poe derived his theory of the aesthetics of poetry.

Apparently the former commanding officer of the cashiered cadet did not reply. In any case Poe seems to have forgotten the desperate gesture almost as soon as he made it. As his manic excitement inevitably descended towards depression, only one place in the world seemed to call to him with the voice of a mother. By the end of March 1831 Poe was back there in Baltimore in the house of Mrs Clemm, his faithful 'Muddy'.

As during his earlier stay, life at Mrs Clemm's was supported by Muddy's work and unfailing maternal warmth, and the brightness of Virginia, now about to celebrate her ninth birthday. All else was sadness, with Henry Clemm, the young stonemason, developing into a brutal drinker, Henry Poe, Edgar's brother, only a few months from death, and old grandmother Poe dying. But there was still his place in the attic room (soon to be his entirely), soup for all, and, that essential of Poe's life, unconditional and unending female affection. Henry died, aged twenty four, in August, the processes of the dread and obscure disease accelerated by his drinking.

His only legacy was a debt for $80 which Edgar accepted. In Baltimore, where the debt laws were strict and one could be confined for owing $5, it was a serious matter. But for the time being Edgar ignored it with Byronic insouciance. The debt was already two years old and, as winter came on, his late brother's creditors would wait no longer. Mrs Clemm managed to find only some $20, so there was no alternative but to appeal to Allan. This Poe did in the most abject terms:

Balt. Dec. 15th, 1831.

Dear Pa,

I am sure you could not refuse to assist me if you were well aware of the distress I am in. How often have you relieved the distress of a perfect stranger in circumstances less urgent than mine, and yet when I beg and entreat you in the name of God to send me succour you will still refuse to aid me. I know that I have no longer any hopes of being again received into your favour, but for the sake of Christ, do not let me perish for a sum of money which you would never miss, and which would relieve me from the greatest earthly misery.... If you wish me to humble myself before you I am humble – Sickness and misfortune have left me not a shadow of pride....

Concerned for his own good name or impelled by some ancient affection for his foster-son, Allan wrote to his Baltimore agent instructing him to 'procure liberation' for Edgar and 'give him $20 besides'. But so ambivalent was Allan towards Poe that though he wrote the letter on 7 December, he forgot to send it until some five weeks later, leaving Edgar to sweat it out over Christmas and into the new year, when liberation finally arrived.

The fear of prison, the latest mortification by Allan, and straitened conditions in the Clemm household, forcing Muddy to go begging for scraps with her big basket over her arm, seemed to have convinced Poe, as nothing till now had done, that a change of direction in his writing was essential. The *Philadelphia Saturday Courier* had announced a short story competition with a prize of $100; clearly there was more to be made from fiction than from poetry. For the time being Poe decided to apply himself totally to the problems of story-writing. In the garret of the Clemm house he wrote several stories which became the basis for his collection, *The Tales of the Folio Club*. He failed to win the prize (which went to a Mrs Bacon for her *Love's Martyr*), but the paper published his *Metzengerstein*. Though his efforts in fiction were obviously influenced by the fashion for gothic tales, Poe knew no German, and later stated that, 'If in many of my productions terror has been the thesis, I maintain that terror is not of Germany, but of the soul.'

It is during this period of intensive application to the writing of terror that Poe became familiar with opium, which was, in the form of tincture of laudanum, a commonly used medicine, effective as an anti-spasmodic and regarded as a specific for pulmonary conditions and 'irritation' of the stomach. It was such stomach 'irritation' that had, at the age of eighteen, made de Quincey into an opium-eater. In his

Thomas de Quincey, like Poe, was addicted to opium.

*Confessions of an Opium Eater* he describes how the drug first increased his working stamina and heightened his imaginative flights: 'In the middle of 1817 this faculty became increasingly distressing to me: at night, when I lay awake in bed, vast processions moved along continually in mournful pomp; friezes of never-ending stories drawn from time before Oedipus or Priam, before Tyre, before Memphis. And, concurrently with this, a corresponding change took place in my dreams; a theatre seemed suddenly opened and lighted up within my brain, which presented nightly spectacles of more than earthly splendour.' The drug also masked hunger, warmed the body and extended the sense of time. Poe, writing in the long, cold, lonely nights in the attic, haunted by his brother's hacking cough, would have welcomed a support at once as inexpensive and creatively rich as opium. It was a stimulant, furthermore, which, taken moderately, did not affect him in the sickening, violent and dangerous way of alcohol. No doubt, too, it had pleasurable and loving associations for him, for he would have seen the divine sick ladies who haunted his memory tremulously sipping their precious drops of laudanum and sinking back, forgetful of pain, into the dream-world. Opium was the drug of the Romantics as tuberculosis was their disease. Edgar Poe was sworn brother sweet to both of them.

## *The Mystery of Mary Devereaux*

Baltimore was proud of its 'Bard'. Poe walked the town from Coale's bookshop on Calvert Street to Widow Meagle's Oyster Parlor on Pratt, sometimes accompanied by a sailor named Tuhey, playing a flute. Enlivened by a visit to a seafarers' tavern,

Poe, his greatcoat worn as a cloak, occasionally drilled street urchins or recited his poetry. Indeed the dark, handsome Byronic poet did all those things which handsome Byronic poets are expected to do, and Baltimore loved him for it. Young ladies showed a particular weakness for Edgar's person and 'legend', and he was not slow to take his opportunities. His attic looked over the rear of Essex Street in the Old Town. Writing one day, he was distracted from the pains of composition by a pretty girl with auburn hair arranged in the fashion of 'frizzed puffs' sitting in a window opposite. Her name was Mary Devereaux and she, with her friend Mary Newman who lived next door, began a handkerchief-waving flirtation with Edgar. They knew the young soldier-poet with his self-made 'legend' well enough by sight, and pursued the game so avidly that Mrs Devereaux asked why Mary was spending so much time upstairs.

One summer afternoon the two Marys were talking together on the front stoop of their houses on Essex Street with a balustrade between them, when Edgar passed on his way home. He bowed to them, but his bright, hypnotic eyes were concentrated upon Miss Devereaux, for Virginia had been to her with his request for a lock of hair and she had complied. No doubt then, the Marys were waiting for the gallant young poet on that hot summer afternoon in 1832. Miss Devereaux told the whole story of that meeting and its consequences in an interview with Augustus Van Cleef in *Harper's* fifty-seven years later. It was a long time to keep a secret but, on the other hand, it was the sort of secret which a lady never allows to lose its brightness. Miss Devereaux's story of her 'affair' with Poe is of particular interest as a first-hand account of the manner in which he conducted himself in a relationship with a woman. Even if Mary's memory of precise dialogue creaks a little, she captures very convincingly the feeling and atmosphere of that lost summer in Baltimore when opium, terror and passion were compounded in Edgar Allan Poe:

Mr Poe, having crossed the street, came up to Newman's stoop. As he did so, I turned my back, as I was then young and bashful. He said, 'How do you do, Miss Newman?' She then turned and introduced him to me, and then happened to be called into the house. Mr Poe immediately jumped across the balustrades separating the stoops, and sat down by me. He told me I had the most beautiful head of hair he ever saw, the hair that poets always raved about.... From that time on, he visited me every evening for a year, and during that time, until the night of our final lovers' quarrel, he never drank a drop, as far as I know.... Affectionate!... he was passionate in his love.... My intimacy with Mr Poe isolated me a good deal. In fact my girl friends were many of them afraid of him and forsook me on his account. I knew more of his male friends. He despised ignorant people, and didn't like trifling and small talk. He didn't like dark-skinned people. When he loved, he loved desperately. Though tender and very affectionate, he had a quick, passionate temper, and was very jealous. His feelings were intense and he had but little control of them. He was not well balanced; he had too much brain. He scoffed at everything sacred and never went to church. If he had had religion to guide him he would have been a better man. He said often that there was a mystery hanging over him he never could fathom. He believed he was born to suffer, and this embittered his whole life. Mrs Clemm also spoke vaguely of some family mystery, of some disgrace.... Mr Poe once gave me a letter to read from Mr Allan, in which the latter said, referring to me, that if he married any such person he would cut him off without a shilling.

Eddie and I never talked of his poetry then or in later years. He would not have done that; he would have considered it conceited. We were young, and only thought of our love. Virginia always carried his notes to me.... Eddie's favourite name was 'Mary', he said. He used often to quote Burns, for whom he had a great admiration. We used to go out walking together in the evenings. We often walked out of the city and sat down on the hills.

One moonlight summer night we were walking across the bridge, which was not far from our house. At the other end of the bridge was a minister's house. Eddie took my arm and pulled me, saying, 'Come, Mary, let us go and get married; we might as well get married now as any other time.' We were then but two blocks from home. He followed, and came in after me. We had no definite engagement, but we understood each other. He was then not in circumstances to marry. When my brother found that Mr Poe was coming so often he said to me: 'You are not going to marry that man, Mary? – I would rather see you in your grave than that man's wife. He can't support himself, let alone you.' I replied, being as romantic as Eddie was, that I would sooner live on a crust of bread with him than in a palace with any other man.... The only thing that I had against him was that he held his head so high. He was proud and looked down on my uncle whose business did not suit him. He always liked my father, and talked with him a good deal....

One evening a friend of my brother's, a Mr Morris, was visiting us. He knew that Mr Poe's favorite song, which I often sang him, was Come Rest in This Bosom. He asked me to sing it in order to tease Mr Poe. I went to the piano to sing. Mr Morris stood by me and turned the leaves. Mr Poe walked with one hand behind his back, up and down the room, biting the nails of the other hand to the quick, as he always did when excited. He then walked over to the piano, and snatched the music and threw it on the floor. I said that it made no matter, and that I could sing the song without music, and did so. Mr Morris, knowing me well, called me 'Mary'. That also made Eddie jealous. He stayed after Mr Morris left, and we had a little quarrel.

Our final lovers' quarrel came about in this way: One night I was waiting in the parlor for Eddie, and he didn't come. My mother came into the room about ten o'clock and said, 'Come Mary, it's bed-time.' The parlor windows were open, and I lay with my head on my arms on one of the window sills. I had been crying. Eddie arrived shortly after my mother spoke to me, and he had been drinking. It was the only time during that year that I ever knew him to take anything. He found the front door locked. He then came to the window where I was, and opened the shutters, which were nearly closed. He raised my head, and told me where he had been. He said he had met some cadets from West Point when on his way across the bridge. They were old friends, and took him to Barnum's Hotel, where they had a supper and champagne. He had gotten away as quickly as possible to come and explain matters to me. A glass made him tipsy. He had more than a glass that night. As to his being an habitual drunkard, he never was as long as I knew him. I went and opened the door and sat on the stoop with him in the moonlight. We then had a quarrel, about whose cause I do not care to speak. The result was that I jumped past him off the stoop, ran around through an alleyway to the back of the house, and into the room where my mother was.

She said, 'Mary! Mary! what's the matter?'

Mr Poe had followed me, and came into the room. I was much frightened, and my mother told me to go upstairs. I did so.

Mr Poe said, 'I want to talk to your daughter. If you don't tell her to come downstairs, I will go after her. I have a right to!'

My mother was a tall woman, and she placed her back against the door of the stairs, and said, 'You have no right to; you cannot go upstairs.'

Mr Poe answered, 'I have a right. She is my wife now in the sight of Heaven!'

My mother then told him he had better go home and to bed, and he went away. He didn't value the Laws of God or man. He was an atheist. He would just as lief have lived with a woman without being married to her as not. . . . I made a narrow escape in not marrying him. I don't think he was a man of much principle.

After the quarrel . . . I broke off all communication with Mr Poe, and returned his letters unopened. My mother also forbade him the house. He sent me a letter by Virginia. I sent it back unopened. He wrote again, and I opened the letter. He addressed me formally as 'Miss Devereaux', and upbraided me in satiric terms for my heartless, unforgiving disposition. I showed the letter to my mother, and she in turn showed it to my grandmother, who was then visiting us. My grandmother read it, and took it to my uncle James. My uncle was very indignant, and resented Mr Poe's letter so much that he wrote him a very severe cutting letter, without my knowledge. Mr Poe also published at the same time in a Baltimore paper a poem of six or eight verses addressed To Mary. The poem was very severe, and spoke of fickleness and inconstancy. All my friends and his knew whom he meant. This also added to my uncle's indignation.

Mr Poe was so incensed at the letter he received that he bought a cowhide, and went to my uncle's store one afternoon and cowhided him. My uncle was a man of over fifty at the time. My aunt and her two sons rushed into the store, and in the struggle to defend my uncle tore his assailant's black frockcoat at the back from the skirts to the collar. Mr Poe then put the cowhide up his sleeve and went up the streets to our house as he was, with his torn coat, followed by a crowd of boys. When he arrived at our house he asked to see my father. He told him he had been up to see his brother, pulled out my uncle's letter, said he resented the insult and had cowhided him. I had been called downstairs, and when Mr Poe saw me, he pulled the cowhide out of his sleeve and threw it down at my feet, saying, 'There, I make you a present of that!'

It is very clear from Miss Devereaux's account that when she says that Poe 'was passionate in his love' and speaks of her 'intimacy' with him, she is talking of a markedly physical relationship. How far she allowed Edgar to go in that 'intimacy' must remain speculative. She has him say, 'I have a right. She is my wife now in

the sight of Heaven!' Now Poe may very well have used such a phrase and certainly it would have conveyed to Mrs Devereaux the information that he and her daughter had proceeded far beyond the bounds of convention in their 'affair'. On the other hand we know that Poe was much given to hyperbole, and as it is most unlikely that he had much physical knowledge and experience of women, he might very well have taken the smallest 'intimacies' as a commitment 'in the sight of Heaven'. Then, of course, we must consider Miss Devereaux's observation that Poe had come from dinner, that he had been drinking champagne and that: 'A glass made him tipsy. He had more than a glass that night.' Drink invariably made Poe violently manic and his posture of 'husband' could reasonably be attributed to its effects. On the other hand Miss Devereaux was convinced that the atheist 'would just as lief have lived with a woman without being married to her as not'. She therefore knew that the passionate Edgar would go a very long way in his courtship if permitted; no doubt she had permitted a degree, or was prepared to let the readers of *Harper's* think she had, something a respectable old lady would hardly be inclined to do for mere bravado. Yet she would surely never have admitted publicly to the 'ultimate intimacy'. We may reasonably conclude therefore that Poe did not have a full sexual liaison with Miss Devereaux, regardless of his invocation of 'Heaven' as a witness to the seriousness of their troth.

Two early twentieth-century illustrations to *Fairyland*, one of Poe's West Point poems: OPPOSITE by Edmund Dulac, and BELOW by W. Heath Robinson.

The investigation into the mystery of Poe's relationship with Mary Devereaux is of considerable importance in studying Poe's sexual behaviour. It suggests strongly that in 1832 Poe certainly felt capable of consummating an 'affair', whether he did so or not. That is to say, he had not yet any reason to suspect himself of the 'impotence' of which many students of his pathology are convinced. In 1832 he was passionate, physical and intensely possessive, and the full effects of opium and alcohol upon his basically disturbed psychology were yet to be seen. In Baltimore he was an assiduous courtier of several pretty girls, signed their albums, recited his poems to a circle of them in the Herring house, and was felt to be attractive, intensely male, and somewhat dangerous. They found him unforgettable, as did Miss Devereaux fifty years later:

Mr Poe was about five feet eight inches tall, and had dark, almost black hair, which he wore long and brushed back in student style over his ears. It was as fine as silk. His eyes were large and full, gray and piercing. He was entirely clean shaven. His nose was long and straight, and his features finely cut. The expression about his mouth was beautiful. He was pale, and had no color. His skin was of a clear beautiful olive. He had a sad, melancholy look. He was very slender . . . but had a fine figure, an erect military carriage, and a quick step. But it was his manner that most charmed. It was elegant. When he looked at you it seemed as if he could read your thoughts. His voice was pleasant and musical but not deep. He always wore a black frock-coat buttoned up, with a cadet or military collar, a low turned-over shirt collar, and a black cravat tied in a loose knot. He did not follow the fashions, but had a style of his own. His was a loose way of dressing as if he didn't care. You would know that he was very different from the ordinary run of young men.

Miss Devereaux was right. Mr Poe was quite extraordinary.

## *A Prize of Gold*

In April 1832 John Allan drew up a detailed will in which there was no mention of Edgar. Allan's dropsy was getting worse and it was known that he might die at any time. Poe knew his condition for he received a constant flow of intelligence from Richmond by one source or another. A printer named Askew carried letters back and forth for him; 'Marse Eddie' kept in touch with friendly house-slaves; Miss Valentine, the Mackenzies and sister Rosalie were all sources of information. From them he knew both Allan's physical condition and the fact that the new Mrs Allan had rapidly presented him with two heirs. Some faint hope that the threat of total disinheritance could be averted by some last personal appeal to Allan brought Poe back to Richmond in June 1832 after a two-year absence.

On arriving, Edgar asked his old friend Dab, the butler, for Miss Valentine, but his loving Aunt Nancy was unfortunately out. He then asked Dab to take his bag up to 'his room'. Dab hesitated. Angrily Edgar repeated his order. Dab, embarrassed, explained that 'Marse Eddie's Room' was now a guest room. Poe, much put out, demanded to see Mrs Allan. Eventually she came down to the parlour, where she found a furious young stranger acting like the favoured scion of the family put out by herself, an interloper. Unable to control himself, Poe attacked her as 'the strange woman' who had usurped his loving 'Ma's' position. Hearing one of the baby heirs crying upstairs infuriated him further, and he included the child in his strictures on Mrs Allan for her mercenary motive in marrying his foster-father. For her part, the strong-charactered lady, white with fury, made it clear that Poe was not a member of her family, but a mere pensioner of her husband's whose Christian philanthropy he had never ceased to insult. Mrs Allan and Edgar hated one another on sight as mortal enemies. Many of the calumnies against Poe as an ingrate drinker, gambler and dishonourable beggar derive from the strong-willed Mrs Allan's unconditional dislike and sharp tongue. For the moment she sent to the office for Mr Allan, adding to her message the statement that 'Edgar Poe and herself could not remain a day under the same roof.' Poe stubbornly stood upon his contested rights and remained pale and immovably seated in the parlour until he heard the approach of John Allan's walking stick. Then, as Allan entered the house, panic seized Poe and he left hurriedly by another door without ever confronting his irate 'Pa'.

Edgar went to the Mackenzies where, in a sympathetic atmosphere, he told them and Rosalie of his latest mortification at the hands of the Allans. Miss Valentine sent him some money, and no doubt the Mackenzies persuaded him to stay, but after the adoration of Baltimore Richmond was unbearable to the proud young man and he departed, leaving behind him the loud murmur of gossip. Rumour soon had it that he had forced himself past the Allan butler, gone to Mrs Allan's room where she lay in bed, a new-born infant in her helpless arms; there he 'reviled' her and the child until servants threw him out; after which he had stood like an insane schoolboy, throwing stones up at the house. Mrs Allan was only saved by her husband's arrival from the mad, drunk poet, the son of dissolute and immoral actors, incapable of the smallest gratitude for Mr Allan's unending generosity. The story was irresistible and took root in the other 'legend' of Edgar Poe, the mad, drunk ingrate, strongly promoted in Richmond and with her husband by the new Mrs Allan.

Back in Baltimore in the autumn of 1832 Mrs Clemm moved from Milk Street to 3 Amity Street, with Edgar as much a part of her family now as little Virginia. During the succeeding winter he worked at odd jobs, contributing to the family resources, while continuing work on the style of tale of which he had successfully placed five in the *Philadelphia Saturday Courier*. But his health was poor, there

The small house on Amity Street, Baltimore, into which the kind-hearted Maria Clemm moved in autumn 1832 with Edgar, Virginia, and the various other invalid members of her family.

was little interest in most of the tales he wrote and, even though he was inspired enough to work on his drama *Politian*, he had no reason to believe that he was approaching success. By early spring the Clemm household was in such despair that Poe wrote the last letter of his life to Allan, explaining that he was utterly without friends and employment, and must perish soon for want of help though he was neither idle nor addicted to any vice, nor had he offended society in any way deserving of such a fate. He concluded his letter, 'For God's sake pity me, and save me from destruction.' There was no reply to his appeal, though Allan noted the letter as a 'precious relict of the Blackest Heart and deepest ingratitude, alike destitute of honor and principle'.

That July Mr and Mrs Allan, Miss Valentine, two baby boys, two nurses, two drivers, five horses and two carriages set out from Richmond for Virginia Hot Springs. Allan was helpless with dropsy but enjoyed the fact that 'we made quite a little cavalcade'. He was at the height of his world with a wife, concubines, heirs and other children, slaves, horses and the envy of his neighbours to buoy up his spirits and help him to enjoy life a little longer. The knowledge that the diabolical Poe was rotting in Baltimore added sauce to it all. But Allan's pleasure in his cavalcade would have been somewhat less if he had known that in that same month Edgar had taken his first great stride towards international fame.

That same July the *Baltimore Saturday Visitor*, a well-read weekly edited by L. A. Wilmer, offered a $50 prize for the best tale, and $20 for the best poem submitted. The judges included J. H. B. Latrobe who left an account of the awards committee in session:

I noticed a small quarto bound book . . . the writing was in Roman characters – an imitation of printing. I remember that while reading the first page to myself . . . I said that we seemed at last to have a prospect of awarding the prize. . . . The first tale finished, I went to the second, then to the next and did not stop till I had gone through the volume. . . . There was genius in everything, no uncertain grammar, no feeble phraseology, no ill-placed punctuation, no worn truisms, no strong thought elaborated into weakness. Logic and imagination were combined in rare consistency. . . . There was an analysis of complicated facts – an unravelling of circumstantial evidence that won the lawyer judges – an account of accurate scientific knowledge that charmed . . . a pure classic diction that delighted all three.

At first *A Descent into the Maelstrom* was preferred, but finally the committee decided to award the first prize to *Ms Found in a Bottle*. Latrobe felt that Poe would have won the poetry prize if he had not already gained the prose award. On 19 October the *Visitor* published Poe's story with the following notice:

. . . Amongst the prose articles were many of various and distinguished merit but the singular force and beauty of those sent by the author of *The Tales of the Folio Club* leave us no

HARRY CLARKE

ABOVE A modern illustration by Wilfried Satty to *MS Found in a Bottle*, a story which won Poe a $50 prize.

OPPOSITE Illustration by Harry Clarke for *A Descent into the Maelstrom*, which was also acclaimed by the judges.

room for hesitation in that department, as well as to the gratification of the community, to publish the entire volume. These tales are eminently distinguished by a wild, vigorous, and poetical imagination, a rich style, a fertile invention, and varied and curious learning.

Signed John P. Kennedy
J. H. B. Latrobe
James H. Miller

It is difficult to appreciate today the importance of a $50 prize awarded by a provincial newspaper, but in 1833 there were few such acts of literary recognition. The attendant publicity was total confirmation for Poe's admirers and a clear signal to readers all over America that a new luminary had risen. The judges were all local men of influence, now committed to support Poe's reputation as a writer, and the Monday after the announcement of the award Poe called upon them severally to thank them. Latrobe left the following revealing account of the interview:

I was seated at my desk on the Monday following the publication of the tale, when a gentleman entered and introduced himself as the writer, saying that he came to thank me as one of the committee, for the award in his favor. Of this interview, the only one I ever had with Poe, my recollection is very distinct, indeed. He was if anything, below the middle size, and yet could not be described as a small man. His figure was remarkably good, and he carried himself erect and well, as one who had been trained to it. He was dressed in black, and his frock coat was buttoned to the throat, where it met the black stock, then almost universally worn. Not a particle of white was visible. Coat, hat, boots, and gloves had evidently seen their best days, but so far as mending and brushing go, everything had been done apparently, to make them presentable. On most men his clothes would have looked shabby and seedy, but there was something about this man that prevented one from criticizing his garments, and the details I have mentioned were only recalled afterwards. The impression made, however, was that the award in Mr. Poe's favor was not inopportune. Gentleman was written all over him. His manner was easy and quiet, and although he came to return thanks for what he regarded as deserving them, there was nothing obsequious in what he said or did. His features I am unable to describe in detail. His forehead was high, and remarkable for the great development at the temple. This was the characteristic of his head, which you noticed at once, and which I have never forgotten. The expression of his face was grave, almost sad, except when he become engaged in conversation, when it became animated and changeable. His voice I remember was very pleasing in its tone and well modulated, almost rhythmical, and his words were well chosen and unhesitating. . . . I asked him whether he was then occupied with any literary labor. He replied that he was then engaged on *A Voyage to the Moon*, and at once went into a somewhat learned disquisition upon the laws of gravity, the height of the earth's atmosphere, and capacities of baloons, warming in his speech as he proceeded. Presently speaking in the first person, he began the voyage . . . leaving the earth, there was a sudden bouleversement of the car and great confusion among its tenants. By this time the speaker had become so excited, spoke so rapidly, gesticulating much, that when the turn upsidedown took place, and he clapped his hands and stamped with his foot by way of emphasis, I was carried along with him.... When he had finished his description he apologized for his excitability which he laughed at himself. The conversation then turned upon other subjects, and soon afterward he took his leave....

Edgar, never slow to follow up encouragement, also began discussions with Mr Wilmer on the possibility of founding a literary magazine in Baltimore. It was the first of many such projects promoted by Poe, as both a financial and a critical power base. To the end of his life he planned 'the great American Periodical', but capital was as short for the project as was the stability needed by its would-be managing director. But Wilmer liked the project and was impressed by Poe's character and talent. In view of the scandalous rumours of Edgar's chronic drunkenness now being circulated by Mrs Allan and her Richmond allies, Wilmer's observations are worth recording:

... His time appeared to be constantly occupied by literary labors;... he lived in a very retired way with his aunt Mrs Clemm and his moral deportment as far as my observations extended was altogether correct.... In his youthful days Poe's personal appearance was delicate and effeminate but never sickly or ghastly, and I never saw him in any dress, which was not fashionably neat with some approximation to elegance. Indeed, I often wondered how he could continue to equip himself so handsomely, considering his pecuniary resources were generally scanty and precarious enough. My intercourse with Poe was almost continuous for weeks together.... His general habits at that time were strictly temperate, and but for one or two incidents I might have supposed him to be a member of the cold-water army....

The 'incidents' referred to were a cadets' supper at the Barnum Hotel and a solitary occasion on which Poe took rum with Wilmer. It would seem, therefore, that in this time of admiration by the literary circles of Baltimore, Poe felt no compulsion to drink. Success was a greater stimulant than alcohol, and Edgar was too much a connoisseur to spoil its rare flavour.

## *Death and Dreams*

Winters are a bad time for impoverished literary men. For Edgar they were always as long and dangerous as a voyage by foot to the North Pole. Even after the success of 1833 the winter was long and hard, warmed only by a flicker of interest from Carey, Lea and Carey, Poe's Philadelphia publishers, in *The Tales of the Folio Club*, and the publication of one of them, *The Visionary*, in *Godey's Lady's Book*. The $50 prize had disappeared into the chronic exigencies of the Clemm household as quickly as the scraps Mrs Clemm collected in her great basket. She tried to add to the family

Silhouette of John Allan, who died at Richmond in 1834.

income by occasional dame-teaching, and her needle never stopped working for pennies. Somehow the strange family in the little brick house on Amity Street survived another hard winter, brightened only by Virginia's precocious emergence into young womanhood and the strengthening of the bond between her and Edgar.

Through his intelligence sources Poe heard in February 1834 that John Allan was undoubtedly dying. He decided to make one last attack upon the Richmond castle before the ogre departed for good. He would, somehow or other, appeal to the old man and secure his 'rights', eloquently pleading the needs, nay, the demands of his genius, pointing to his latest success and his imminent prospects. Surely a man on his deathbed would forgive one who had been as close as any true son could be. As always in his fantasies of his relationship with Allan, Edgar was forgetful of the facts, especially his last violent encounter with Mrs Allan. Otherwise he would surely have found it quite beyond reason that Allan, his wife deeply antipathetic, his true heirs crying in the nursery, would ever again soften towards Edgar, that 'Blackest Heart'.

Arriving at the Allan house Edgar forced his way in and ran up to Allan's large front bedroom. John Allan was lying helpless with dropsy, his cane beside him, propped with pillows, reading a newspaper. But his merchant eyes were still sharp and shrewd, and when they recognized the black-dressed Edgar, an unwelcome ghost in the doorway, Allan reacted as if violently attacked, lifting his cane and waving it at Edgar and cursing. Mrs Allan and the servants rushed to the room, and Poe was bundled out while Allan exhausted himself shouting so violently that even Edgar finally realized the profundity of the old man's hatred, and the totality of the loss of any prospects he might ever have had. When Allan died a month or so later there was no mention at all of Edgar in his will, not even a curse or a reproach. The document, confusedly written, was to be much contested, but with it Poe's unwilling 'Pa', that hated, feared and apparently immovable rock on which he had so often been washed aground, was certainly sunk for ever so far as his foster-son was concerned. Edgar would never again need to compose a wheedling, pitiful, hopeful, begging letter to the Merchant of Richmond.

Poe now threw himself upon the patronage of Mr Kennedy, one of his literary judges, of whose good opinion he was confident:

Dr Sir, – I have a favor to beg of you which I thought it better to ask in writing, because, sincerely, I had not the courage to ask it in person. I am indeed well aware that I have no claim whatever to your attention, and that even the manner of my introduction to your notice was, at best equivocal. Since the day you first saw me my situation in life has altered materially. At that time I looked forward to the inheritance of a large fortune, and in the meantime was in receipt of an annuity sufficient for my support. This was allowed to me by a gentleman of Virginia (Mr Jno Allan) who adopted me at the age of two years (both my parents being dead) and who, until lately always treated me with the affection of a father. But a second marriage on his part, and I daresay many follies on my own at length ended in a quarrel between us. He is now dead and has left me nothing. I am thrown entirely upon my own resources with no profession, and very few friends. Worse than all this, I am at length penniless. In deed no circumstances less urgent would have induced me to risk your friendship by troubling you with my distresses. But I could not help thinking that if my situation was stated – as you could state it – to Carey and Lea, they might be led to aid me with a small sum in consideration of my Ms. now in their hands. This would relieve my immediate wants, and I could then look forward more confidently to better days. At all events receive the assurance of my gratitude for what you have already done.

Most respy, yr obt. st.,
Edgar Allan Poe.

Mr Kennedy responded like a prince. He encouraged Carey and Lea, who, though they were unwilling to risk an advance, sold one of the *Tales* to the *Souvenir* at a dollar a page, totalling $15, and hoped that other stories would win similar serialization rewards. Kennedy's support and encouragement were constant. Poe asked him to help him obtain a job as a schoolmaster. Kennedy replied at once positively and with an invitation to dinner. Poe sent Virginia to him with the following note:

Dr Sir, – Your kind invitation to dinner today has wounded me to the quick. I cannot come – and for reasons of the most humiliating nature in my personal appearance. You may conceive my deep mortification in making this disclosure to you – but it was necessary. If you will be my friend so far as to loan me $20, I will call on you tomorrow – otherwise it will be impossible and I must submit to my fate.

Sincerely yours, E. A. Poe

The *Southern Literary Messenger* building on 15th and Main Streets, Richmond. Poe started working for its editor, Thomas Wylkes White, in the summer of 1835.

Kennedy was so touched that not only did he help Poe with this and other 'loans' and frequent invitations to meals, but he also lent him a horse, a generous lift to his confidence. He also strongly recommended him to Thomas Wylkes White, now editing the Richmond *Southern Literary Messenger*:

Baltimore, Apr. 13 1835

Dear Sir, – Poe did right in referring to me. He is very clever with his pen – classical and scholar-like. He wants experience and direction, but I have no doubt he can be made very useful to you. And, poor fellow, he is very poor. I told him to write something for every number of your magazine, and that you might find it to your advantage to give him some permanent employ. . . . The young fellow is highly imaginative and a little *terrific*. He is at work upon a tragedy, but I have turned him to drudging upon whatever may make money. . . .

White agreed with Kennedy about Poe's potential value to the *Messenger* and encouraged him to contribute correspondence, stories, reviews and articles. He even suggested that Poe might join the staff, to which Poe replied 'I have been desirous for some time past of paying a visit to Richmond, and would be glad of any reasonable excuse of so doing.' Apart from Poe's memories of unhappy, painful and violent scenes in the Allan house, he still had strong positive ties with Richmond. There were young ladies there whom he wished to look up again; his sister and the Mackenzies would always welcome him; and he had an understandable desire to flaunt his new status as a writer before the snobbish friends of the late John Allan. But for the moment Richmond must wait, for the *Messenger* could not take him on yet, his grandmother was dying and, in the late spring of 1835, Poe himself was 'too unwell to go abroad ... so ill ... in a state of complete exhaustion....'

The 'complete exhaustion' from which Poe suffered at this time must be carefully considered. From 1831 to 1834 there are few records of his life and activities, and for a large part of that time none whatsoever. He seems to have become a recluse, totally committed to the 'drudging upon whatever may make money' to which Kennedy had advised him to turn his talents and energies. Yet even if intense concentration upon writing and poor health are to account for Edgar's absence from society for such an extended period, they cannot totally explain it. He had stopped drinking almost entirely, and even if an extended depressed phase could account for his reclusiveness, Poe's depressions alternated with periods of high manic excitement. But through these years there are few accounts of the violent, impulsive man who thrust himself, uninvited, into his dying foster-father's presence. Certainly Poe had a 'weak heart', certified later by a doctor and a nurse, and possibly its enervating effects were especially marked at this time, yet a more dominant fact is that the excessive use of laudanum renders the heart's action feeble, and the pulse small, irregular and slow. It also induces drowsiness and, eventually, a sense of 'complete exhaustion'. Yet the clearest evidence of Poe's increasing use of opium through these years is to be found in his work. *The Tales of the Folio Club* are full of opiate fantasies, as Baudelaire recognized years later, as he wept over stories which embodied his own dreams. Hervey Allen, Poe's most exhaustive, sympathetic, yet unbiased biographer, notes: 'Such stories as *Ligeia* and *Berenice* ... provide not only direct references to the drug, but the imagery, the irrational associations, and the very use of words [which] are characteristic. To those who have no knowledge or familiarity with the effects of opium, and they are, of course, the majority, the evidence may seem insufficient; to those who have, the turning of these pages tells an irrefutable tale.' In *Berenice* Poe described the effects of 'this monomania, if I must so term it', very clearly:

To muse for long unwearied hours with my attention riveted to some frivolous device on the margin, or in the typography of a book; to become absorbed for the better part of a summer's day, in a quaint shadow falling aslant upon the tapestry, or upon the door; to

Berenice, like Morella and Ligeia in Poe's fiction, and like his mother and Virginia in reality, was one of his tragic, consumptive heroines. Illustration by Harry Clarke.

lose myself for an entire night in watching the steady flame of a lamp, or the embers of a fire; to dream away whole days over the perfume of a flower; to repeat monotonously some common word, until the sound, by dint of frequent repetition, ceased to convey any idea whatever to the mind; to lose all sense of motion or physical existence, by means of absolute bodily quiescence long and obstinately persevered in – such were a few of the most common and least pernicious vagaries by a condition of the mental faculties, not, indeed, altogether unparalleled, but certainly bidding defiance to anything like analysis or explanation.

Though a dependence upon opium could and would be kept more secret than a drinking habit, Poe was seen taking it in Philadelphia; in 1847 he attempted suicide with laudanum; and Rosalie Poe recorded the fact that in 1848, at Fordham, he 'begged for morphine'. In 1884 Dr John Carter of Baltimore, whose brother had treated Poe in 1849, wrote: 'I may state, in a matter of so leading importance, that I incline to the view that Poe began the use of drugs in Baltimore, that his periods of abstinence from liquor were periods of at least moderate indulgence in opium....' Poe's abstinence from liquor is very much indicative of the availability of opium which, when taken with care in measured and controlled quantities, would have assisted in the release of those powerful, frequently necrophilic, fantasies which came to be Poe's most individual contribution to literature. Certainly the years 1831–5 saw the production of a great *corpus* of extraordinary work, all of which has the unmistakable opiate quality. But opium markedly reduces sexual drive, and Hervey Allen considers that it is at this time that Poe, capable of intense physical passion towards Mary Devereaux in 1832, was much lowered in his sexuality, and was beginning to show the impotence symptoms so often deduced by students of his pathology. So reduced and aberrant had he become that, in 1835, he was able to marry the thirteen-year-old Virginia. It was a marriage which, if it ever was consummated, certainly remained virgin until some years later.

Many admirers of Poe's work have felt it necessary to deny his use of opium, just as they have found it necessary to argue that he was neither an alcoholic, nor a dipsomaniac, nor possessed of a morbid love of death and the dead. Possibly some mistaken notion that his afflictions somehow lessened Poe's virtues as an artist has compelled commentators to defend him against his 'vices'. But a moralistic attitude towards artists, which urges that they are better equipped for doing good work by being 'good' men, has always been difficult to sustain against the facts. Poe was an extremely disordered personality, but though his disorders are the manifest substance of his work they are not its art and craft. Yet it is impossible to understand truly the content of his work without making an approach to the psychopathology embodied in it. If in the process one discovers that, quite often, great artists are disordered and unlikeable personalities, the only conclusion one may reasonably come to is that it is better to be the recipients of their work than the injured victims of their temperaments.

# CHAPTER FIVE
# 1835–1842

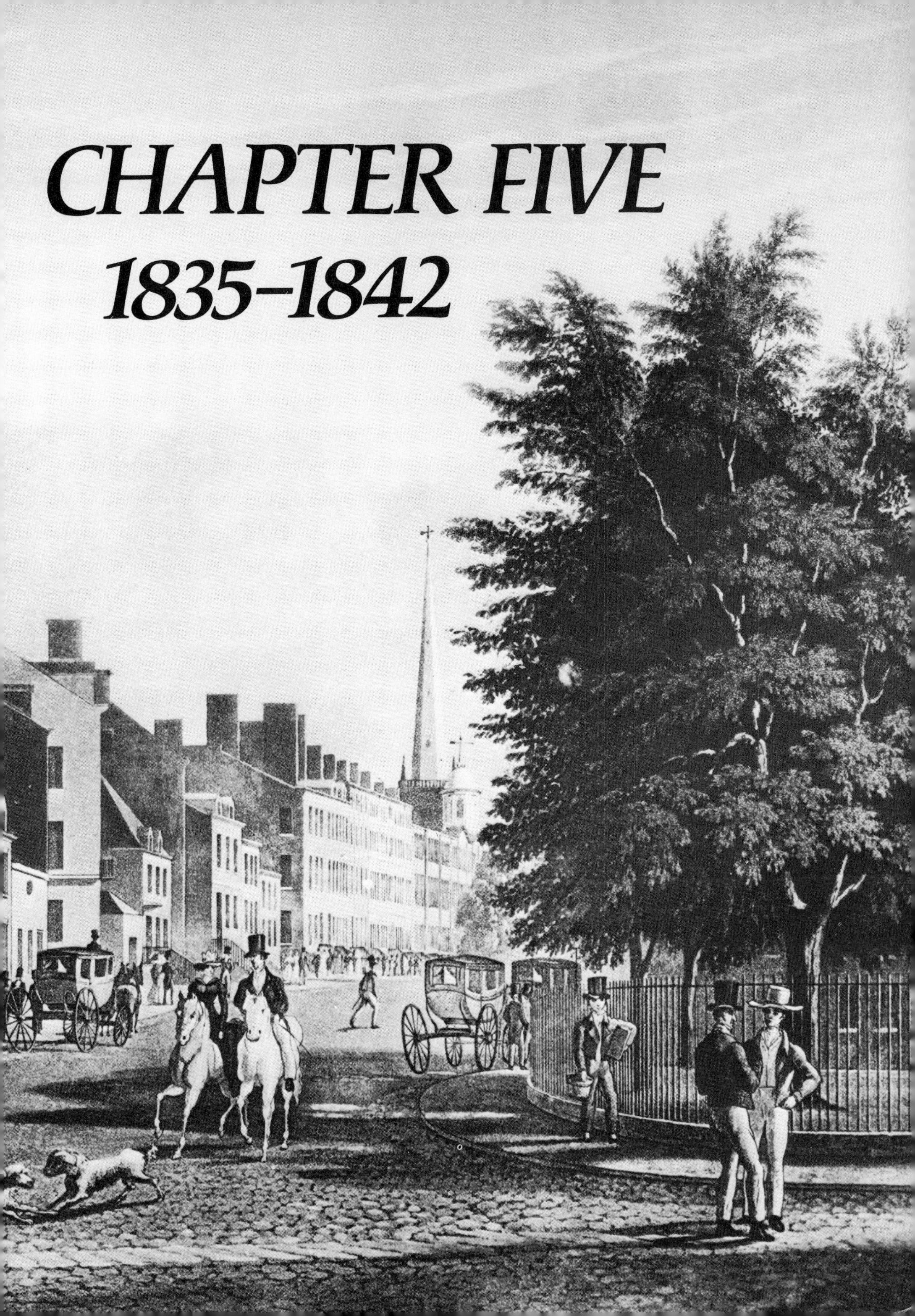

## *Marriage in Secret*

In August 1835 Edgar Poe returned to Richmond to work for Thomas Wylkes White on the *Southern Literary Messenger*. His figure, black as a raven, shabbily but carefully dressed in Byronic style, his haunted blue-grey eyes superbly intelligent above a mouth twisted with pain and bitterness, was noteworthy upon the quiet streets of Richmond. The brilliant local poet was home again, and his scandalous 'legend' and reputation were talked about by many who found his writing far above their heads. At first he stayed with the Mackenzies where Aunt Nancy, now comfortably off with $300 a year and her board and laundry provided under John Allan's will, came to see him and to bestow small presents. Edgar kept his distance from the sharp-tongued widow in the Allan mansion, and soon he moved to the greater privacy of lodgings with a Mrs Poore on Bank Street. From there he lived the literary life, with invitations to dine and recite, and platonic flirtations including one with Mr White's daughter Eliza, who had 'remarkable eyes' and could 'recite elegantly'. But Poe was already more interested in unavailable loves than in those who might be courted and won. His painfully lost Elmira, now Mrs A. Barrett Shelton, was in Richmond and Edgar made certain she knew he was back. Shortly after his return the *Messenger* published a poem signed 'Sylvio', intended to make Elmira as unhappily nostalgic as possible, Mr Shelton extremely uncomfortable, and stimulate talk among the knowing:

TO SARAH

The silvery streamlet gurgling on,
The mock-bird chirping on the thorn,
    Remind me, love, of thee.
They seem to whisper thoughts of love,
As thou didst when the stars above
    Witnessed thy vows to me;–

PREVIOUS PAGES *Broad Way from the Bowling Green*, an aquatint of New York by William Bennett.

OPPOSITE The December 1835 issue of the *Southern Literary Messenger*, announcing Poe's arrival on the staff.

# SOUTHERN LITERARY MESSENGER.

VOL. II. RICHMOND, DECEMBER, 1835. No. 1.

T. W. WHITE, PROPRIETOR. FIVE DOLLARS PER ANNUM.


## PUBLISHER'S NOTICE.

☞ The gentleman, referred to in the ninth number of the Messenger, as filling its editorial chair, retired thence with the eleventh number; and the intellectual department of the paper is now under the conduct of the Proprietor, assisted by a gentleman of distinguished literary talents. Thus seconded, he is sanguine in the hope of rendering the second volume which the present number commences, *at least* as deserving of support as the former was: nay, if he reads aright the tokens which are given him of the future, it teems with even richer banquets for his readers, than they have hitherto enjoyed at his board.

Some of the contributors, whose effusions have received the largest share of praise from critics, and (what is better still) have been read with most pleasure by that larger, unsophisticated class, whom Sterne loved for reading, and being pleased "they knew not why, and care not wherefore"—may be expected to continue their favors. Among these, we hope to be pardoned for singling out the name of Mr. EDGAR A. POE; not with design to make any invidious distinction, but because such a mention of him finds numberless precedents in the journals on every side, which have rung the praises of his uniquely original vein of imagination, and of humorous, delicate satire. We wish that decorum did not forbid our specifying other names also, which would afford ample guarantee for the fulfilment of larger promises than ours: but it may not be; and of our other contributors, all we can say is—"by their fruits ye shall know them."

It is a part of our present plan, to insert *all original communications* as editorial; that is, simply to omit the words "For the Southern Literary Messenger" at the head of such articles:—unless the contributor shall especially desire to have that caption prefixed, or there be something which requires it in the nature of the article itself. *Selected articles*, of course, will bear some appropriate token of their origin.

With this brief salutation to patrons and readers, we gird up ourselves for entering upon the work of another year, with zeal and energy increased, by the recollection of kindness, and by the hopes of still greater success.

---

## SKETCHES OF THE HISTORY

### AND PRESENT CONDITION OF TRIPOLI, WITH SOME ACCOUNTS OF THE OTHER BARBARY STATES.

NO. IX.—(Continued.)

of Algiers, large quantities of grain on credit, for the subsistence of its armies in Italy, and the supply of the Southern Department where a great scarcity then prevailed. The creditors endeavored to have their claims on this account satisfied by the Directory, but that incapable and rapacious Government had neither the principle to admit, nor the ability to discharge such demands; every species of chicanery was in consequence employed by it in evading them, until the rupture with Turkey produced by the expedition to Egypt placing the Barbary States either really or apparently at war with the French Republic, a pretext was thus afforded for deferring their settlement indefinitely. Under the Consular *regime* however, a treaty of peace was concluded with Algiers on the 17th of December 1801, by the thirteenth article of which, the Government of each State engaged to cause payment to be made of all debts due by itself or its subjects to the Government or subjects of the other; the former political and commercial relations between the two countries were re-established, and the Dey restored to France the territories and privileges called the *African Concessions*, which had been seized by him on the breaking out of the war. This treaty was ratified by the Dey on the 5th of April 1802, and after examination of the claims on both sides, the French Government acknowledged itself debtor for a large amount to the Jewish mercantile house of Bacri and Busnach of Algiers, as representing the African creditors. Of the sum thus acknowledged to be due, only a very small portion was paid, and the Dey Hadji Ali seeing no other means of obtaining the remainder, in 1809 seized upon the *Concessions;* they were however of little value to France at that time, when her flag was never seen in the Mediterranean, and their confiscation merely served as a pretext for withholding farther payment. In 1813, when the star of Napoleon began to wane, and he found it necessary to assume at least the appearance of honesty, he declared that measures would be taken for the adjustment of the Algerine claims; but he fell without redeeming his promise, and on the distribution of his spoils, the Jewish merchants had not interest enough to obtain their rightful portion, which amounted to fourteen millions of francs.

Upon the return of the Bourbons to the throne of France, the government of that country became desirous to renew its former intercourse with the Barbary States, and to regain its ancient establishments and privileges in their territories, which were considered important from political as well as commercial motives. For this purpose, M. Deval a person who was educated in the East and had been long attached to the French Em-

The gentle zephyr floating by,
In chorus to my pensive sigh,
Recalls the hour of bliss,
When from thy balmy lips I drew
Fragrance as sweet as Hermia's dew,
And left the first fond kiss....

Edgar and Elmira met only once, at a reception to which Poe knew she was going. He waited. She came up the stairs alone, the afternoon sun catching her auburn hair. It seemed (she remembered later), as if there were nothing else in the room except the shadows of longing and reproach. Then Mr Shelton arrived, and, immediately recognizing the danger, took his wife home at once. Poe did not see his lost Lenore again till ten years later.

To earn his $10 a week writing every kind of material for the *Messenger*'s 700 subscribers, Poe went to the office on the corner of Main and 15th Streets daily. It was not the first time he had worked in that area, for next door were the premises of Ellis and Allan. As Poe sat playing editor during Mr White's constant absences, he must have missed John Allan in his office nearby, waxing furious over Edgar's success, for, no doubt about it, successful he was. The circulation figures of the *Messenger*, the surest indicator of success, were rising, speeded by the distinction of Poe's work and the publicity surrounding his personality. In a few months the *Messenger* gained several thousand new readers, a startling achievement for a young journalist in his first editorial job at $520 per annum. But the intensive activity made great demands upon Poe's erratic energy resources. In 1835 alone he published in the paper nine stories, four poems, extracts from his drama *Politian*, critical notes, editorials, and thirty-seven reviews. In order to sustain the hectic social and writing activities demanded by the *Messenger* Edgar required a support, a stimulant. Opium could not help him perform these new duties; she was the private addiction, the companion of the unending nights, the queen of darkness with her court of curious dreams. For the extrovert world of the *Messenger* the feasible support was the familiar, easily available, and socially acceptable crutch – liquor. After three years of almost total abstinence Poe began to drink again. Without Muddy and Sis to support him with their unflagging love and adoration, the drinking quickly became habitual, its after-effects blackened by remorse and anxiety for the plight of the loved ones back in Baltimore to whom he could not, 'success' though he was, offer the slightest support and comfort. By September Poe was wretched, as an appealing letter to John Kennedy, his generous patron and friend, reveals:

Richmond, Sept. 11.

Dr Sir, – I received a letter yesterday from Dr Miller in which he tells me you are in town [Baltimore]. I hasten therefore to write you, – and express by letter what I have always found impossible to express orally – my deep sense of gratitude for your frequent and effectual assistance and kindness. Through your influence Mr White has been induced to employ me in assisting him with the Editorial duties of his Magazine – at a salary of $520 per annum. The situation is agreeable to me for many reasons – but alas! it appears to me that nothing can now give me pleasure – or the slightest gratification. Excuse me, my Dear Sir, if in this letter you find much incoherency. My feelings at this moment are pitiable indeed. I am suffering under a depression of spirits such as I have never felt before. I have struggled in vain against the influence of this melancholy – you will believe me when I say that I am still miserable in spite of the great improvement in my circumstances. I say you will believe me, and for this simple reason, that a man who is writing for effect does not write thus. My heart is open before you – if it be worth reading, read it. I am wretched, and know not why. Console me – for you can. But let it be quickly – or it will be too late. Write me immediately. Convince me that it is worth one's while, that it is necessary to live, and you will prove yourself my friend. Persuade me to do what is right. I do not mean this – I do not mean that you should consider what I now write you a jest – oh pity me! for I feel that my words are incoherent – but I will recover myself. You will not fail to see that I am suffering under a depression of spirits which will ruin me should it be long continued. Write me then, and quickly. Urge me to do what is right. Your words will have more weight with me than the words of others – for you were my friend when no one else was. Fail not – as you value your peace of mind hereafter.

E. A. Poe

Behind Poe's suicidal agony was the fear that Virginia, his little Sis, was declining in his absence, and would be lost to him for ever, like all the women he had ever loved. As she entered adolescence the bright girl was developing the 'delicate' characteristics of the mysterious, fashionable and romantic disease by which Poe was haunted all his life. Her complexion showed the waxen whiteness with high colour of the cheeks and unnatural largeness of the eyes, the typical appearance of the heroines of his writings. Virginia was maturing into a pawn of the Red Death like Eleanora, Ligeia, Eulalie, Morella and Berenice:

Berenice and I were cousins, and we grew up together in my paternal halls. Yet differently we grew – I, ill of health, and buried in gloom – she, agile, graceful, and overflowing with energy.... O gorgeous yet fantastic beauty! O sylph amid the shrubberies of Arnheim.... And then – then all is mystery and terror, and a tale which should not be told. Disease, a fatal disease, fell like the simoom upon her frame; and even while I gazed upon her, the spirit of change swept over her, pervading her mind, her habits, and her character, and, in a manner the most subtle and terrible, disturbing even the identity of her person....

In *Morella* the mother and daughter are unified; 'I shudder at its too perfect identity.... My *child*, and my *love*, were the designations usually promoted by a father's affection, and the rigid seclusion of her days precluded all other intercourse.' Mother and daughter are finally unified, the one replacing the other in Morella's tomb.

ABOVE Illustration by Harry Clarke for *Morella*: 'The earth grew dark, and its figures passed by me, like flitting shadow, and among them all I beheld only – Morella.'

OPPOSITE The death of Ligeia, by Wilfried Satty: 'And now, as if exhausted with emotion, she suffered her white arms to fall, and returned solemnly to her bed of death.'

Haunted by his archetypal loves, all rapidly becoming invested in the maturing person of Virginia Clemm, Poe fretted and worried and drank. Kennedy's advice was positive enough, but showed little comprehension of Edgar's psychological problems:

Baltimore, Sept. 19, 1835

My Dear Poe, I am sorry to see you in such a plight as your letter shows you in. – It is strange that just at the time when everybody is praising you and when Fortune has begun to smile upon your hitherto wretched circumstances you should be invaded by these villainous blue devils. – It belongs, however, to your age and temper to be thus buffeted, but be assured it only wants a little resolution to master the adversary forever, – Rise early, live generously, and make cheerful acquaintances and I have no doubt you will send these misgivings to the Devil. – You will doubtless do well henceforth in literature and add to your comforts as well as to your reputation which, it gives me great pleasure to tell you, is everywhere rising in popular esteem. Can't you write some farces after the manner of the French Vaudevilles? If you can – (and I think you can) you may turn them to excellent account by selling them to the managers in New York. I wish you would give your thoughts to this suggestion....

But Edgar had already left Richmond for Baltimore, compelled to resolve the anxieties which tortured him. In his absence Mr White wrote confirming the sack in the kindest possible way, simultaneously offering to take him back if he gave up drinking:

Richmond, Sept. 29, 1835

Dear Edgar, – Would that it were in my power to unbosom myself to you in language such as I could on the present occasion, wish myself master of. I cannot do it – and therefore must be content to speak to you in my plain way.

That you are sincere in all your promises, I firmly believe. But Edgar, when you once again tread these streets, I have my fears that your resolves would fall through, – and that you would sip the juice, even till it stole away your senses. Rely on your own strength and you are gone! Look to your Maker for help, and you are safe.

How much I regretted parting with you, is unknown to anyone on this earth, except myself. I was attached to you – and am still, and willingly would I say return, if I did not dread the hour of separation very shortly again.

If you could make yourself contented to take up your quarters in my family, or any other private family, where liquor is not used, I should think there were hopes for you. – But, if you go to a tavern, or to any other place where it is used at table, you are not safe. I speak from experience.

You have fine talents, Edgar, – and you ought to have them respected as well as yourself. Learn to respect yourself, and you will very soon find that you are respected. Separate yourself from the bottle, and bottle companions, forever!

Tell me if you can and will do so – and let me hear that it is your fixed purpose never to yield to temptation.

If you should come to Richmond again, and again be an assistant in my office, it must be expressly understood by us that all engagements on my part would be dissolved, the moment you get drunk.

No man is safe who drinks before breakfast! No man can do so, and attend to business properly....

I am your true Friend
T. W. White.

E. A. Poe, Esq.

A few days before Mr White's letter arrived, Edgar dealt with his problems in characteristically compulsive manner.

On 22 September 1835, Poe married his thirteen-year-old cousin secretly in St Paul's Episcopal Church, Baltimore. Mrs Clemm was the only witness and the minister did not enter the occasion in the parish register. The only proof of the clandestine marriage is in the city licences record and in Mrs Clemm's assurance that it happened. She had always wanted Edgar for a son and perhaps felt the marriage to be more the achievement of her own fantasy than a radical change in Virginia's status. Furthermore, she now needed the protection and small income which Edgar, with his new-found success and 'stability', would offer. He, for his part, wanted to feel that he was totally committed to the most important people in his life. It is unlikely that any of the three principals in the ceremony consciously considered the sexual implications. It was a confirmation of the family relationships between the Clemms and Poe; a consummation of a 'sister-love' too young to threaten Edgar's sexual uncertainty. At the same time it compounded into Poe's disturbed needs the 'pale suggestion of incest'. Thus, with his extraordinary requirements secured for the moment, Edgar felt 'safe' enough to give up drinking before breakfast, and return to the Richmond *Messenger*. Muddy and Sis were soon to follow, the three taking up residence together, for all the world a devoted mother with her brilliant son and sweet, gentle and curiously pale daughter.

## *Marriage in Richmond*

Edgar Poe, ostensibly still a bachelor, moved into Mrs Yarrington's two-storey brick house with green shutters on Bank and 11th Streets in Richmond, with his aunt and little cousin as dependants. Virginia was a pale, good-natured schoolgirl, small for her age, plump but not especially pretty, with a child's simplicity and the gentle manner which she kept all her short life. Her playmate was Rosalie Poe, now twenty-five but mentally still thirteen. Rosalie adoringly followed 'Buddie' (as Edgar was now called by his family) about, and she and Virginia played like sisters at the Mackenzies or at Mrs Yarrington's. But Mrs Mackenzie was somewhat shocked to observe the 'abandon' with which Virginia greeted 'Buddie' when he came one day to fetch her home.

Whenever Edgar could take time out from his work, he was happy to be with Sis, teaching her French, the harp and to sing bird-like trills. Resettled in the *Messenger* office, he had drink under control, and was comparatively affluent partly through his own efforts, but also because of the support of distant wealthy relatives whose assistance he had solicited 'to help Mrs Clemm'. Because Virginia could not be relied upon to conceal her 'abandon' indefinitely, and since Poe had now secured the assistance of his relatives, (who would have disapproved of the union), a second and unsecret marriage was now arranged. The bond was signed in the Hustings Court of the City of Richmond on 16 May 1836, where it was witnessed on oath that 'Virginia E. Clemm is of the full age of twenty-one years.' Sis was, in fact, thirteen years, nine months and one day old, and could only have been taken for a woman of twenty-one on the most earnest assurances of her mother. That assurance was given and convinced Richmond, though many thought the liaison 'queer'. The wedding party was

A *carte-de-visite* photograph of Poe's sister, Rosalie, taken late in life. As a grown woman Rosalie still retained the mental age of a child.

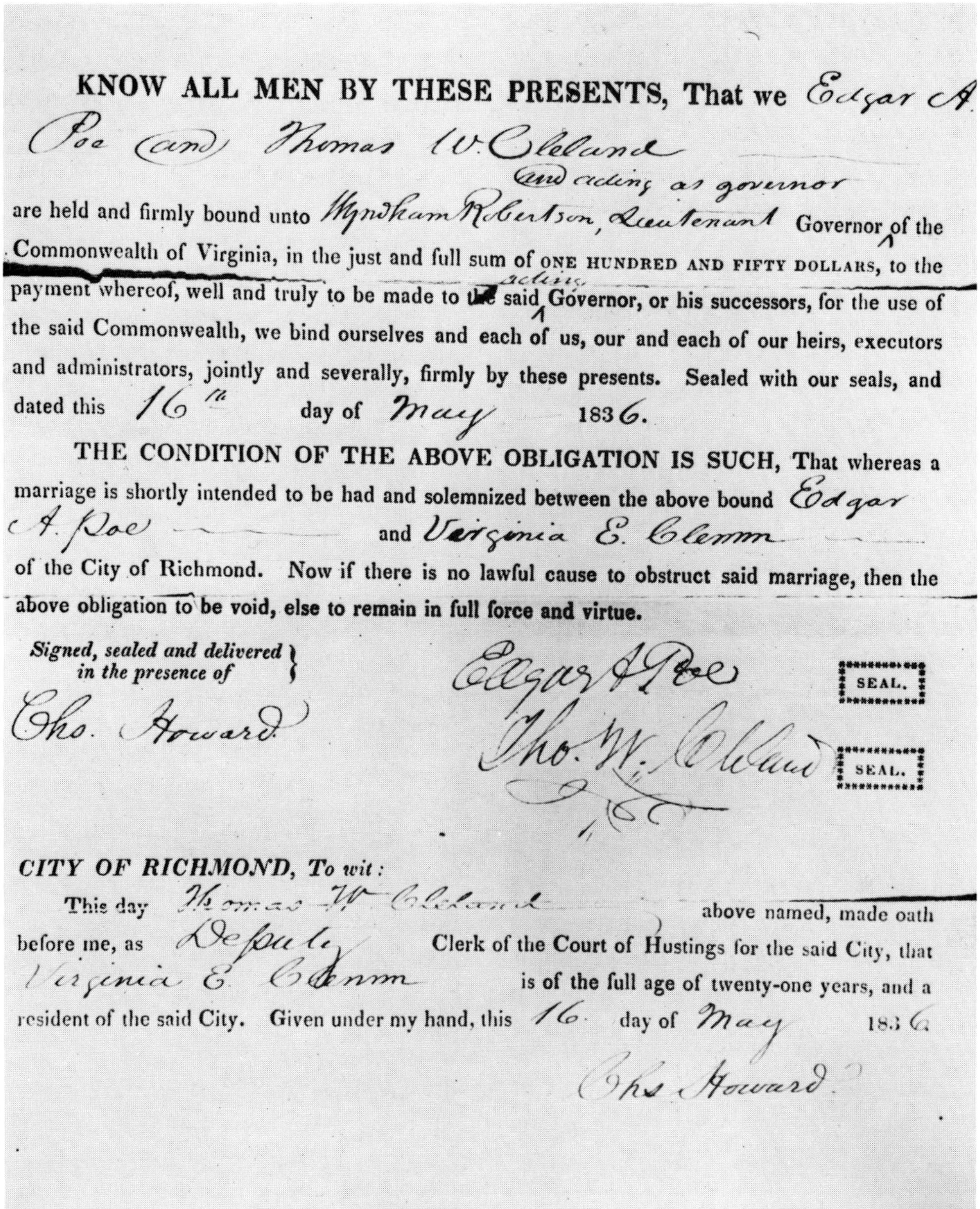

**KNOW ALL MEN BY THESE PRESENTS,** That we Edgar A Poe and Thomas W. Cleland are held and firmly bound unto Wyndham Robertson, Lieutenant Governor and acting as governor of the Commonwealth of Virginia, in the just and full sum of ONE HUNDRED AND FIFTY DOLLARS, to the payment whereof, well and truly to be made to the said acting Governor, or his successors, for the use of the said Commonwealth, we bind ourselves and each of us, our and each of our heirs, executors and administrators, jointly and severally, firmly by these presents. Sealed with our seals, and dated this 16th day of May 1836.

**THE CONDITION OF THE ABOVE OBLIGATION IS SUCH,** That whereas a marriage is shortly intended to be had and solemnized between the above bound Edgar A. Poe and Virginia E. Clemm of the City of Richmond. Now if there is no lawful cause to obstruct said marriage, then the above obligation to be void, else to remain in full force and virtue.

*Signed, sealed and delivered in the presence of*
Chs. Howard

Edgar A Poe [SEAL.]
Tho. W. Cleland [SEAL.]

***CITY OF RICHMOND,*** *To wit:*

This day Thomas W. Cleland above named, made oath before me, as Deputy Clerk of the Court of Hustings for the said City, that Virginia E. Clemm is of the full age of twenty-one years, and a resident of the said City. Given under my hand, this 16 day of May 1836

Chs Howard

The marriage bond of Poe and Virginia Clemm, dated 16 May 1836. Virginia was stated to be 'of the full age of twenty-one years', but was in fact only thirteen.

attended by Mr White and his daughter, Mr Cleland who had witnessed the marriage, the printers from the *Messenger* and other friends, together with the Rev. Amasa Converse, the Presbyterian minister who had officiated at the afternoon ceremony in the parlour of the Yarrington house. Jane Foster, a friend of Mrs Yarrington's, was present and gave an account to her niece who passed it on to Hervey Allen:

Virginia was dressed in a travelling dress and a white hat with a veil; Poe was, as usual, in a black suit and the omnipresent black stock. Jane Foster, who was herself scarcely more than a child, remembered the very youthful appearance of Virginia. The nuptial scene was reflected in a looking glass on the parlor wall, and little Miss Foster was surprised to note that the mirror did not show Virginia to be any older when she passed out than when she walked in. Marriage, she was sure in her naïve way, would magically remedy the contrast between the little bride and the mature bridegroom, for Poe was twenty-seven. The Reverend Amasa Converse remarked that the bride had a pleasing air, but did seem young. Mrs Clemm he noted as 'being polished, dignified, and agreeable in her bearing' and that she gave Virginia away 'freely'. In the parlor after the ceremony Mrs Clemm was in her element when her fellow boarders were called in while the happy event was announced, and wine and cake were served. It was doubtless then that the Reverend Amasa noted that the widow was 'agreeable in her bearing'. . . . After the felicitation, a hack was called to the door, and Virginia and Edgar drove off together on their honeymoon.

The Poes spent their official honeymoon at the house of Mr Haines, a journalist in Petersburg, where they were entertained at a round of parties, Virginia's charming appearance and Poe's brilliant conversation making the couple a great success. They returned at the end of the month with Edgar's status sufficiently enhanced for Mr White to promise him a rise in salary to $20 a week 'after November'.

That summer was idyllic, a 'Valley of the Many-Colored Grass' as Poe described it in *Eleonora*:

She whom I loved in youth, and of whom I now pen calmly and distinctly these remembrances, was the sole daughter of the only sister of my mother long departed. Eleonora was the name of my cousin. We had always dwelled together, beneath a tropical sun, in the Valley of the Many-Colored Grass. No unguided footstep ever came upon the vale; for it lay far away among a range of giant hills. . . . Thus it was that we lived all alone, knowing nothing of the world without the valley, – I, and my cousin, and her mother.

The idyll was possible because of Virginia's youth and 'sister' quality, and because she was of the tubercular type which fascinated Poe. Large- and liquid-eyed with a high forehead (not unlike his own), and hair of the raven darkness he adored, she typified the immature but ageless women of his fantasies. Though he was to court many other women, he was always 'faithful' to Sis, yet it is doubtful whether he ever had physical relations with her. At first he 'respected' her youth, and turned his drives upon training her to embody even more perfectly his ideal. That 'respect' continued until Virginia grew actually ill, whereupon it was elevated to 'duty'. It would not occur to the totally innocent Virginia that there was something strange about a husband who never attempted to possess her physically. On the contrary, he would be the dearer and gentler for it. As for Muddy, she always insisted that Eddy had loved Sis only 'as a dear cousin'. Poe's biographers argue about the reasons for the non-consummation of his marriage with Virginia, but while some favour the explanation that opium rendered him impotent, and others consider that this 'impotence' was psychic in origin, the result of a fixation upon his mother, and others yet again accept Marie Bonaparte's theory that he was necrophilic, there is little doubt among them that his ten years of marriage to Virginia remained celibate.

Poe was, of course, aware of mysteries and profound contradictions in himself. His depressions and the 'emptiness' which accompanied them seemed to him a form of deep 'mourning' for a lost loved one who had been lowered into a death which always remained for him a dubious condition. In his stories the dead raise the lids of their coffins, or sit up and talk, or are discovered to be in a state of suspended animation, or, as phantoms, hold colloquies on the future of the world. For Poe to feel at all secure the loved one must be with him, constantly available and totally devoted. It was as if the soon-to-be dead sister–mother wife was already, in essence, a corpse sustaining a post-mortem marriage with her brother–son husband. At first Poe's marriage was an opium dream of timeless contradictions without the help of laudanum. But soon the drug itself was needed to fill the 'emptiness' which still depressed him from time to time. Under opium, he could stay at home, be nursed and dream of fulfilling his horrific needs. To quote Princess Bonaparte again: 'Opium, in fact, established this perfect compromise. It intensely evoked the object on which his grim desires were fixated while depriving him of power to unleash his dire instincts, for his love object remained imaginary while he, the subject, continued impotent and inert before it. Opium, for him, thus opened the dream world of inaction in which our worst instincts may find satisfaction.'

With the autumn Edgar was deep into the social and editorial life of the *Messenger*. He had written to Kennedy with a new editorial adroitness:

> Our *Messenger* is thriving beyond all expectations, and I myself have every prospect of success. It is our design to issue, as soon as possible, a number of the Magazine consisting entirely of articles from our most distinguished literati. . . . Could you not do me so great a favor as to send me a scrap, however small, from your portfolio? Your name is of the greatest influence in that region where we direct our greatest efforts – in the South.
>
> Any little reminiscence, tale, jeu d'esprit, historical anecdote, – anything, in short, with your name, will answer all our purposes. I presume you have heard of my marriage.

Apart from obtaining contributions from distinguished writers, Poe had drawn attention to the *Messenger* with attacks on fashionable writers. His biting violence

Charles Dickens did much to help establish copyright protection for authors – it would have made Poe rich from *The Raven*. A daguerreotype taken in America in 1843.

was unusual at a time when the general principle was to say something pleasant or not speak at all. Theodore Fay, one of the writers he attacked, was much respected in the north, a member of the famous 'Knickerbocker' cabal. With a review of Fay, Poe achieved those essentials of a *littérateur*'s reputation: he became feared, hated, admired and read.

Poe was now editor of the *Messenger* and earning some $800 a year. Though *The Tales of the Folio Club* had been rejected both by Carey and Lea and by Harper Brothers, many of the stories were appearing in the *Messenger* and building his reputation as an original and frightening teller of tales. But, as in his previous experience of journalism, the social pressures pushed him towards drink which was constantly available, continually offered, and often needed to stimulate brilliant dialogue with dull people and the energy required by an intensely active editor and contributor. Here, in his professional world of men, drink was a support and a defence against total immolation by opium and Virginia. Here drink supported the flight from women to the safety of a masculine world of aggressive competition. But drink still exercized an instant effect upon him, a single glass changing depression into hypomanic euphoria, and little more than a glass making him violent and soon helpless. Useless for Mr White to advise him: 'Separate yourself from the bottle, and bottle companions, forever.' Pointless for relatives to exhort him to shun the demon, 'that great enemy of our family', reminding him of its dire effects on his father and brother. When Virginia's spell failed to hold him, and opium withdrew its arms, he was driven to the tavern; as Marie Bonaparte observed: 'Virginia, opium, the "fugues", drink, were thus so many weapons Poe used to combat the intolerable depressions to which his manic-depressive constitution, his crushing sense of bereavement and his constant struggle against his repressed and fearful sexuality, condemned him.'

The response his stories received, the example of Dickens' great success with serializations, and the advice that 'a Tale in a couple of volumes' would solve all his money problems, encouraged Poe to begin work on his only long narrative, *Arthur Gordon Pym*. He would first publish it in parts in the *Messenger* and then as a book. It was the first new fiction he had undertaken since returning to Richmond, though he had written numerous essays, the most important of which was *Maelzel's Chess-Player*, in which he exposed by deductive reasoning methods anticipating those of his detective Dupin how an 'automatic' chess-player was being operated. This exposé created great interest, since Maelzel was generally regarded as an automaton-builder of genius. But the very excitement of his successes exacerbated the drinking into which the journalistic life inevitably drew him. Mr White reminded him time and again of his principle regarding drink before breakfast. Poe himself admitted: 'I certainly did give way to the temptation held out on all sides by the spirits of Southern conviviality. My sensitive temperament could not stand an excitement which was an every day matter to my companions. In short, it sometimes happened that I

Engraving of New York in the 1830s, looking towards the harbour.

was completely intoxicated. For some days after each excess I was invariably confined to bed.' On such occasions Mrs Clemm would send a note, explaining that 'dear Eddy's health was too bad for him to get down to the office today.' Poe's friend Kennedy put it kindly, observing that, 'He was irregular, eccentric, and querulous, and soon gave up his place.' The fact is that 'his place' was closed to him by Mr White in January 1837 when the *Southern Literary Messenger* published, more in sorrow than in anger, the following notice: 'Mr Poe's attention being called in another direction, he will decline, with the present number, the Editorial duties on the *Messenger*. His Editorial Notices for this month end with Professor Anthon's *Cicero* – what follows is from another hand. With the best wishes to the Magazine, and to its few foes as well as many friends, he is now desirous of bidding all parties a peaceable farewell.'

Poe left the paper, having made it in a little more than a year into an important literary magazine with a large circulation. Yet though his reputation as a tale-teller of frightening propensities and a critic of savage style were so augmented that his boast of years before, 'The world shall be my theater!', seemed now to be justified, Edgar Poe left Richmond as financially bedevilled as ever he had been. Mr White tried to be helpful, but he had financial problems himself:

...You are certainly as well aware as I am, that the last $20 I advanced to you was in consideration of what you were to write for me by the piece. I also made you a promise

The house at 113½ Carmine Street, New York, where Poe, Muddy, Sis and their various lodgers lived during 1837.

on Saturday that I would do something for you today... and though it is entirely out of my power to send you up anything this morning, yet I will do something more sure, before night or early tomorrow if I have to borrow it from my friends.

T.W.W.

It seemed that even when good fortune was with Poe it could never be strong enough to expel the devil he always encountered in Richmond.

## *Grotesques and Gents*

On their way to New York the Poe family stayed with friends in Baltimore and Philadelphia, Edgar seeking sufficient financial reason to remain; but though he now had a national reputation, there was nothing for him. Furthermore the Poes arrived in New York at the end of February, in the middle of a financial crisis caused by President Jackson's free-handed fiscal policy and the 'wild cat' paper issues of state banks which it encouraged. It was a poor time to look for support for Poe's ambition to found an important national literary magazine. The strange trio – the Byronic man, the pale, lovely girl and the motherly Mrs Clemm – took lodgings in Manhattan in a crumbling house on 6th Avenue and Waverley Place, where a well-known bookseller, William Gowans, who admired Poe's work, shared his floor with them. Gowans was to remain Edgar's most valuable friend and contact throughout his short New York stay, and the bookshop on Broadway became his office and meeting-place.

Poe hoped that the New York *Review* would provide him with the basis of a living, but due to the crisis the *Review* was suspended, as were numerous other magazines and newspapers. For the moment publishers were inclined towards the safest and best-known authors; furthermore Poe's bitter *Messenger* reviews had made him enemies who were now happy to do him whatever harm they could. Mrs Clemm saved the financial situation by taking in boarders, and in order to increase facilities the Poes moved to 113½ Carmine Street, near St John's Church, a sad-looking house with a high roof, but large enough to take several boarders. Mrs Clemm's first lodger was William Gowans, 'the wealthy and eccentric bibliopolist' who wrote of life with the Poes:

> For eight months or more one house contained us, as one table fed! During that time I saw much of him [Poe], and had an opportunity of conversing with him often, and I must say, that I never saw him the least affected by liquor, nor ever descend to any known vice, while he was one of the most courteous, gentlemanly, and intelligent companions I have met with during my journeyings, and haltings through divers divisions of the globe; besides, he had an extra inducement to be a good man as well as a good husband, for he had a wife of matchless beauty and loveliness; her eye could match that of any houri, and her face defy the genius of Canova to imitate; a temper and disposition of surpassing sweetness; besides she seemed as much devoted to him as a young mother is to her first-born.... Poe had a remarkably pleasing and prepossessing countenance, which the ladies would call decidedly handsome.

Clearly Virginia was maturing into a desirable young woman, and Edgar was happy to be seen taking twilight walks with her in the graveyard of nearby St John's Church.

Gowans introduced Poe to the many literary men among his clientele and acquaintance, taking him to a dinner at which the influential 'Knickerbocker' writers were present in force. But though Poe found that the New York literary world knew and respected or feared his pen, it had little to offer him in the way of commissions. In consequence, the year in New York was a creative one. In spite of the severe winter, debts, and a bad cold which sent him to the Northern Dispensary for 'medicine' (probably opium-based), Poe completed his single long work, *The Narrative of Arthur Gordon Pym*, and several grotesque tales. Of these *Siope*, considered by some critics to be his most 'majestic prose', was published in the *Baltimore Book*, while the *American Monthly Magazine* published *Von Jung, the Mystific*. In July 1838 Harpers announced the publication of the long story:

*The Narrative of Arthur Gordon Pym, of Nantucket*; comprising the Details of a Mutiny and Atrocious Butchery on board the American Brig Grampus, on her Way to the South Seas – with an Account of the Recapture of the Vessel by the Survivors; their Shipwreck, and subsequent Horrible Sufferings from Famine; their Deliverance by means of the British Schooner Jane Gray; the brief Cruise of this latter Vessel in the Antarctic Ocean, her Capture, and the massacre of her Crew among a Group of Islands in the 84th Parallel of Southern Latitude; together with the incredible Adventures and Discoveries still further South, to which that distressing Calamity gave rise.
12 mo., pp. 198 New York: Harper and Brothers, 1838.

While *Pym* is an attempt to exploit the public taste for German-style horror combined with the type of sea adventure which Captain Marryat had made popular, in its uninhibited delineation of horrors from supernatural fear to cannibalism, the novella is all Poe. He based the book upon the expedition of J.N. Reynolds, an Antarctic explorer, who exercized an enormous influence upon his imagination by the courage and terror of his projected confrontation with the great wall of ice in the remote south. Poe's imagination soared over that wall, for the Antarctic, the coldest depth of all, was, like death and the grave, endlessly attractive to him. Poe so identified with Reynolds that, sixteen years later as he lay dying, he spoke his name several times. Containing the unconscious symbols was, however, well-judged commercial material. Poe used Coleridge's *Ancient Mariner* as an inspiration, adding to it the public's interest in real-life adventures at sea which he supported with Morrell's *Narrative of Four Voyages to the South Sea and the Pacific*, and *The Mutiny on the Bounty* which Harpers themselves had published. But it is Poe's very personal avidity for horror and violence which heightens and transforms the material of his book. The note on hieroglyphs at the end of the story he took from the Mount Sinai material described in Stephen's *Travels in Arabia Petraea*, which he read and reviewed at this time, and it is the first indication of his interest in ciphers. Yet with all its powerful inventions and ingenuities *Pym* had little success, and Poe's financial problems were not to be solved, as he had been assured they would, by a longer tale.

The New York period is quiet and poorly documented, and like many of Poe's times of intense writing activity supported by opium rather than alcohol, but, apart from Gowans, the Poes became very friendly with an English writer of children's stories, James Pedder, and his family. Pedder was appointed editor of the Philadelphia *Farmer's Cabinet* in 1838, and his recommendation of the greater literary possibilities of the Quaker city brought Poe there that summer. Pedder's sisters kept a boarding house on 12th Street and the Poe family moved in there with their friends for the time being, the financing of the move being arranged by Mrs Clemm, now a skilful borrower. Pedder quickly arranged literary introductions, which in Philadelphia were of a much more practical nature since the city had

ABOVE Engraving of Philadelphia by William Birch, showing Congress Hall and the New Theatre in Chestnut Street. Poe went to Philadelphia, the centre of printing and publishing in America, in the summer of 1838. While there he completed the collection of stories published in 1840 as *Tales of the Grotesque and Arabesque.*

OPPOSITE Aubrey Beardsley's drawing of Roderick Usher, from a limited edition published in 1894–5. *The Fall of the House of Usher* was first published in 1839.

been, since Benjamin Franklin's day, the centre for printing and publishing; periodicals appeared continually, making it the hub of the magazine world. A few weeks later he moved closer to the publishing district, to Quaker Mrs Parker's boarding house on 4th and Mulberry Streets. For the next few months Poe worked there preparing *Tales of the Grotesque and Arabesque*, completing the work in a 'small house' on 16th Street which he took in September.

Here on 16th Street, Philadelphia, Poe was to spend his few short years of relative success and prosperity, though it was typical of his perverse luck that a commercial assignment which earned a mere $50 turned against him. Copyright in the name of Edgar A. Poe is registered on an unexpected book, his fifth, entitled *The Conchologist's First Book: or, a System of Testaceous Malacology*. Designed for schools and published in 1839 by Haswell, Barrington and Haswell, the book is largely a rearrangement of the work of others, a hack work which Poe hoped would earn him further income as a school textbook. Pedder had introduced him to the publishers who provided the research for the work. It had a preface and

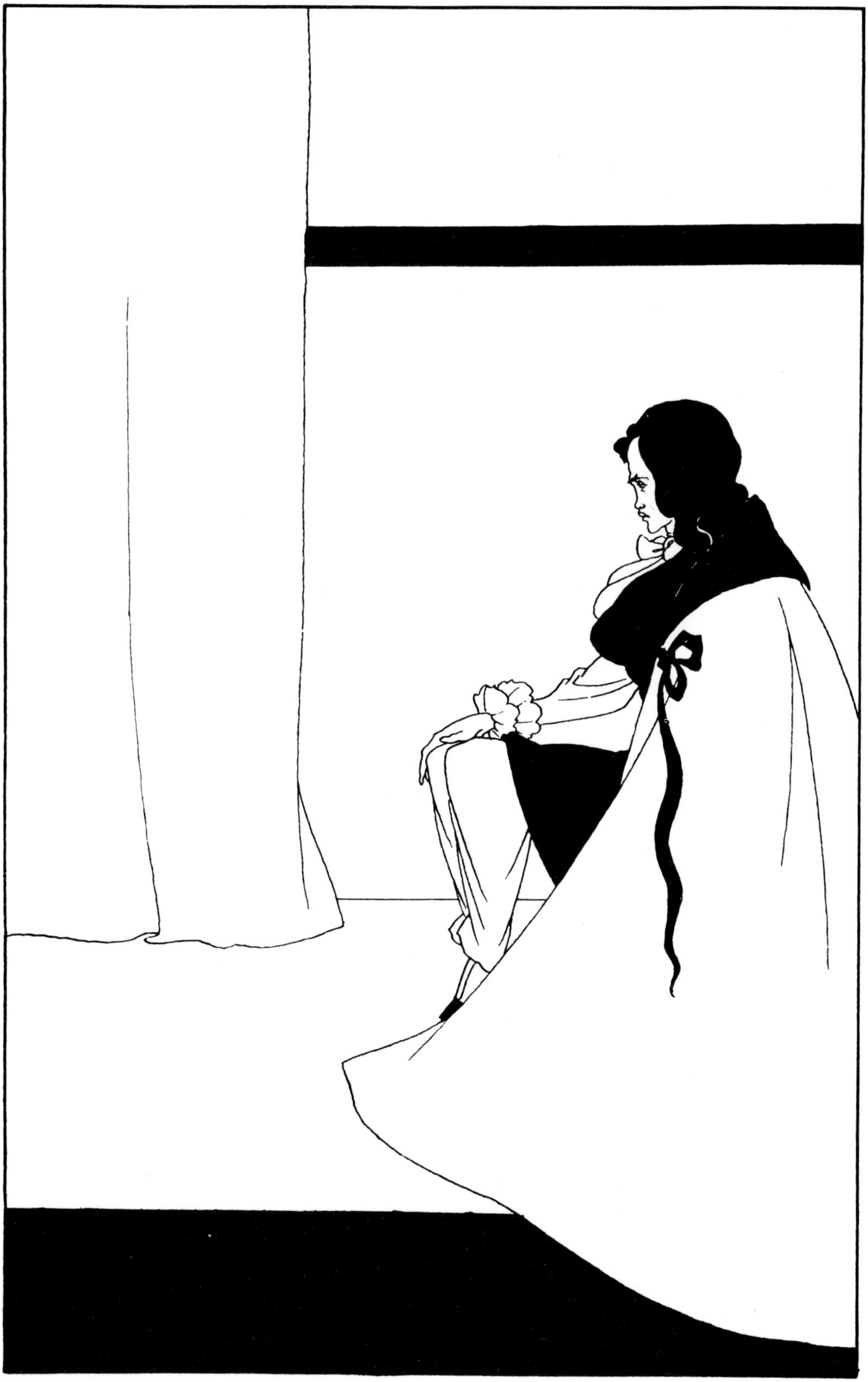

introduction written by Poe acknowledging his sources, and the body of the book was paraphrase. Yet, though it was to be a considerable success during Poe's life with a second edition in 1840, a third in 1845 and an English reprint, *The Conchologist's First Book* quickly brought accusations of plagiarism. Poe replied sensibly, 'I wrote the Preface and Introduction and translated from Cuvier the accounts of the animals, etc. *All* school-books are necessarily made in a similar way.' He pointed out that he had never implied the work was original, but the many enemies he had made through his reviewing and editorial activities were pleased to see him embarrassed, and harried him. Yet it was and is a sad truth of the writer's profession that commissions like *The Conchologist's First Book* frequently earn more money than his original work. Surely only those who love literature and hate writers will criticize Poe for attempting to live in order to continue writing the original work they admire so greatly.

Of Poe's original works, the grotesque story *The Devil in the Belfry* was published in the *Saturday Evening Chronicle* and the poem *The Haunted Palace* in the *Baltimore Museum*. The same poem was reprinted in the famous tale, *The Fall of the House of Usher*, in which the description of Roderick Usher is a self-portrait of the writer at thirty:

> The character of his face had been at all times remarkable. A cadaverousness of complexion, an eye large, liquid, and luminous beyond comparison; lips somewhat thin and very pallid, but of a surprisingly beautiful curve, a nose of a delicate Hebrew model, but with a breadth of nostril unusual in similar formations; a finely moulded chin, speaking, in its want of prominence, of a want of moral energy; hair of a more than web-like softness and tenuity; – these features, with an inordinate expansion above the regions of the temple, made up altogether a countenance not easily to be forgotten.

*The Fall of the House of Usher* is also autobiographical in that it is tinctured with opium, referring notably to 'the morbid condition of the auditory nerve'. The story also characterizes Virginia, now beginning to show the unmistakable signs of tuberculosis. She is embodied in the dying Lady Madeline whose disease 'had long baffled the skill of the physicians, with her settled apathy . . . a gradual wasting away of the person'. The story captures for ever Poe's fears for his dying cousin–wife. Yet there was also the morbid satisfaction of having his own 'most perfect subject for poetry', his own beautiful dying woman. Virginia's 'baffling disease' did not prevent him opportunistically pursuing his fame and reputation.

The notion of starting his own magazine was ever with Poe but, biding the financial opportunity, he was prepared to be an editor again. Even though W. E. Burton, publisher and editor of the *Gentleman's Magazine*, had reviewed *Pym* less than enthusiastically, Poe now approached him with a proposition. The John Bullish Englishman replied enthusiastically:

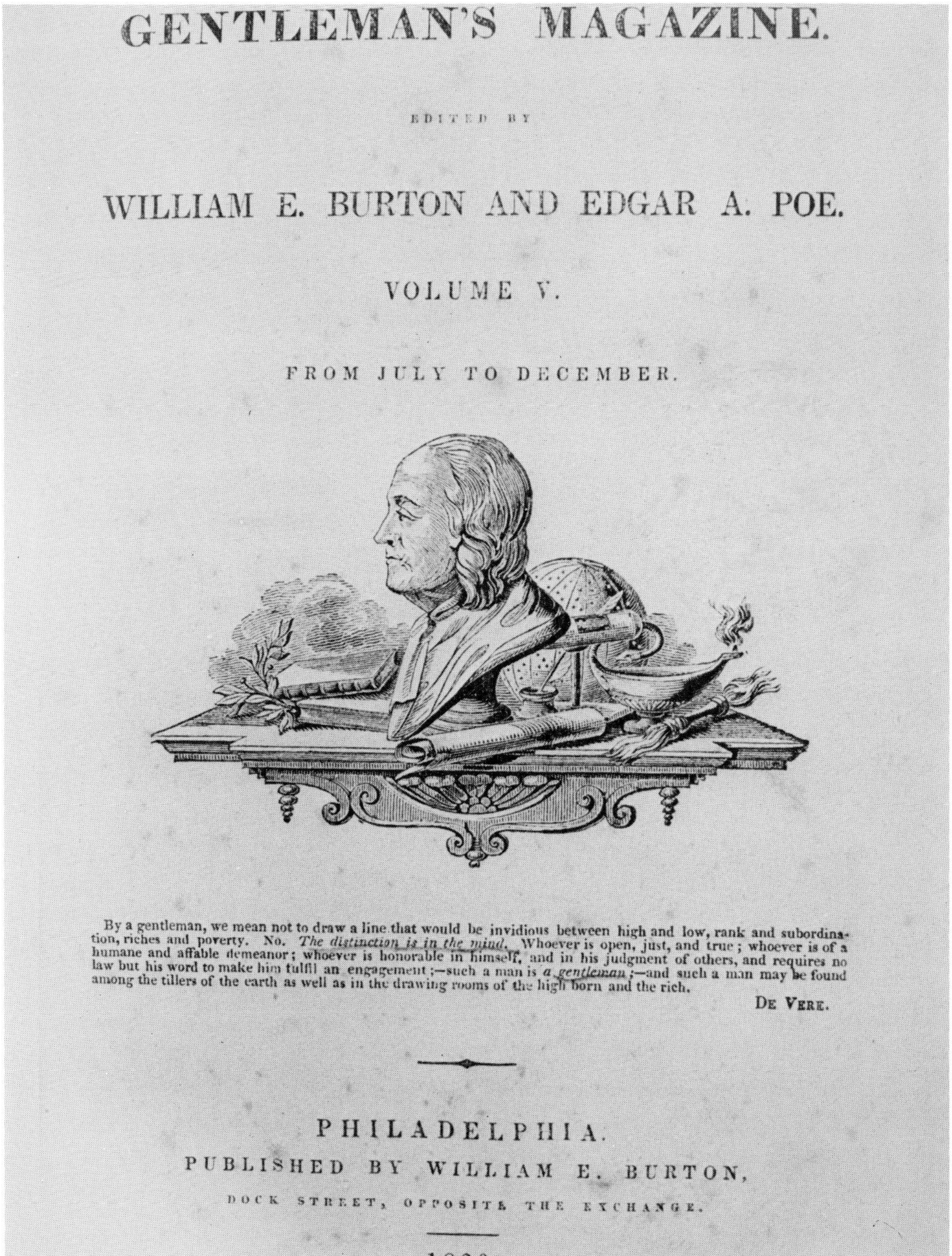

GENTLEMAN'S MAGAZINE.

EDITED BY

WILLIAM E. BURTON AND EDGAR A. POE.

VOLUME V.

FROM JULY TO DECEMBER.

By a gentleman, we mean not to draw a line that would be invidious between high and low, rank and subordination, riches and poverty. No. *The distinction is in the mind.* Whoever is open, just, and true; whoever is of a humane and affable demeanor; whoever is honorable in himself, and in his judgment of others, and requires no law but his word to make him fulfil an engagement;—such a man is *a gentleman*;—and such a man may be found among the tillers of the earth as well as in the drawing rooms of the high born and the rich.

De Vere.

PHILADELPHIA.
PUBLISHED BY WILLIAM E. BURTON,
DOCK STREET, OPPOSITE THE EXCHANGE.

1839.

The cover of Volume v of Burton's *Gentleman's Magazine*, which appeared in July 1839, bore Poe's name as co-editor alongside that of Burton. Burton was to publish some of Poe's best stories in the magazine.

I have given your proposal a fair consideration. I wish to form some such engagement as that which you have proposed, and know of no one more likely to suit my views than yourself. The expenses of the Magazine are already awfully heavy; more so than my circulation warrants. I am certain that my expenditure exceeds that of any publications now extant, including the monthlies which are double in price. Competition is high – new claimants are daily arising.

Shall we say ten dollars per week for the remaining portion of the year. Should we remain together, which I see no reason to negative, your proposition shall be in force for 1840. A month's notice to be given on either side previous to a separation.

Two hours a day except occasionally, will, I believe, be sufficient for all required except in the production of any article of your own. At all events you could easily find time for any other light avocation – supposing that you did not exercise your talents in behalf of any publications interfering with the prospect of the G.M.

I shall dine at home today at 3. If you will cut your mutton with me, good. If not, write or see me at your leisure.

I am, my dear Sir, your obedt. Servt.
W.E. Burton.

The literary gentlemen 'cut their mutton' together and in July 1839 Burton's *Gentleman's Magazine* appeared with Edgar A. Poe's name on the cover as co-editor, although he was actually contributing editor, being in no way tied to the office as he was in his first editorial job with Mr White. Mr Burton was altogether more amiable and amusing than Mr White with his continuous advice about drink. He was keen on the theatre, with a reputation as an excellent comic actor, and wanted his magazine to be worthy of a place 'upon the parlour table of every gentleman in the United States'. A contemporary actor, Joseph Jefferson, described Burton as: 'Thoughtful and saturnine . . . one of the funniest creatures that ever lived . . . As an actor of the old broad farce comedy Mr Burton had no equal in his day. . . . "Captain Cuttle", and "Micawber" were his great achievements; his face was a huge map on which was written every emotion that he felt. . . .'

Unfortunately Burton's comedy did not appeal to the gloomy, serious Edgar Poe who despised what he called the 'buffoon' in the man. Certainly Burton was no brilliant editor, casting his net wide rather than exercizing any sharp literary discriminations. He was also happy to steal from British authors, especially favouring Leigh Hunt. Poe's *Tales* in this literary rag-bag have the green glow of real emeralds in a chest of theatrical props. He dismissed the magazine as 'the Gent's Mag', but made it immortal with such stories as *The Man that was Used Up*; *The Fall of the House of Usher*; *William Wilson*; *Morella*; and *The Conversation of Eiros and Charmion.*

During his time with Burton, Poe tried hard to avoid drink. He wrote in 1841 to his doctor: 'I pledge you, before God, the solemn word of a gentleman, that I am temperate even to rigor. From the hour in which I first saw this basest of calumniators

[Burton] to the hour in which I retired from his office in uncontrollable disgust at his chicanery, arrogance, ignorance and brutality, nothing stronger than water ever passed my lips.' Mrs Clemm confirms that Poe took no wine during the period in question, yet he did frequently absent himself from the office, partly because his original agreement specifically allowed him such freedom, but also because he was using the small security the magazine gave as a base for preparing his own paper, *The Penn Magazine*, and completing his first collection of stories, *Tales of the Grotesque and Arabesque*, for Lea and Blanchard.

Time too was taken up with cryptograms and hieroglyphics, part of the evolution of his hero-figure, 'the infallible ratiocinator', eventually embodied in Dupin, the literary ancestor of Sherlock Holmes and unending generations of clinically impeccable detectives. This preoccupation of Poe's with a character which would embody the triumph of reason and logic acted as a kind of balance to his other growing preoccupation with terror and the irrational. In January 1840 he challenged 'the universe' in Alexander's *Weekly Messenger* to provide a cipher which he could not solve. The 'universe' of the paper in question was only a few hundred readers, but quite a number of cryptograms came in. Poe solved them all, but again it took time, and since Burton was now frequently away from the office, either performing as a comic or trying to trade his magazine for a theatre, the editorial desk grew heaped with unfinished business. Soon Burton discovered that Poe was planning a new paper, while Poe heard that Burton was trying to sell the *Gentleman's Magazine*. Burton accused Poe of stealing his subscription lists; Poe counter-accused that Burton had given him no warning of his intention to sell and that he had allowed the whole work of the magazine to devolve upon him, against the spirit of his agreement and without additional salary. As a protest Poe stayed away from the office, while letters and manuscripts continued to pile up. Burton returned and in a theatrical rage threw everything into a cab and drove to the house of a friend where he spent the night catching up with work which he firmly believed it was Poe's duty to do. The magazine appeared on time, but Poe never entered the office of the 'Gent's Mag' again, moving soon after the incident to the other end of town, to a house overlooking the Schuylkill River.

The inevitable correspondence followed, Poe setting out his claims, defences and complaints at length, concluding:

Upon the whole I am not willing to admit that you have greatly overpaid me. That I did not do four times as much as I did for the Magazine was your own fault. At first I wrote long articles, which you deemed unadmissable, and never did I suggest any to which you had not some immediate and decided objection. Of course, I grew discouraged, and could feel no interest in the journal.

I am at a loss to know why you call me selfish. If you mean that I borrowed money of you – you know that you offered it, and you know that I am poor... Place yourself in my situation and see whether you would not have acted as I have done. You first 'enforced', as you say, a deduction of salary; giving me to understand thereby that you thought of parting company. You next spoke disrespectfully of me behind my back – this is an habitual thing; to those whom you supposed your friends, and who punctually reported to me, as a matter of course, every ill-natured word you uttered. Lastly, you advertised your magazine for sale without saying a word to me about it. I felt no anger at what you did – none in the world. Had I not firmly believed in your design to give up your journal, with a view of attending to the Theatre, I should never have dreamed of attempting one of my own. The opportunity of doing something for myself seemed a good one – (and I was about to be thrown out of business) – and I embraced it. Now I ask you, as a man of honor and as a man of sense, – what is there wrong in all this? What have I done at which you have any right to take offence? . . . . The charge of $100 I shall not admit for an instant. If you persist in it our intercourse is at an end, and we can each adopt our own measures.

Burton's rejection had come at a bad time, since Poe was in the middle of one of his 'nervous collapses', a condition which was not helped by his decision to settle his nerves by drinking 'hard cider'. But even if Edgar was frequently 'nervous', the new house on Coates Street beside the river was the most charming and comfortable he had known since leaving the Allan mansion. Life in the country (even though it was only three miles from the town centre), relaxed him. There he could swim or shoot waterfowl, while Virginia, though her energies were erratic, gardened, filling the small house with flowers. In the evenings she sang in her small, pure soprano, while Mrs Clemm radiated maternal benevolence and their kitten Catarina played with Muddy's wool. In these relatively idyllic circumstances Mr Burton put on his *Pickwick* make-up and responded to a despairing letter from Poe with grace and charm, reinstating him as a contributor to the *Gentleman's Magazine*:

I am sorry you have thought it necessary to send me such a letter. Your troubles have given a morbid tone to your feelings which it is your duty to discourage. I myself have been as severely handled by the world as you can possibly have been, but my sufferings have not tinged my mind with melancholy, nor jaundiced my views of society. You must rouse your energies, and if care assail you, conquer it. I will gladly overlook the past. I hope you will as easily fulfill your pledges for the future. We shall agree very well, although I cannot permit the magazine to be made a vehicle for that sort of severity which you think 'so successful with the mob'! . . . I accept your proposition to recommence your interrupted avocations with the Maga. Let us meet as if we had not exchanged letters. Use more exercise, write when feelings prompt, and be assured of my friendship. You will soon regain a healthy activity of mind and laugh at your past vagaries.

Burton's renewed support encouraged Poe to complete his serial story, *The Journal of Julius Rodman*, which appeared in the magazine, unsigned, from January to June 1840. It follows the pattern of *Pym*, being the adventures of a young Kentucky traveller on a trapping expedition up the Missouri in the 1790s, and has little vitality or originality. But Poe's sixth book, *Tales of the Grotesque and Arabesque*, appeared at the same time in two volumes with the famous preface in which Poe defended himself against 'Germanism', maintaining that his terror was 'not of Germany, but of the soul' and that he had deduced this terror only 'from its legitimate sources'. His horror, he insisted, was the true thing, not the pseudo-terror of the gothic tale-tellers. He had experienced it himself and he wished people to re-experience it in reading the *Tales*. With them the immortal writer of mystery and imagination had at last arisen from the tomb of provincial American writing. His readers felt the authentic breath of his terror upon their necks; they recognized that his was true horror from the depths of the psyche, both Poe's and their own. But the readers of the *Tales* were very few. Lea and Blanchard complained that, 'the state of affairs is such as to give little encouragement to undertakings'. Poe received a few complimentary copies and added brightness to his fame. Since his death that brightness has shone in almost every language of the world, for the *Tales* are the basis of Edgar Poe's countlessly reprinted collection, *Tales of Mystery and Imagination.*

## *A Magazine of My Own*

The American literary scene was controlled from Boston, New York, Philadelphia and Baltimore, each centre having its magazines. Poe planned to disregard these cabals, with their back-scratching and internecine warfare, and establish a periodical which would be both national and international. This, the first project of its kind in American letters, he was able to visualize because of his unusual awareness of the literary movements in England and in Europe. Only two magazines in America had had any pretensions to such knowledge, the *North American Review* and the *Knickerbocker*, representing the new England and Manhattan literary groups. Poe's Southern background and personal animosities had made him intensely hostile to both of them. Their pretensions as the literary mandarins of the New World and their conspiracy to support one another's reputations had produced that 'severity' of critical attack which Mr Burton found too much for his magazine. The New Englanders were well able to take care of themselves and their reputations. Emerson, their oracle, dismissed Poe as a 'jingle man'; he was condemned as a drunkard and, when French interest in his work was heard of, 'immoral'. In fact, Poe was becoming the first artist of international significance the United States had produced. He knew it, and realized his talents needed an arena. The *Penn Magazine* was to be it. Its *Prospectus*, published on New Year's Day 1841, sets out Poe's ambitions for himself and American letters:

TO THE PUBLIC

Since resigning the conduct of the Southern Literary Messenger, at the commencement of its third year, I have always had in view the establishment of a Magazine which should retain some of the chief features of that journal, abandoning or greatly modifying the rest. Delay, however, has been occasioned by a variety of causes, and not until now have I found myself at liberty to attempt the execution of the design.

I will be pardoned for speaking more directly of the Messenger. Having in it no proprietary right, my objects too being at variance in many respects with those of its very

*The Murders in the Rue Morgue*, first published in *Graham's Magazine* in 1841, is a horrific story of a giant ape which goes berserk and commits a number of brutal murders. Aubrey Beardsley's ape (ABOVE) is evil and decadent, while Harry Clarke's version (OPPOSITE) stresses the violence and savagery in Poe's tale.

worthy owner, I found difficulty in stamping upon its pages that individuality which I believe essential to the full success of all similar publications. In regard to their permanent influence, it appears to me that a continuous definite character, and a marked certainty of purpose, are requisites of vital importance; and I cannot help believing that these requisites are only attainable when one mind alone has the general direction of the undertaking. Experience has rendered obvious – what might indeed have been demonstrated *a priori* – that in founding a Magazine of my own lies my sole chance of carrying out to completion whatever peculiar intentions I may have entertained.

To those who remember the early days of the Southern periodical in question, it will be scarcely necessary to say that its main feature was a somewhat overdone causticity in its department of Critical Notices of new books. The Penn Magazine will retain this trait of severity insomuch only as the calmest yet sternest sense of justice will permit. Some years since elapsed may have mellowed down the petulance without interfering with the vigor of the critic. Most surely they have not yet taught him to read through the medium of a publisher's will, nor convinced him that the interests of letters are unallied with the interests of truth. It shall be the first and the chief purpose of the Magazine now proposed to become known as one where may be found at all times, and upon all subjects, an honest and a fearless opinion. It shall be a leading object to assert in precept, and to maintain in practice, the rights, while in effect it demonstrates the advantages, of an absolutely independent criticism; a criticism self-sustained; guiding itself only by the purest rules of Art; analyzing and urging these rules as it applies therein; holding itself aloof from all personal bias; acknowledging no fear save that of outraging the right; yielding no point either to the vanity of the author, or to the assumptions of critical prejudice, or those organized cliques which, hanging like nightmares upon American literature, manufacture, at the nod of our principal booksellers, a pseudo-public opinion by wholesale. These are objects of which no man need be ashamed. They are purposes, moreover, whose novelty at least will give them interest. For assurance that I will fulfill them in the best spirit and to the very letter, I appeal with confidence to those friends, and especially to those Southern friends, who sustained me in the Messenger, where I had but a very partial opportunity of completing my own plans.

In respect to the other characteristics of the Penn Magazine a few words here will suffice.

It will endeavor to support the general interests of the republic of letters, without reference to particular regions – regarding the world at large as the true audience of the author. Beyond the precincts of literature, properly so called, it will leave in better hands the task of instructions upon all matters of very grave moment. Its aim chiefly shall be to please – and this through means of versatility, originality, and pungency. It may be as well here to observe that nothing said in this Prospectus should be construed into a design of sullying the Magazine with any tincture of the buffoonery, scurrility, or profanity, which are the blemish of some of the most vigorous of the European prints. In all branches of the literary department, the best aid, from the highest and purest sources, is secured.

To the mechanical execution of the work the greatest attention will be given which such a matter can require. In this respect it is proposed to surpass, by very much, the ordinary Magazine style. The form will somewhat resemble that of the Knickerbocker; the paper will be equal to that of the North American Review; pictorial embellishments are promised only in the necessary illustration of the text.

The Penn Magazine will be published in Philadelphia, on the first of each month; and will form, half-yearly, a volume of about 500 pages. The price will be $5 per annum, payable in advance, or upon receipt of the first number which will be issued on the First of March, 1841. Letters addressed to the Editor and Proprietor,

Edgar A. Poe
Philadelphia, January 1, 1841.

The *Prospectus* sketches Poe's basic theory that the purpose of art is 'to please' – the writer himself, he meant, not the public or the cliques. But Poe's financial resources were, as ever, barely sufficient to provide for the modest needs of his family, let alone indulge fully the luxury of art for art's sake. Reactions to the *Prospectus* were encouraging, and there was some hope of the magazine appearing within the year, but then came the 'nervous attack' and the breach with Burton.

Poe did not find the mythical backer for whom all writers languish, but in F. W. Thomas, the young author of the novel *Clinton Bradshaw* which depicted life in Baltimore, he found a supporter for his project and a lifelong friend. Both men were writers, poets and editors, raised in the South, inimical to the New England literary spirit, and suffering from poor health. Thomas was crippled, probably through tuberculosis of the bones, and had struggled as consistently as Poe to make a living as a literary man. They shared Whig political ideas, and wrote political songs together, and when Thomas eventually gained a political appointment he tried to use his influence in Poe's interest. He was the only friend Poe never turned against. 'You have shown yourself, from the first hour of our acquaintance, that *rara avis in terris* – a true friend. Nor am I the man to be unmindful of your kindness', wrote Poe, responding with what literary favours he could. His relationship with Thomas is taken by those who resent the suggestion that he was incapable of maintaining normal friendships as a clear indication that, when unthreatened, he could do so. But perhaps the relationship with Thomas is best explained by the fact that he had been a friend of Poe's brother, Henry. They had been rivals in a love affair, though friendly ones, and Thomas brought back the lost brother for whom Edgar had mourned so deeply. The friendship helped to sustain him through the 'nervous collapse' which followed the trouble with Burton.

In October 1840 Burton sold the *Gentleman's Magazine* for $3,500 to George R. Graham, who owned a pale monthly called *Atkinson's Casket*. With the cash he bought Cook's Olympic Circus in Philadelphia, satisfying his lifelong ambition to be a manager and star performer, though as both he was soon to fail completely. Graham meanwhile merged his two magazines into a new publication, *Graham's Magazine*, with a circulation of some 5,000. Kindly Mr Burton, having completed his deal with Graham, had added, 'There is one thing more. I want you to take care of my young editor.' Graham did so, and Poe took care of him in return, for within a few months he had built up *Graham's* circulation to over 37,000, making it the first of the large-circulation American magazines and the largest-selling monthly in the world.

Graham's policy was to 'find a mean between the uninteresting and severe literature that only Tories read and the namby-pambish writing which is the ruling note of the age'. He also, very sensibly and unusually, believed in paying authors well, as high as $1,800 for a Fenimore Cooper story and $50 for a Longfellow poem. He also spent money on engravings, printing and good quality paper, but unfortunately Mr Graham saw no reason to overpay his young editor. Poe received $800 a year and a small sum per page in addition for his own writings. He therefore began his work on the new paper with resentment, for Mr Graham had promised considerably more than he delivered. Poe's disappointment with being a successful editor for White and Burton was being repeated. He was also soon to repeat the pattern of 'irregularity', his usual reaction to the pressures of success and the frustrations of resentment.

The offices of *Graham's Magazine* were at 3rd and Chestnut Street on the top floor of an old newspaper building. Here Poe was expected to attend every day, and though such routine irked him, his commitment to the editorial chair forced out of him a constant flow of reviews and stories. Mr and Mrs Graham would call in the course of the morning to open the mail, taking out any cash for subscriptions, and leaving the less profitable correspondence to Poe. They would then exit happily with the money, disgusting Poe even more with his miserly share in the fruits of his labour. By July 1841 Mr Graham had grossed $60,000 for the first half-year of the magazine's operation, and by the end of the year his profit was some $15,000. Poe was tired, fretting and frustrated, and some mere $500 the richer for all his hard work and great success. Yet he was not denied some part in the Grahams' new-found wealth.

The Grahams spent a great deal of their magazine profits supporting an impressive house on Arch Street, where they gave brilliant and generous dinner parties. Mr Graham, with a sure sense of promotion, knew that a generous display of affluence always goes down rather well with men of letters, most of whom are happy to exchange profound dialogue for excellent dinners with copious wine. Poe was expected to appear at these parties and more than hold his own in the dialogues. Given his characteristic behaviour, it was a commitment to drink. Graham could hardly have realized that this friendly supplement to his meagre salary was a mortal danger to Poe, for Edgar was not the only literary mandarin who drank deep before stumbling from the generous table in Arch Street.

Graham wrote a posthumous defence of Poe in the magazine in 1850. Though it was also a defence of his own parsimony towards his tragically dead editor, it reveals, clearly enough, genuinely warm feelings towards the Poes:

*The Dinner Party*, a painting by the American artist Henry Sargent. The Grahams' generous hospitality at their house on Arch Street encouraged Poe to continue drinking.

One of the French artist Gustave Doré's famous series of engravings of *The Raven*: 'Get thee back into the tempest and the night's Plutonian shore.'

I shall never forget how solicitous of the happiness of his wife and mother-in-law he was, whilst one of the editors of Graham's Magazine, his whole efforts seemed to be to procure the comfort and welfare of his home. Except for their happiness and the natural ambition of having a magazine of his own, I never heard him deplore the want of wealth. The truth is he cared little for money, and knew less of its value, for he seemed to have no personal expenses! What he received from me in regularly monthly instalments went directly into the hands of his mother-in-law for family comforts; and twice only I remember his purchasing some rather inexpensive luxuries for his house, and then he was nervous to the degree of misery until he had, by extra articles, covered what he considered an imprudent indebtedness. His love for his wife was a sort of rapturous worship of the spirit of beauty which he felt was fading before his eyes. I have seen him hovering around her when she was ill, with all the fond fear and tender anxiety of a mother for her first born – her slightest cough causing in him a shudder, a breast chill that was visible....

Throughout that year of prosperity, 1841, Virginia declined and Poe shuddered and ran from the unbearable vision of her lovely decline. Both success and the glittering Graham salon, and the Red Death, familiar of the Poe family at home once more, sent him back to drink. Hervey Allen suggests that the opium influence is present in *The Colloquy of Monos and Una*, written at this time, but there can be no doubt that the prosperous year generally saw Poe driven in a 'fugue' back to the bottle.

Edgar's companion in the 'male' activity of drinking was a charming and amusing young lawyer, Henry Beck Hirst, who shared his interest in revising international copyright laws, which, being more deficient in America than anywhere else, resulted in uncontrolled piracy of authors' rights by publishers. Poe knew that Charles Dickens was equally interested in the subject and hoped eventually to establish a contact with him which would help to create an international lobby for improvement of the copyright laws. He also hoped that Dickens might help him to find a publisher in London; but Dickens was not to visit Philadelphia until the following year. When he did, he was impressed by Poe but did little for him. Meanwhile, Poe discussed the problems and planned their solutions with Hirst and, in his enthusiasm, even entered himself as a law student. Hirst was also intensely interested in ornithology and poetry and made an ideal walking companion for Poe. He had unusual friends, the most eccentric of whom was a young writer who habitually dressed in a blue coat very tight at the waist, with a scalloped velvet collar, and wore his hair in long, shaggy locks. He was George Lippard, who spent his nights in a hundred-roomed abandoned building near Franklin Square which was occupied by weird squatters. There Lippard, no stranger to opium, dreamed dreadful dreams, the recounting of which made him sympathetic to Poe, who encouraged him in his writing of a gothic novel of a rather ordinary kind called *The Quaker City or the Monks of Monk Hall*. The novel had grinning skulls, ghostly figures and strange shadows in the moonlight, but nothing frighteningly original. Lippard, a confused protestor, attacked upright Quaker Philadelphia as a Sodom. He eventually married by moonlight in Indian style.

With his fellow eccentrics Poe regularly visited the printing offices of John Sartain, an absinthe drinker. Hirst was friendly with Napoleon's brother, the exiled ex-King Joseph Bonaparte, who had built a palace near Trenton on the proceeds of the royal regalia he had smuggled out of Europe. From him Hirst had learnt about brandy, and, in order to satisfy all tastes, the drinking brothers adopted as their staple the fatal mixture of absinthe and brandy. Perhaps if F. W. Thomas, his best and most loved friend, had been around, Poe might have avoided some of these fatal sessions. But Thomas now had a political job in Washington, and Edgar's new habitués brought him into the lower depths of Philadelphia where Poe, in an intense, drink-induced excitement which was close to madness, often recited lines from his doom-haunted poem *The Raven* which, encouraged by a bird-loving lawyer and a gothic lunatic, was beginning to cast the shadow of its black wings over his life.

# CHAPTER SIX
# 1842–1846

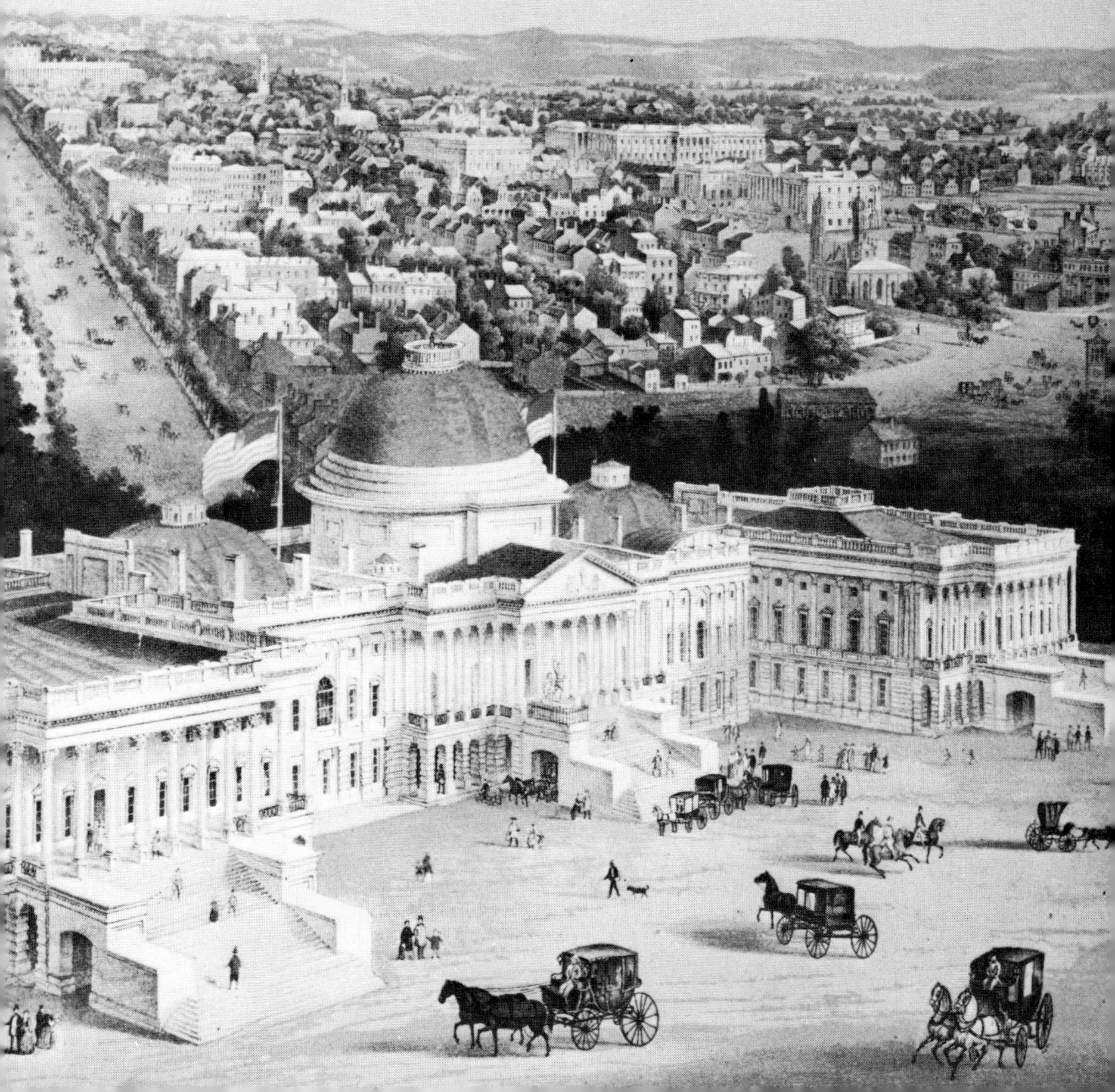

## *The Coming of the Red Death*

On an evening towards the end of January 1842 a modest supper party was much enjoyed at the house of Edgar Poe in Coates Street. Poe's cousins, the Herrings, who had come from Baltimore, were delighted to find the strange, gloomy, sometimes frightening Eddy so happy for once. A fire burned in the grate, a generous coal fire, symbol of Poe's new-found relative prosperity; there had been a well-set table, prepared and supervised by a happy Mrs Clemm who now went to the kitchen to make coffee, followed by the cat, Catarina. The tame birds slept in their covered cage as Virginia sat down at her harp, a pale, great-eyed child-woman, wearing a pure white dress. Poe leaned forward, tense and expectant as he always was when Virginia sang. He adored her voice which, he said, was the voice of the strange women of his dreams. Virginia struck the strings of the harp and began to sing in her true, clear soprano. Then as the nightingale trills which Poe had helped her to perfect mounted higher, she suddenly stopped, catching her breath. She coughed violently and, as in a Poe nightmare, a vessel broke in her chest and blood spouted from her mouth. It flushed through the whiteness of her dress, staining it like the cape of the Red Death.

Poe cried out as he sprang to catch Virginia. Mrs Clemm hurried in from the kitchen as he carried her up to the bedroom. He left Muddy to nurse her with cold compresses while he took a cab across town to collect Dr Mitchell. Poe's state itself must have given the doctor cause for concern, for what little stability he had depended upon Virginia. She was for him the last link with reality, and the possibility of her death opened the door to insanity. Yet the loss of Virginia was a tragic inevitability which he had often anticipated and fled from to his 'irregularities'.

Now that Virginia's condition had declared itself to be the shameful disease which no one understood, it could no longer be considered a delicate, poetic, rather fashionable condition. Virginia's 'decline' had been succeeded by 'a consumption', and now was, patently, the fatal malady itself, 'the terrible evil', tuberculosis. Poe for his part grew more unstable, his drinking increasing as he fled Virginia's relapses, sometimes disappearing for days on end, coming home filthy and disordered to be cleaned up

PREVIOUS PAGES View of Washington in the mid-nineteenth century, with the White House in the foreground. Poe moved to the Spring Garden area of the city in 1842.

and nursed by Muddy. His heart trouble returned and he entered into the dark maze of the last confused years of his life. A year after Sis's death he wrote of this dreadful time:

You say, 'Can you hint to me what was the "terrible evil" which caused the "irregularities" so profoundly lamented?' Yes, I can do more than hint. This "evil" was the greatest which can befall a man. Six years ago, a wife, whom I loved as no man ever loved before, ruptured a blood-vessel in singing. Her life was despaired of. I took leave of her forever and underwent all of the agonies of her death. She recovered partially, and I again hoped. At the end of a year, the vessel broke again. I went through precisely the same scene.... Then again – again – again – and even once again, at varying intervals. Each time I felt all the agonies of her death – and at each accession of the disorder I loved her more dearly and clung to her life with more desperate pertinacity. But I am constitutionally sensitive – nervous in a very unusual degree, I became insane, with long intervals of horrible sanity. During these fits of absolute unconsciousness, I drank – God only knows how often or how much. As a matter of course, my enemies referred the insanity to the drink, rather than the drink to the insanity. I had, indeed, nearly abandoned all hope of a permanent cure, when I found one in the death of my wife. This I can endure as becomes a man. It was the horrible never-ending oscillation between hope and despair which I could not longer have endured, without total loss of reason. In the death of what was my life, then, I receive a new but – Oh, God! – how melancholy an existence.

There was no possibility of 'a permanent cure' for Poe and in observing that 'the drink resulted from the insanity' he knew it well. What he could not allow himself to know was why drink was his only refuge. He was convinced that his anguish and fear of loss were the reasons, and the convention of such grief is convincing to all but the most perceptive. Baudelaire wrote of Poe's drinking bouts:

The poet Charles Baudelaire translated Poe into French.

It is easy enough, for that matter, to suppose that a man so truly solitary and so profoundly unhappy ... it is natural ... to suppose that this poet ... at times, sought the luxury of forgetfulness in the bottle. Literary animosities, the vertigoes inspired by the cosmos, misery at home and poverty's lash – from all these Poe fled into the night of drunkenness, as though into a premature tomb. But however sound this explanation may seem, I do not find it sufficiently inclusive, and distrust it as deplorably simple.

Princess Bonaparte, Poe's post-mortem Freudian analyst, also found the over-simplification 'deplorable', seeing in the ambivalence of Poe's behaviour at this time clear clues to his profoundest disturbance:

If Poe, at every crisis in Virginia's illness, loved her the more, it was not so much because each threatened him with her loss, but because every crisis, every haemoptysis, deeply reactivated his terrible unconscious infantile memories and converted Virginia into an ever more lifelike and, as it were, superimposed portrait of his dying and never forgotten mother. And if, then, he sought respite in drink from his intolerable anxiety, it was because that anxiety arose not so much from sorrow, as from the terrible temptations which – given his sado-necrophilist drives – Virginia would rouse in him at such times.

That Poe was a potential sado-necrophilist all his work shows and only his most purely literary devotees would deny it. Lauvrière, in his work on Poe, well realized this, though with no inkling, naturally, of its infantile roots. Given these circumstances, it must be admitted that Poe had good reason to fly from his dying wife and her haemorrhages, for she then realized his sexual ideal.

The sinister element in Poe's horror stories is depicted in Beardsley's illustration of *The Black Cat* (ABOVE) and Harry Clarke's *The Mystery of Marie Rogêt* (OPPOSITE).

Poe's writing during this period is highly revealing. In *The Mystery of Marie Rogêt*, the only story he ever wrote with an overtly criminal sexual content, the body of the dead perfumery girl is described in great physical detail:

The face was suffused with dark blood, some of which issued from the mouth. No foam was seen, as in the case of the merely drowned. There was no discoloration in the cellular tissue. About the throat were bruises and impressions of fingers. The arms were bent over on the chest, and were rigid. The right hand was clenched; the left partially open. On the left wrist were two circular excoriations, apparently the effect of ropes, or of a rope in more than one volution. A part of the right wrist, also, was much chafed ... the flesh of the neck was much swollen ... a piece of lace was found tied so tightly around the neck as to be hidden from sight; it was completely buried in the flesh....

The immensely detailed observation of a dead body lends substance to the tales of Poe's haunting of mortuaries.

*The Black Cat*, the horrific story which came to him as he watched Virginia sick in bed with Catarina curled up beside her, has obvious autobiographical content:

I married early and was happy to find in my wife a disposition not uncongenial with my own. Observing my partiality for domestic pets, she lost no opportunity of procuring those of the most agreeable kind. We had birds, gold-fish, a fine dog, rabbits, a small monkey, and a *cat*... Pluto – this was the cat's name – was my favourite pet and playmate.... Our friendship lasted in this matter for several years, during which my general temperament and character – through the instrumentality of the Fiend Intemperance – had (I blush to confess it) experienced a radical alteration for the worse. I grew, day by day, more moody, more irritable, more regardless of the feelings of others. I suffered myself to use intemperate language to my wife. At length, I even offered her personal violence. My pets of course were made to feel the change in my disposition. I not only neglected, but ill-used them. For Pluto, however, I still retained sufficient regard to restrain me from maltreating him, as I made no scruple of maltreating the rabbits, the monkey, or even the dog, when by accident, or through affection, they came in my way. But my disease grew upon me – for what disease is like Alcohol? and at length even Pluto, who was now becoming old, and consequently somewhat peevish – even Pluto began to experience the effects of my ill-temper.

One night, returning home much intoxicated, from one of my haunts about town, I fancied that the cat avoided my presence. I seized him; when, in his fright at my violence, he inflicted a slight wound upon my hand with his teeth. The fury of a demon instantly possessed me. I knew myself no longer. My original soul seemed at once to take its flight from my body, and a more than fiendish malevolence, gin-nurtured, thrilled every fibre of my frame. I took from my waistcoat-pocket a penknife, opened it, grasped the poor beast by the throat, and deliberately cut one of its eyes from the socket! I blush, I burn, I shudder, while I pen the damnable atrocity.

The story thus, with painful clarity, conveys the love-hate ambivalence which so characterized Poe. For him, the tendency to be drawn irresistibly into hatred of the love-object was the cause of his 'final and irrevocable overthrow', the victory of 'the spirit of PERVERSENESS'. This was the spirit of which 'philosophy takes no account'. He was certain that 'perverseness is one of the primitive impulses of the human heart – one of the indivisible primary faculties, or sentiments, which gives direction to the character of Man. Who has not, a hundred times, found himself committing vile or silly actions for no other reason than because he knows he should *not*!'

Certainly the spirit of perverseness was much abroad at this time. It even occasionally soured Poe's relationship with his bosom drinking friends, Hirst and Lippard. Poe and Hirst were to accuse one another of plagiarism, and Hirst, years later, his mind destroyed by drink, publicly claimed that he had written *The Raven*! But for the time being, in spite of sporadic differences, Poe needed his drinking brothers badly and clung to them. Perverseness, however, confused his judgment when he pursued a close acquaintanceship with one Rufus Wilmot Griswold, whom he was to make his literary executor.

In the spring of 1841 the Rev. Mr Griswold, a printer's ex-apprentice who had become a Baptist clergyman, was preparing for publication his immensely popular anthology, *Poets and Poetry of America.* Griswold had discovered all the superficial formulae which enable a man to become a *littérateur* without ever committing literature. He had become a highly competent and commercially successful editor, compiler, anthologist and profile writer. No author of any ability in the United States was unknown to him and his capacity for gaining introductions and exploiting them would have made him a successful journalist at any time. Griswold had a certain insight into writers and their ways of work, but an even greater understanding of what the public wanted to believe. He was often attacked as, in Lowe's words, 'an ass, and what's more, a Knave', and Poe made his contempt for the Reverend's own poetry quite clear; yet he desperately wanted to appear in the anthology, believing that it could lead to the reprinting of the three early volumes of poetry which he had revised. Poe, as he invariably did when his mind and will were devoted to it, succeeded in cultivating Griswold, and when the anthology appeared in March it contained his poem *The Haunted Palace*, together with a brief and misleading sketch of Edgar A. Poe. It was little enough, but if Griswold's collection was the popular American Parnassus then Edgar had ensured a position for himself somewhat below the summit. It flattered and supported his vanity, but he was to pay dearly for it.

Through the spring Virginia deteriorated and so did Edgar. He became even more difficult to work with, hypersensitive and quarrelsome, and his attendances at the office of *Graham's Magazine* were increasingly erratic. His tendency to pontificate on literary and all other matters, in combination with his growing unreliability as an editor, grew insufferable to his colleagues. Charles Peterson, his editorial associate, was fairly opinionated himself, and resented being subordinate to Poe. He was one day discovered in violent argument with his editor by Mr Graham, who was highly embarrassed but forced to intervene. Poe must have been in the wrong because Graham, much as he wanted to keep his brilliant editor, for commercial reasons if no other, came down on Peterson's side. Graham concluded that, 'either Peterson or Poe would have to go – the two could not get along together.' Graham well knew Poe's tragic domestic background and was sympathetic. He wrote later, 'It was this hourly anticipation of her loss that made him a sad and thoughtful man,' but unfortunately it made him a violent and unreliable one too, and Graham clearly felt that his paper came first. One April morning Poe turned up at the office after an unexplained absence to find his anthologist 'friend' the Rev. Griswold in his chair. Without a word Poe left the office and never returned. He gave his own account of the termination of his editorship some months later:

... My connection with Graham's Magazine ceased with the May number, which was completed by the first of April – since which period the conduct of the journal has rested with Mr Griswold.... I have no quarrel with either Mr Graham or Mr Griswold – although I hold neither in especial respect. I have much aversion to communicate with them in any way, and perhaps it would be best that you should address them yourself. . . . I am making earnest although secret exertions to resume my project of the Penn Magazine, and I have every confidence that I shall succeed in issuing the first number on the first of January [1843]. You may remember that it was my original design to issue it on the first of January 1842. I was induced to abandon the project at that period by the representations of Mr Graham. He said that if I were to join him as a salaried editor, giving up for the time my own scheme, he himself would unite with me at the expiration of six months, or certainly at the end of a year. As Mr Graham was a man of capital and I had no money, I thought it most prudent to fall in with his views. The result has proved his want of faith and my own folly. In fact I was continually laboring against myself. Every overture made by myself for the benefit of Graham, by rendering that Magazine a greater source of profit, rendered its owner at the same time less willing to keep his word with me. At the time of our bargain (a verbal one), he had 6,000 subscribers – when I left him he had 40,000. It is no wonder that he has been tempted to leave me in the lurch.

Neither the new editor nor the paper's owner seems to have resented Poe, and he, in spite of blaming Graham for not supporting his *Penn Magazine* project, contributed some fifty items to the magazine after being discharged from its editorship. The most important and significant of these is the horrifyingly lush *The Masque of the Red Death*, the emblematic story of his destined subjection to tuberculosis. In *The Masque* a dreadful, mysterious and irresistible pestilence attacks the country of the 'happy and dauntless and sagacious Prince Prospero':

The 'Red Death' had long devastated the country. No pestilence had ever been so fatal, or so hideous. Blood was its Avatar and its seal – the redness and horror of blood. There were sharp pains, and sudden dizziness, and then profuse bleeding at the pores, with dissolution. The scarlet stains upon the body and . . . face of the victim, were the pest ban which shut him out from the aid and from the sympathy of his fellow-men. And the whole seizure, progress, and termination of the disease, were the incidents of half an hour.

Prince Prospero seals off his magnificent palace and, with all his court, dancers, musicians, 'beauty and wine', he stages a masked ball which will go on until the pestilence has left the country. So the revellers exhaustingly pursue their desperate orgy, costumed and concealed from the frightening reality of life outside the palace, until there appears amongst them an uninvited guest whose costume is that of the Red Death itself:

The figure was tall and gaunt, and shrouded from head to foot in the habiliments of the grave. The mask which concealed the visage was made so nearly to resemble the countenance of a stiffened corpse that the closest scrutiny must have had difficulty in detecting the cheat. And yet all this might have been endured, if not approved by the mad revellers around. But the mummer had gone so far as to assume the type of the Red Death. His vesture was dabbled in *blood* – and his broad brow, with all the features of the face, was besprinkled with the scarlet horror.

The revellers at the ball, drawn by Beardsley to illustrate
*The Masque of the Red Death*.

Prince Prospero orders the 'blasphemous mockery' to be seized and unmasked, but no one dares to do it. The Prince himself draws his dagger and attacks the strange figure. But the weapon falls from his hand on to the sable carpet, and the Prince himself falls dead. Whereupon the revellers, seizing the mummer:

... whose tall figure stood erect and motionless within the shadow of the ebony clock, gasped in unutterable horror at finding the grave cerements and corpse-like mask which they handled with so violent a rudeness, untenanted by any tangible form.

And now was acknowledged the presence of the Red Death. He had come like a thief in the night. And one by one dropped the revellers in the blood-bedewed halls of their revel, and died each in the despairing posture of his fall. And the life of the ebony clock went out with that of the last of the gay. And the flames of the tripods expired. And Darkness and Decay and the Red Death held illimitable domination over all.

So Poe allegorized his conviction that the 'mysterious malady' was the inescapable destiny of all he loved, and his own as well. He was wrong about himself. Destiny had in mind for him a charade more macabre than even *The Masque of the Red Death*.

## *Sensation in Washington*

Early in 1842 the Poes moved to the Spring Garden area, to former servants' quarters on a rear lot at 234 North 7th Street. It was the setting for the last days of Poe's short time of prosperity, a two-storey house with a charming little low-ceilinged bedroom with three casement windows and an open fireplace which became Sis's room. Edgar's was the front room on the ground floor, which had a black slate mantel. There he wrote or dreamt, sometimes locked in by Mrs Clemm to make sure he could not escape to a tavern with its inevitably dire results. But generally the house was happy, with Virginia, in spite of the dark places in her life, still sustaining her bright, often merry and gregarious nature, sometimes singing comic songs which she composed with a young girlfriend who kept her company. Mrs Clemm still entertained the frequent visitors with 'excellent repasts served on snowy cloths', even though Poe's income since the loss of his job was small and erratic. And Edgar himself was not always moody or locked up like a madman. He described his behaviour between times, defining his problem succinctly:

My habits are vigorously abstemious, and I omit nothing of the natural regimen requisite for health – i.e., I rise early, eat moderately, drink nothing but water, and take abundant and regular exercise in the open air. But this is my private life – my studious and literary life – and of course escapes the eye of the world. The desire for society comes upon me only when I have become excited by drink. Then only I go – that is, at these times only I have been in the practice of going among my friends; who seldom, or in fact never, having seen me unless excited, take it for granted that I am always so. Those who really know me, know better. . . .

In such times of 'natural regimen' in his room with the black mantel, Poe wrote *The Gold Bug*, certainly one of his more 'rational' constructions. Writing in the garden in the afternoons he would hear Virginia laughing and singing with her friend upstairs. Sometimes he talked with guests among the flowers, and it seemed that the wild poet from Baltimore was settling into a conventional early middle age. The talk would be of poetry and criticism, with Poe often achieving eloquence without any stimulation other than the admiration of his listeners, among whom even the Rev. Griswold waxed highly complimentary:

His conversation was at times almost supra-mortal in its eloquence. His voice was modulated with astonishing skill, and his large and variably expressive eyes looked repose or shot fiery tumult into theirs who listened, while his own face glowed or was changeless in pallor, as his imagination quickened his blood, or drew it back frozen to his heart. His imagery was from the worlds no mortal can see but with the vision of genius – Suddenly starting from a proposition exactly and sharply defined in terms of utmost simplicity and clearness, he rejected the forms of customary logic, and in a crystalline process of accretion, built up his ocular demonstrations in forms of gloomiest and ghostliest grandeur, or in those of the most airy and delicious beauty, so minutely, and so distinctly, yet so rapidly, that the attention which was yielded to him was chained till it stood among his wonderful creations, till he himself dissolved the spell, and brought his hearers back to common and base existence, by vulgar fancies or by exhibitions of the ignoble passions. . . .

Other less 'supra-mortal' afternoons were spent walking with Hirst with his pistol, shooting at random marks. Poe 'once shot a chicken on the wing at 50 yards', which suggests that Hirst brought a bottle with him. With Hirst, Poe also indulged in enthusiastic discussion of the great days ahead for the *Penn*. Thus the long summer passed, in what seemed to be an idyll of a successful author's life. But Mrs Clemm was supporting the dream with aid from a charitable society and by selling and pawning the household furnishings.

About the middle of the summer Virginia had a relapse which drove Poe out of the house on an odyssey of public houses. Mrs Clemm eventually found him and brought him home. The sympathetic Dr Mitchell saw Poe delirious from drink, remorse and opium, and decided that he must be sent away for a rest. He knew a local lady with a house at Saratoga Springs, the fashionable spa, and she was happy to have Edgar as a guest. So in August he went off to Saratoga, there to be seen driving around and taking the waters with a married lady well known in Philadelphia. The scandalous talk inevitably began and took so well that it eventually contributed to Poe's decision to leave the Quaker city. For the moment the Saratoga visit seemed to help him, and when he returned he was not drinking. But the total abstinence from stimulants could not last. Mrs Warden, one of his Herring cousins, who was often at the house, wrote that: '... she had often seen him [Poe] decline to take even one glass of wine but... that for the most part, his periods of excess were occasioned by a free use of opium.... During these attacks he was kept entirely quiet, and they did all possible to conceal his faults and failures.'

Occasional mad sprees coloured the summer of 1842. One such was reported by his earlier love, Mary Devereaux, now married and living in New York. Poe, drunk and wild, crossed and re-crossed on the Jersey ferry boat several times, asking all and sundry for Mary's address. With the success that usually crowned his extraordinary persistence, he obtained it. Later that day he found his way to her house, and broke in. Mary described the scene that followed:

> When Mr Poe reached our house I was out with my sister, and he opened the door for us when we got back. We saw he was on one of his sprees, and he had been away from home for several days. He said to me: 'So you have married that cursed –! Do you love him truly? Did you marry him for love?' I answered, 'That's nobody's business; that is between my husband and myself.' He then said, 'You don't love him. You do love me. You know you do.'

Poe stayed for one cup of tea, after which he took a dish of radishes and a knife and 'cut them up so violently the pieces flew over the table, to everybody's amusement'. He then demanded that Mary sing his favourite song, *Come Rest in this Bosom*, after which he left as suddenly as he had arrived. This flight to an old love suggests that Poe needed desperately to feel loved by a woman. Virginia, suffering a relapse, which brought her nearer to his dead mother, now had the reduced ability to project love of those whose energies are concentrated upon sustaining the small spark of life in themselves.

A few days after this episode Mrs Clemm, searching for 'Eddy dear', finally tracked him to Mary's house, and she, Mary and some neighbours went out to search the woods for the famous author. They found him, filthy, starving and out of his mind. Mary reports: 'He was wandering about like a crazy man. Mrs Clemm took him back with her to Philadelphia.'

Poe had continued his friendship with F. W. Thomas, now in a political position in Washington, through regular correspondence. Between them they hatched a plot to provide Poe with a means of support through Thomas' political contacts. The centrepiece of their plan was Robert Tyler, the President's son, who knew and admired Poe's work. Poe's first ploy was to publish a good critical opinion of one of Tyler's poems. This Thomas drew to Tyler's attention at the White House, later writing to Poe: '... Robert Tyler expressed himself highly gratified with your favorable opinion of his poems which I mentioned to him. He observed that he valued your opinion more than any other critic's in the country – to which I subscribed. I am satisfied that any aid he could extend to you would be extended with pleasure.

Write me frankly upon the subject....' From this point the conspirators planned to involve Robert Tyler in Poe's magazine project, the *Penn Magazine*, now renamed *The Stylus*. It was hoped that Tyler might help them obtain government printing for the magazine. When this proved impossible Poe changed his objective to an appointment at the Philadelphia Custom House. Robert Tyler supported the idea, and Thomas wrote to Poe:

... last night I was speaking of you [to Robert Tyler], and took occasion to suggest that a situation in the Custom House, Philadelphia, might be acceptable to you, as [Charles] Lamb had held a somewhat similar appointment, etc., etc., and as it would leave you leisure to pursue your literary pursuits. Robert replied that he felt confident that such a situation could be obtained for you in the course of two or three months at farthest, as certain vacancies would then occur. What say you to such a plan? Official life is not laborious – and a situation that would suit you and place you beyond the necessity of employing your pen, he says he can obtain for you there....

Poe was delighted with the progress of the plan so far, replying: '... Could I obtain such an appointment, I would be enabled thoroughly to carry out all my ambitious projects. It would relieve me of all care as regards a mere subsistence, and thus allow me time for thought, which, in fact, is action.' On the basis of his hopes Poe pressed on with plans to launch *The Stylus*, soliciting support from financial and literary contacts, and continuing to seek the backing of political tyros, even though he was nervous and depressed, still recovering from his summer breakdown, and worried about Sis: 'My poor wife still continues ill, I have scarcely a faint hope of her recovery.' Thomas visited the Poes in the autumn. J.H.Whitty gives Thomas' account of the visit:

Poe was living in a little home on the rural outskirts of the city in a house that is described by Thomas as small but quite comfortable within. Although the whole aspect of the cottage testified to the poverty of its tenants, the rooms impressed the visitor as being neat and orderly. Thomas arrived quite late in the morning but found Mrs Clemm busy cooking Poe's breakfast. The caller produced quite an evident confusion by his sudden advent, and there was some difficulty in arranging to include him at the board. In the meanwhile, Virginia entertained the guest. Thomas found the poet's wife to be both graceful and agreeable, and he remarked not only her regular and well-formed features but the most expressive pair of eyes that had ever gazed upon him. Nevertheless, her excessive pallor, a consumptive cough, and the deep facial lines caused him to look upon her as a victim to be claimed by an early grave. Both Virginia and Mrs Clemm were much concerned about their 'Eddie', and made it quite plain to Thomas that they hoped most ardently that the head of the house might soon be able to secure some steady work.

Poe, who had evidently just arisen, now appeared to greet his friend. A mop of dark hair tangled carelessly over his high forehead, and contrary to his general habit, his clothes were rather slovenly. Poe's greeting to Thomas was cordial, although a little

THE

# STYLUS

A

Monthly Journal of Literature Proper
The Fine Arts And The Drama.

Aureus aliquando STYLUS, ferreus aliquando.

Paulus Jovius.

---

EDITED BY

EDGAR A. POE

restrained, and Thomas noted that his friend complained of feeling unwell. Poe told him that he had gone to New York to find employment, and also remarked that an effort to publish a new edition of his tales had been unsuccessful. Like so many others who visited the Poes, Thomas was forever impressed by Poe's pathetic tenderness and loving manner toward Virginia, but the visitor from Washington could not help but observe at the same time, and with the deepest regret, that his friend had again been yielding to intemperate habits. Thomas was so worried as to venture to remonstrate with Poe who admitted that he had lately been drinking 'while in New York' – and then changed the subject by relating a humorous dialogue of Lucian.

Later on during the same day, the two friends visited town together. Thomas says that Poe was sober when they parted and they were to meet by appointment next day.

Thomas' visit encouraged Poe in believing that the Custom House appointment would materialize, and although Edgar was 'taken with a severe chill and fever' (probably the results of drink or opium), and could not attend Thomas' political meeting at Independence Hall, Philadelphia, or say goodbye to him before he left, his friend's support remained firm. But when on 19 November the Custom House appointments were announced Poe's name was not among them. He wrote to Thomas, hurt, amazed, and indignant: '... Some of the papers announced four removals and appointments. Among the latter I observed the name of – Pogue. Upon inquiry among those behind the curtain, I soon found that no such person as – Pogue had any expectation of an appointment, and that the name was a misprint or rather a misunderstanding of the reporters, who had heard my own name spoken of at the Customs House.' Poe characteristically persisted in pursuing the appointment, calling several times upon a Mr Smith, who was responsible for swearing in appointees. Mr Smith took to avoiding him, but Poe finally caught up with him and reported the following exchange:

'Have you no good news for me?'

'No, I am instructed to make no more removals.'

'But I have heard from a friend, from Mr Robert Tyler, that you were requested to appoint me.'

'From whom [*sic*] did you say?'

'From Mr Robert Tyler.'

(I wish you could have seen the scoundrel, – for scoundrel, my dear Thomas, in your private ear, he is –)

'From Mr Robert Tyler!' says he – 'Hem! I have received orders from President Tyler to make no more appointments, and shall make none.

OPPOSITE The *Penn Magazine*, later re-named *The Stylus*, was Poe's lifelong ambition for a magazine of his own, which would give him complete editorial freedom. This was Poe's own suggested design for the cover.

In fact there was another appointment, but it was not for Poe, and he was furious:

> You can have no idea of the low ruffians and boobies – men, too, without a shadow of political influence or caste – who have received office over my head. If Mr Smith had the feelings of a gentleman, he would have perceived that from the very character of my claim, – by which I mean want of claim – he should have made my appointment an early one.... I would write more, my dear Thomas, but my heart is too heavy. You have felt the misery of hope deferred, and will feel for me....

So renewed disappointments saw the year out and though the autumn also brought publication of *The Tell-Tale Heart* and other pieces in Lowell's important new magazine, the *Pioneer*, and the beginning of a warm relationship with the *doyen* of American letters, the auspices for the New Year were not all that the summer had promised. Yet Poe's own magazine was nearer to materialization than ever.

In the first months of 1843 Poe and Hirst were often at the house of a wealthy publisher and editor, Thomas C. Clarke, persuading him to back *The Stylus.* Thomas also brought his influence to bear upon Clarke, and soon the publisher agreed to support Poe's project. An agreement was drawn up for F.O.C. Darley, an illustrator, to provide drawings, indicating the extent of the practical plans entered into, but the completion and successful resolution of those plans still rested with Poe. He was promoted as an important literary figure in association with the announcements of the new magazine. Hirst wrote a sketch of him which was published with a portrait in the *Saturday Museum*, and the item was enthusiastically picked up by other papers. The Philadelphia *Spirit of the Times* commented: 'We look upon Mr Poe as one of the most powerful, chaste, and erudite writers of the day, and it gives us pleasure to see him placed through the public press in his proper position before the world.' The publicity impressed Washington, and with Robert Tyler's support assured, Poe was invited to give a lecture there, to be received at the White House, and to collect endorsements and subscriptions from well-known people and government officials. It was the greatest opportunity of his life. A successful Washington campaign would establish his reputation and his security, perhaps for life. Mr Clarke paid the expenses and on 8 March Poe caught the train for Washington, excited and nervous but typically full of confidence.

On arriving in Washington Poe called on Thomas, who lived at Fuller's Hotel. Unfortunately Thomas was ill and passed him over to a friend, J.E. Dow, whose character had given him the nickname, sinister for Poe, of 'Rowdy' Dow. It was further bad luck that the owner of the hotel, delighted to meet the famous writer, invited Poe to a party that very evening. There Poe resisted liquor until the very end of the meal when, according to Dow, he was 'over-persuaded' to take port. The next day found him ill after a long, drunken night which left him without enough coins to pay for a shave. He wrote to Clark with a very hangover air.

*The Tell-Tale Heart*, first published in 1842 in the *Pioneer*, contains a highly credible description of a heart attack. Illustration by Harry Clarke.

Washington, March 11, 1843

My Dear Sir, – I write merely to inform you of my well doing, for, so far, I have done nothing.

My friend, Thomas, upon whom I depended, is sick. I suppose he will be well in a few days: In the meantime I shall have to do the best I can.

I have not seen the President yet.

My expenses were more than I thought they would be, although I have economized in every respect, and this delay (Thomas being sick) puts me out sadly. However, all is going right. I have got the subscriptions of all the departments, President, etc. I believe that I am making a sensation which will tend to the benefit of the magazine.

Day after tomorrow I am to lecture. Rob Tyler is to give me an article, also Upsher. Send me $10 by mail as soon as you get this. I am grieved to ask you for money in this way, but you will find your account in it twice over.

Very truly yours,
Edgar A. Poe.

Thos. C. Clarke, Esq.

Poe was certainly a 'sensation' in Washington. His reception at the White House was ruined by the fact that he was drunk, so that Robert Tyler decided not to introduce him to his father, the President. Edgar's appearance was curious to say the least, for he had taken to wearing his coat inside out like a cloak. 'Rowdy' Dow was understandably worried and wrote to Clarke:

Washington, March 12, 1843

Dear Sir, – I deem it to be my bounden duty to write you this hurried letter in relation to our mutual friend E. A. P.

He arrived here a few days since. On the first evening he seemed somewhat excited, having been over-persuaded to take some port wine.

On the second day he kept pretty steady, but since then he has been, at intervals, quite unreliable.

He exposes himself here to those who may injure him very much with the President, and thus prevent us from doing for him what we wish to do if he is himself again in Philadelphia. He does not understand the ways of politicians nor the manner of dealing with them to advantage. How should he?

Mr Thomas is not well and cannot go home with Mr P. My business and the health of my family will prevent me from so doing.

Under all circumstances of the case, I think it advisable for you to come on and see him safely back to his home. Mrs Poe is in a bad state of health, and I charge you, as you have a soul to be saved, to say not one word to her about him until he arrives with you. I shall

OPPOSITE Illustration by Edmund Dulac to the poem *To —*.

FOLLOWING PAGES *The City of Washington from behind the Navy Yard*, by William Bennett after George Cooke, 1833.

*View of the City of Washington*, a lithograph made in 1836
by F.H.Lane.

expect you or an answer to this letter by return mail.

Should you not come, we will see him on board the cars bound for Philadelphia but we fear he might be detained in Baltimore and not be out of harm's way.

I do this under a solemn responsibility. Mr Poe has the highest order of intellect, and I cannot bear that he should be the sport of senseless creatures, who, like oysters, keep sober, and gape and swallow everything.

I think your good judgment will tell you what course you ought to pursue in the matter, and I cannot think it will be necessary to let him know that I have written you this letter; but I cannot suffer him to injure himself here without giving you this warning.

Yours respectfully,
J.E.Dow

To Thos. C. Clarke, Esq.,
Philadelphia, Pa.

'A little port' had made Poe too rowdy for Dow who evokes, painfully, a picture of the genius making a fool of himself before idiots. Of course the lecture which was to launch Poe and *The Stylus* had to be cancelled, but the revels continued. At a party in the house of Brady, the photographer, Poe was involved in a fight with a hot-blooded Spaniard and he had to be taken, roaring, back to Fuller's. It was hardly the image of the 'most powerful, chaste, and erudite writer of the day', and scarcely the 'sensation' that had been planned. The 'oysters' could not believe that the noisy, hectoring drunk was a great man of literature. On the thirteenth, the day he was to have brought Washington to his feet with a brilliant lecture, Poe was furtively despatched home.

As he sobered up, taking his time returning to Philadelphia, Poe began to compose

OPPOSITE Illustration by Dulac to *Eldorado*.

his apologies and a pattern of explanation for his behaviour. Muddy, terribly worried, met him at the station and was somewhat surprised at his appearance, which he described as 'quite decent'. She took him home, fed him and got him into a bath. Later, he did his best to appease Sis, who was as near to losing her habitual good temper as she ever had been. As soon as he could be called on Clarke, about whom he wrote to Thomas and Dow: 'I never saw a man in my life more surprised to see another. He thought by Dow's epistle that I must not only be dead but buried.... I told him what had been agreed upon – that I was a little sick.... This morning I took medicine, and as it is a snowy day, would avail myself of the excuse to stay at home so that by to-morrow I shall be *really* as well as ever.' No doubt the 'medicine' gave him that total rest with which laudanum habitually compensated him for the excesses induced by its enemy, alcohol.

Though Edgar's apologies for his Washington fiasco were charming and copious, he could not bid time return. The opportunity was lost, and sadly he knew it. 'I blame no one but myself', he wrote to his friends, 'what a confounded business I have got myself into.' To Dow he wrote: 'My dear fellow, thank you a thousand times for your kindness and forbearance, and don't say a word about the cloak turned inside out or other peccadilloes of that nature.... Call, also, at the barber's shop just above Fuller's and pay for me a levy which I believe I owe. And now, God bless you, for a nobler fellow never lived.' His long-suffering, ever-faithful friend Thomas, he begged for forgiveness:

> My dear friend, forgive me my petulance and don't believe I meant, all I said. Believe me, I am very grateful to you for your many attentions and forbearances, and the time will never come when I shall forget either them or you. Remember me to the Don whose mustachios I do admire after all, and who was about the finest figure I ever beheld.... Please express my regret to Mr Fuller for making such a fool of myself in his house, and say to him (if you think necessary) that I should not have got so drunk on his port wine but for the rummy coffee with which I was forced to wash it down. I should be glad, too, if you would take an opportunity of saying to Mr Rob Tyler that if he can look over matters and get me the inspectorship I will join the Washingtonians forthwith. I am serious as a judge – and much more so than many. I think it would be a feather in Mr Tyler's cap to save from the perils of mint julep – and 'Port Wines' – a young man of whom all the world thinks so well and who thinks so remarkably well of himself.

The sad little hope at the end of the letter was scarcely taken seriously by either Edgar or his friends. An even sadder postscript to the Washington visit was

OPPOSITE *The Pit and the Pendulum*, one of the most famous of Poe's stories, has inspired many dramatics and film-makers. First published in 1843 in *The Gift*, it relates the plight of a victim of the fiendish tortures of the Spanish Inquisition.

LEFT President John Tyler, the chance of whose patronage Poe threw away.

reported by Thomas. On 26 March he had an interview with President Tyler at the White House. The President asked in a kindly way after Poe, whereupon his other son, John, said he wished that he would appoint Poe to an office in Philadelphia. In that moment all the evil effects of Poe's sensational visit to Washington might have been wiped out, but before the President could reply he was called out of the room and Poe's business was forgotten for ever.

F.W.Thomas wrote a note on Poe's apologetic letter expressing his chagrin and sadness, together with his regretful sense that his good offices had been wasted upon the errant winds of Poe's uncontrollable disposition:

While his friends were trying to get Poe a place he came on to Washington in the way he mentions. He was soon quite sick, and while he was so Dow wrote to one of his friends in Philadelphia about him! Poor fellow. A place had been promised his friends for him, and in that state of suspense which is so trying to all men, and particularly to men of imagination, he presented himself in Washington certainly not in a way to advance his interests. I have seen a great deal of Poe, and it was his excessive and at times marked sociality which forced him into his 'frolics', rather than any morbid appetite for drink, but if he took but one glass of weak wine or beer or cider, the rubicon of the cup had been passed with him, and it almost always ended in excess and sickness. But he fought against the propensity as hard as ever Coleridge fought against it, and I am inclined to believe, after his sad experience, and suffering, if he could have gotten office with a fixed salary, beyond the need of literary labour, that he would have redeemed himself at least this time.... His was one of those temperaments whose only safety is total abstinence.

Hervey Allen makes the point that this temperament of Poe's was of a recognizable type in nineteenth-century American society, that of the 'proud, quixotic, cavalierly-manner, and superficial Southerner with a little military training; more specifically a Virginian of a certain brand'. He observes that this type of pseudo-aristocrat was bred out of the slave and plantation society, and that there was in the gentlemen it produced 'a smouldering hostility rooted in fear'. Poe often took up this cavalier position, and pre-eminent among the props of the type was drink. Poe, in his guise of 'a Bad Man from Virginia on a spree', was living out one of the characterizations reserved for Southerners by north American society.

Marie Bonaparte adds her conclusion to the affair:

This Washington trip is the clearest example of how Poe always managed to spoil any chance of success. Some will say that, as a dipsomaniac, he was hardly 'responsible' for his acts and cannot therefore have desired a disaster which ruined his dearest hopes. Such a remark, however, would rest on the common tendency to confuse conscious and unconscious design. Poe was assuredly not 'responsible' but, for that matter, who is? If he was not, his acts were all the more psychically determined and his unconscious, by urging him to the saloon instead of the White House, doubtless had its own objects. There is no such thing as chance to the psycho-analyst, even in the psyche's utmost depths.

Thus Poe ruined any chance of success just when it seemed nearest.

The Washington 'sensation' stands as a set-piece epitomizing Poe's pattern of 'fugue'. It was not to be excelled as a demonstration until his final flight to Baltimore and death a few years after he was too drunk to be received by the President.

## *The Flight of the Raven*

Thomas Clarke could hardly have been expected to maintain confidence in *The Stylus* after Poe's Washington débâcle. He decided to cut his losses and withdraw from the project, for clearly the editor was a dangerous man to venture with. At the same time Poe's friend Lowell's new paper the *Pioneer*, which had been available to Edgar as a platform and a small source of income, also collapsed, leaving Lowell bankrupt. Once again Poe's financial situation was as bad as it could be, Virginia was ill again, and Mrs Clemm was at the end of her local charity resources. Poe swallowed his Southern pride and appealed to Griswold for the loan of $5. To his credit the Reverend paid up, although Poe had satirized him as 'Dr Driswold', much to his annoyance, and he had, furthermore, just suffered the appalling experience of marrying an ugly woman who was supposed to be wealthy, only to find out that she was not. Griswold was also having difficulties, as editor of *Graham's Magazine*, with Peterson, the colleague with whom his differences had precipitated Poe's exit from the magazine. The Reverend suspected that Graham was thinking of offering the editorial chair back to Poe. In such circumstances one feels that even $5 was a generous contribution. Now, too, the scandal which had begun concerning the lady at Saratoga Springs came home to roost in Philadelphia. Spring Garden Street no longer seemed the setting for an author's idyll.

The only notable success of 1843 came to Poe through *The Gold Bug*, which he had completed and held for *The Stylus*. Now he offered it to Graham, who accepted it with alacrity, for with its cool, controlled narrative, its strong evocation of place, combining the excitement of a pirate treasure story with Poe's very personal cryptographic interest, it was a perfect popular magazine item. But *The Dollar Newspaper*, housed in the same building as *Graham's*, suddenly announced the considerable prize of $100 for the best short story submitted. Edgar replaced *The Gold Bug* in *Graham's* editorial stock with a critical article, and entered the story for the competition. The judges had no difficulty in awarding him the prize, and the story appeared in the newspaper in June and was reprinted there a month later. *The Dollar Newspaper* had a wide circulation, making *The Gold Bug* effectively the first of Poe's stories immediately to win a relatively large readership. But he was too deteriorated both physically and mentally to be able to take advantage of the success. Though he had time on his hands and might have pursued the opportunities opened up by *The Gold Bug*, he wrote little, much of his energy going into contention. He accused Henry Hirst of parodying his work, and terminated their friendship. He was persecuted by rumours of his association with the lady from Saratoga Springs. An anonymous article, which Poe suspected was by Griswold, appeared in a local newspaper attacking him. He was also much put out by another 'attack' on him by his Baltimore friend, L.A.Wilmer. Of this betrayal he wrote: 'I have reason to believe that I have been maligned by some envious scoundrel in this city, who has written you a letter respecting myself. I believe I know the villain's name. It is Wilmer. In Philadelphia no one speaks of him. He is avoided by all as a reprobate of the lowest class....' Poe's comment on Wilmer was certainly much more

OPPOSITE *The Gold Bug* in *The Dollar Newspaper*, 1843.

# THE DOLLAR NEWSPAPER.

A FAMILY PERIODICAL,—Devoted to Literature, Domestic and Foreign News, Agriculture, Education, Finance, Amusements, &c.—INDEPENDENT ON ALL SUBJECTS.

PUBLISHED BY A. H. SIMMONS & CO., S. W. CORNER THIRD AND CHESNUT STREETS.—$1 PER YEAR, IN ADVANCE.

NO. 23. PHILADELPHIA, WEDNESDAY MORNING, JUNE 28, 1843. VOL. I.


[COMMUNICATED FOR THE "DOLLAR NEWSPAPER."]

STANZAS FOR MUSIC.

## THE OLD NIGHT OWL.

BY JAMES REES.

The old owl sat in the hollow tree,
While the winds they passed him fearfully;
His eye, like a demon's, glar'd around,
And from his throat came this mournful sound—
Ha, woo! ha, woo!

'T was a lonely spot, and clust'ring trees
Sigh'd sweetly there to the evening breeze;
But clearer them soar'd the old owl's notes,
Far, far aloft, on the night-wind floats—
Ha, woo! ha, woo!

A fearful bird is the old Night Owl,
His screech is like the wolf's fierce howl,
He meets no kin in his woody bound,
But to himself all night doth chaunt—
Ha, woo! ha, woo!

The darkest shade is the old owl's nest,
When the day-light warns him to his rest;
For a hundred years has the old owl long
Been heard in this lonely dell to sing—
Ha, woo! ha, woo!

Philad., June 20.

# ORIGINAL STORIES.

## THE GOLD-BUG.

A PRIZE STORY.

[WRITTEN EXPRESSLY FOR "THE DOLLAR NEWSPAPER."]

BY EDGAR A. POE, ESQ.,

*And for which the First Premium of One Hundred Dollars was paid.*

What ho! what ho! this fellow is dancing mad!
He hath been bitten by the Tarantula.
*All in the Wrong.*

Many years ago I contracted an intimacy with a Mr. William Legrand. He was of an ancient Huguenot family, and had once been wealthy; but a series of misfortunes had reduced him to want. To avoid the mortification consequent upon his disasters, he left New Orleans, the city of his forefathers, and took up his residence at Sullivan's Island, near Charleston, South Carolina.

This Island is a very singular one. It consists of little else than the sea sand, and is about three miles long. Its breadth at no point exceeds a quarter of a mile. It is separated from the main land by a scarcely perceptible creek, oozing its way through a wilderness of reeds and slime, a favorite resort of the marsh hen. The vegetation, as might be supposed, is scant, or at least dwarfish. No trees of any magnitude are to be seen. Near the western extremity, where Fort Moultrie stands, and where are some miserable frame buildings, tenanted, during summer, by the fugitives from Charleston dust and fever, may be found, indeed, the bristly palmetto; but the whole island, with the exception of this western point and a line of hard white beach on the sea-coast, is covered with a dense undergrowth of the sweet myrtle so much prized by the horticulturists of England. The shrub here often attains the height of fifteen or twenty feet, and forms an almost impenetrable coppice, burthening the air with its fragrance.

In the inmost recesses of this coppice, not far from the eastern or more remote end of the island, Legrand had built himself a small hut, which he occupied when I first, by mere accident, made his acquaintance. This soon ripened into friendship—for there was much in the recluse to excite interest and esteem. I found him well educated, with unusual powers of mind, but infected with misanthropy, and subject to perverse moods of alternate enthusiasm and melancholy. He had with him many books, but rarely employed them. His chief amusements were gunning and fishing, or sauntering along the beach and through the myrtles, in quest of shells or entomological specimens;—his collection of the latter might have been envied by a Swammerdamm. In these excursions he was usually accompanied by an old negro, called Jupiter, who had been manumitted before the reverses of the family, but who could be induced, neither by threats nor by promises, to abandon what he considered his right of attendance upon the footsteps of his young "Massa Will." It is not improbable that the relatives of Legrand, conceiving him to be somewhat unsettled in intellect, had contrived to instil this obstinacy into Jupiter, with a view to the supervision and guardianship of the wanderer.

The winters in the latitude of Sullivan's Island are seldom very severe, and in the fall of the year it is a rare event indeed when a fire is considered necessary. About the middle of October, 18—, there occurred, however, a day of remarkable chilliness. Just before sunset I scrambled my way through the evergreens to the hut of my friend, whom I had not visited for several weeks—my residence being, at that time, in Charleston, a distance of nine miles from the Island, while the facilities of passage and re-passage were very far behind those of the present day. Upon reaching the hut I rapped, as was my custom, and, getting no reply, sought for the key where I knew it was secreted, unlocked the door and went in. A fine fire was blazing upon the hearth. It was a novelty and by no means an ungrateful one. I threw off an overcoat, took an arm-chair by the crackling logs, and waited patiently the arrival of my hosts.

Soon after dark they arrived, and gave me a most cordial welcome. Jupiter, grinning from ear to ear, bustled about to prepare some marsh-hens for supper. Legrand was in one of his fits—how else shall I term them?—of enthusiasm. He had found an unknown bivalve, forming a new genus, and, more than this, he had hunted down and secured, with Jupiter's assistance, a *scarabæus* which he believed to be totally new, but in respect to which he wished to have my opinion on the morrow.

"And why not to-night?" I asked, rubbing my hands over the blaze and wishing the whole tribe of *scarabæi* at the devil.

"Ah, if I had only known you were here!" said Legrand, "but it's so long since I saw you; and how could I foresee that you would pay me a visit this very night of all others? As I was coming home I met Lieutenant G——, from the fort, and, very foolishly, I lent him the bug; so it will be impossible for you to see it until the morning. Stay here to-night, and I will send Jup down for it at sunrise. It is the loveliest thing in creation!"

"What?—sunrise?"

"Nonsense! no!—the bug. It is of a brilliant gold color—about the size of a large hickory-nut—with two jet black spots near one extremity of the back, and another, somewhat longer, at the other. The *antennæ* are"—

"Dey aint no tin in him, Massa Will, I keep a tellin on you," here interrupted Jupiter; "de bug is a goole bug, solid, ebery bit of him, inside and all, sep him wing—neber feel half so hebby a bug in my life."

"Well, suppose it is, Jup," replied Legrand, somewhat more earnestly, it seemed to me, than the occasion demanded, "is that any reason for your letting the birds burn? The color"—here he turned to me—"is really almost enough to warrant Jupiter's idea. You never saw a more brilliant metallic lustre than the scales emit—but of this you cannot judge till to-morrow. In the mean time I can give you some idea of the shape." Saying this, he seated himself at a small table, on which were a pen and ink, but no paper. He looked for some in a drawer, but found none.

"Never mind," said he at length, "this will answer;" and he drew from his waistcoat pocket a scrap of what I took to be very dirty foolscap, and made upon it a rough drawing with the pen. While he did this I retained my seat by the fire, for I was still chilly. When the design was complete, he handed it to me without rising. As I received it a loud growl was heard, succeeded by a scratching at the door. Jupiter opened it, and a large Newfoundland, belonging to Legrand, rushed in, leaped upon my shoulders, and loaded me with caresses; for I had shown him much attention during previous visits. When his gambols were over I looked at the paper, and, to speak the truth, found myself not a little puzzled at what my friend had depicted.

"Well!" I said, after contemplating it for some minutes, "this is a strange *scarabæus*, I must confess: new to me: never saw anything like it before—unless it was a skull, or a death's-head—which it more nearly resembles than anything else that has come under my observation."

"A death's-head!" echoed Legrand—"Oh—yes—well, it has something of that appearance upon paper, no doubt. The two upper black spots look like eyes, eh? and the longer one at the bottom like a mouth—and then the shape of the whole is oval."

"Perhaps so," said I; "but, Legrand, I fear you are no artist. I must wait until I see the beetle itself, if I am to form any idea of its personal appearance."

"Well, I don't know," said he, a little nettled, "I draw tolerably—*should* do it at least—have had good masters, and flatter myself that I am not quite a blockhead."

"But, my dear fellow, you are joking then," said I, "this is a very passable *skull*—indeed, I may say that it is a very *excellent* skull, according to the vulgar notions about such specimens of physiology—and your *scarabæus* must be the queerest *scarabæus* in the world if it resembles it. Why, we may get up a very thrilling bit of superstition upon this hint. I presume you will call the bug *scarabæus caput hominis*, or something of that kind—there are many similar titles in the Natural Histories. But where are the *antennæ* you spoke of?"

"The *antennæ*!" said Legrand, who seemed to be getting unaccountably warm upon the subject; "I am sure you must see the *antennæ*. I made them as distinct as they are in the original insect, and I presume that is sufficient."

"Well, well," I said, "perhaps you have—still I don't see them;" and I handed him the paper without additional remark, not wishing to ruffle his temper; but I was much surprised at the turn affairs had taken; his ill humor puzzled me—and, as for the drawing of the beetle, there were positively *no antennæ* visible, and the whole *did* bear a very close resemblance to the ordinary cuts of a death's-head.

He received the paper very peevishly, and was about to crumple it, apparently to throw it in the fire, when a casual glance at the design seemed suddenly to rivet his attention. In an instant his face grew violently red—in another as excessively pale. For some minutes he continued to scrutinize the drawing minutely where he sat. At length he arose, took a candle from the table, and proceeded to seat himself upon a sea-chest in the farthest corner of the room. Here again he made an anxious examination of the paper; turning it in all directions. He said nothing, however, and his conduct greatly astonished me; yet I thought it prudent not to exacerbate the growing moodiness of his temper by any comment. Presently he took from his coat pocket a wallet, placed the paper carefully in it, and deposited both in a writing-desk, which he locked. He now grew more composed in his demeanor; but his original air of enthusiasm had quite disappeared. Yet he seemed not so much sulky as abstracted. As the evening wore away he became more and more absorbed in reverie, from which no sallies of mine could arouse him. It had been my intention to pass the night at the hut, as I had frequently done before, but, seeing my host in this mood, I deemed it proper to take leave. He did not press me to remain, but, as I departed, he shook my hand with even more than his usual cordiality.

It was about a month after this (and during the interval I had seen nothing of Legrand) when I received a visit, at Charleston, from his man, Jupiter. I had never seen the good old negro look so dispirited, and I feared that some serious disaster had befallen my friend.

"Well, Jup," said I, "what is the matter now?—how is your master?"

"Why, to speak de troof, massa, him not so berry well as mought be."

"Not well! I am truly sorry to hear it. What does he complain of?"

"Dar! dat's it!—him neber plain ob notin—but him berry sick for all dat."

"*Very* sick, Jupiter!—why didn't you say so at once? Is he confined to bed?"

"No, dat he aint!—he aint find nowhar—dat's just whar de shoe pinch—my mind is got to be berry hebby bout poor Massa Will."

"Jupiter, I should like to understand what it is you are talking about. You say your master is sick. Hasn't he told you what ails him?"

"Why, massa, taint worf while for to git mad bout de matter—Massa Will say noffin at all aint de matter wid him—but den what make him go about looking dis here way, wid he head down and he soldiers up, and as white as a gose? And den he keep a syphon all de time"—

"Keeps a what, Jupiter?"

"Keeps a syphon wid de figgurs on de slate—de queerest figgurs I ebber did see. Ise gittin to be skeered, I tell you. Hab for to keep mighty tight eye pon him noovers. Todder day he gib me slip fore de sun up and was gone de whole ob de blessed day. I had a big stick ready cut for to gib him d—n good beating when he did come—but Ise sich a fool dat I had n't de heart arter all—he look so berry poorly."

"Eh?—what?—ah yes!—upon the whole I think you had better not be too severe with the poor fellow—don't flog him, Jupiter—he can't very well stand it—but can you form no idea of what has occasioned this illness, or rather this change of conduct? Has anything unpleasant happened since I saw you?"

"No, massa, dey aint bin noffin onpleasant *since* den—'twas *fore* den, I'm feared—'twas the berry day you was dare."

"How? what do you mean?"

"Why, massa, I mean de bug—dare now."

"The what?"

"De bug—I'm berry sartain dat Massa Will bin bit somewhere bout de head by dat goole-bug."

"And what cause have you, Jupiter, for such a supposition?"

"Claws enuff, massa, and mouff too. I nebber did see sich a d—n bug—he kick and he bite ebery ting what cum near him. Massa Will cotch him fuss, but had for to let him go gin mighty quick, I tell you—den was de time he must ha got de bite. I didn't like de look ob de bug mouff, myself, no how, so I wouldn't take hold ob him wid my finger, but I cotch him wid a piece ob paper dat I found. I rap him up in de paper and stuff piece ob it in he mouff—dat was de way."

"And you think, then, that your master was really bitten by the beetle, and that the bite made him sick?"

"I don't tink noffin bout it—I nose it. What make him dream bout de goole so much, if taint cause he bit by de goole-bug? Ise heerd bout dem goole-bugs fore dis."

"But how do you know he dreams about gold?"

"How I know?—why cause he talk about it in he sleep—dat's how I nose."

"Well, Jup, perhaps you are right; but to what fortunate circumstance am I to attribute the honor of a visit from you, to-day?"

"What de matter, massa?"

"Did you bring any message from Mr. Legrand?"

"No, massa, I bring dis here pissel;" and here Jupiter handed me a note which ran thus:

My Dear ——,

Why have I not seen you for so long a time? I hope you have not been so foolish as to take offence at any little *brusquerie* of mine; but no, that is improbable.

Since I saw you I have had great cause for anxiety. I have something to tell you, yet scarcely know how to tell it, or whether I should tell it at all.

I have not been quite well for some days past, and poor old Jup annoys me, almost beyond endurance, by his well-meant attentions. Would you believe it?—he had prepared a huge stick, the other day, with which to chastise me for giving him the slip, and spending the day, *solus*, among the hills on the main land. I verily believe that my ill looks alone saved me a flogging.

I have made no addition to my cabinet since we met.

If you can, in any way, make it convenient, come over with Jupiter. *Do* come. I wish to see you *to-night*, upon business of importance. I assure you that it is of the *highest* importance.

Ever yours,

WILLIAM LEGRAND.

There was something in the tone of this note which gave me great uneasiness. Its whole style differed materially from that of Legrand. What could he be dreaming of? What new crotchet possessed his excitable brain? What "business of the highest importance" could *he* possibly have to transact? Jupiter's account of him boded no good. I dreaded lest the continued pressure of misfortune had, at length, fairly unsettled the reason of my friend. Without a moment's hesitation, therefore, I prepared to accompany the negro.

Upon reaching the wharf, I noticed a scythe and three spades, all apparently new, lying in the bottom of the boat in which we were to embark.

"What is the meaning of all this, Jup?" I inquired.

"Him syfe, massa, and spade."

"Very true; but what are they doing here?"

"Him de syfe and de spade what Massa Will sis pon my buying for him in de town, and de debbil's own lot of money I had to gib for em."

"But what, in the name of all that is mysterious, is your 'Massa Will' going to do with scythes and spades?"

"Dat's more dan *I* know, and debbil take me if I don't blieve 'tis more dan he know, too. But it's all cum ob de bug."

Finding that no satisfaction was to be obtained of Jupiter, whose whole intellect seemed to be absorbed by "de bug," I now stepped into the boat and made sail. With a fair and strong breeze we soon ran into the little cove to the northward of Fort Moultrie, and a walk of some two miles brought us to the hut. It was about three in the afternoon when we arrived. Legrand had been awaiting us in eager expectation. He grasped my hand with a nervous *empressement* which alarmed me and strengthened the suspicions already entertained. His countenance was pale, even to ghastliness, and his deep-set eyes glared with unnatural lustre. After some inquiries respecting his health, I asked him, not knowing what better to say, if he had yet obtained the *scarabæus* from Lieutenant G——.

"Oh, yes," he replied, coloring violently, "I got it from him the next morning. Nothing should tempt me to part with that *scarabæus*. Do you know that Jupiter is quite right about it?"

"In what way?" I asked, with a sad foreboding at heart.

"In supposing it to be a bug of *real gold*." He said this with an air of profound seriousness, and I felt inexpressibly shocked.

"This bug is to make my fortune," he continued, with a triumphant smile, "to reinstate me in my family possessions. Is it any wonder, then, that I prize it? Since Fortune has thought fit to bestow it upon me, I have only to use it properly and I shall arrive at the gold of which it is the index. Jupiter, bring me that *scarabæus*!"

"What! de bug, massa? I'd rudder not go fer trubble dat bug—you mus git him for your own self." Hereupon Legrand arose, with a grave and stately air, and brought me the beetle from a glass case in which it was enclosed. It was a beautiful *scarabæus*, and, at that time, unknown to naturalists—of course a great prize in a scientific point of view. There were two round black spots near one extremity of the back, and a long one near the other. The scales were exceedingly hard and glossy, with all the appearance of burnished gold. The weight of the insect was very remarkable, and, taking all things into consideration, I could hardly blame Jupiter for his opinion respecting it; but what to make of Legrand's concordance with that opinion, I could not, for the life of me, tell.

"I sent for you," said he, in a grandiloquent tone, when I had completed my examination of the beetle, "I sent for you, that I might have your counsel and assistance in furthering the views of Fate and of the bug"—

"My dear Legrand," I cried, interrupting him, "you are certainly unwell, and had better use some little precautions. You shall go to bed, and I will remain with you a few days, until you get over this. You are feverish and"—

"Feel my pulse," said he.

I felt it, and, to say the truth, found not the slightest indication of fever.

"But you may be ill and yet have no fever. Allow me, this once, to prescribe for you. In the first place, go to bed. In the next"—

"You are mistaken," he interposed, "I am as well as I can expect to be under the excitement which I suffer. If you really wish me well, you will relieve this excitement."

"And how is this to be done?"

"Very easily. Jupiter and myself are going upon an expedition into the hills upon the main land, and, in this expedition, we shall need the aid of some person in whom we can confide. You are the only one we can trust. Whether we succeed or fail, the excitement which you now perceive in me will be equally allayed."

"I am anxious to oblige you in any way," I replied; "but do you mean to say that this infernal beetle has any connection with your expedition into the hills?"

"It has."

"Then, Legrand, I can become a party to no such absurd proceeding."

"I am sorry—very sorry—for we shall have to try it by ourselves."

"Try it by yourselves! The man is surely mad!—but stay!—how long do you propose to be absent?"

"Probably all night. We shall start immediately, and be back, at all events, by sunrise."

"And will you promise me, upon your honor, that when this freak of yours is over, and the bug business (good God!) settled to your satisfaction, you will then return home and follow my advice implicitly, as that of your physician?"

"Yes; I promise; and now let us be off, for we have no time to lose."

With a heavy heart I accompanied my friend. We started about four o'clock—Legrand, Jupiter, the dog, and myself. Jupiter had with him the scythe and spades—the whole of which he insisted upon carrying—more through fear, it seemed to me, of trusting either of the implements within reach of his master, than from any excess of industry or complaisance. His demeanor was dogged in the extreme, and "dat d—n bug" were the sole words which escaped his lips during the journey. For my own part, I had charge of a couple of dark lanterns, while Legrand contented himself with the *scarabæus*, which he carried attached to the end of a bit of whip-cord; twirling it to and fro, with the air of a conjuror, as he went. When I observed this last plain evidence of my friend's aberration of mind, I could scarcely refrain from tears. I thought it best, however, to humor his fancy, at least for the present, or until I could adopt some more energetic measures with a chance of success. In the mean time I endeavored, but all in vain, to sound him in regard to the object of the expedition. Having succeeded in inducing me to accompany him, he seemed unwilling to hold conversation upon any topic of minor importance, and to all my questions vouchsafed no other reply than "we shall see!"

We crossed the creek at the head of the island by means of a skiff, and, ascending the high grounds on the shore of the main land, proceeded in a northwesterly direction, through a tract of country excessively wild and desolate, where no trace of a human footstep was to be seen. Legrand led the way with decision; pausing only for an instant, here and there, to consult what appeared to be certain landmarks of his own contrivance upon a former occasion.

In this manner we journeyed for about two hours, and the sun was just setting when we entered a region infinitely more dreary than any yet seen. It was a species of table-land, near the summit of an almost inaccessible hill, densely wooded from base to pinnacle, and interspersed with huge crags that appeared to lie loosely upon the soil, and in many cases were prevented from precipitating themselves into the valleys below merely by the support of the trees against which they reclined. Deep ravines, in various directions, gave an air of still sterner solemnity to the scene.

The natural platform to which we had clambered was thickly overgrown with brambles, through which we soon discovered that it would have been impossible to force our way but for the scythe; and Jupiter, by direction of his master, proceeded to clear for us a path to the foot of an enormously tall tulip-tree, which stood, with some eight or ten oaks, upon the level, and far surpassed them all, and all other trees which I had then ever seen, in the beauty of its foliage and form, in the wide spread of its branches, and in the general majesty of its appearance. When we reached this tree, Legrand turned to Jupiter, and asked him if he thought he could climb it. The old man seemed a little staggered by the question, and for some moments made no reply. At length he approached the huge trunk, walked slowly around it, and examined it with minute attention. When he had completed his scrutiny, he merely said,

"Yes, massa, Jup climb any tree he ebber see in he life."

"Then up with you as soon as possible, for it will soon be too dark to see what we are about."

"How far mus go up, massa?" inquired Jupiter.

"Get up the main trunk first, and then I will tell you which way to go—and here—stop! take this beetle with you."

"De bug, Massa Will!—de goole bug!" cried the negro, drawing back in dismay—"what for mus tote de bug way up de tree?—d—n if I do!"

"If you are afraid, Jup, a great big negro like you, to take hold of a harmless little dead beetle, why you can carry it up by this string—but, if you do not take it up with you in some way, I shall be under the necessity of breaking your head with this shovel."

"What de matter now, massa?" said Jup, evidently shamed into compliance; "always want for to raise fuss wid old nigger. Was only funnin any how. *Me* feered de bug! what I keer for de bug?" Here he took cautiously hold of the extreme end of the string, and, maintaining the insect as far from his person as circumstances would permit, prepared to ascend the tree.

In youth, the tulip-tree, or *Liriodendron Tulipiferum*, the most magnificent of American foresters, has a trunk peculiarly smooth, and often rises to a great height without lateral branches; but, in its riper age, the bark becomes gnarled and uneven, while many short limbs make their appearance on the stem. Thus the difficulty of ascension, in the present case, lay more in semblance than in reality. Embracing the huge cylinder, as closely as possible, with his arms and knees, seizing with his hands some projections, and resting his naked toes upon others, Jupiter, after one or two narrow escapes from falling, at length wriggled himself into the first great fork, and seemed to consider the whole business as virtually accomplished. The *risk* of the achievement was, in fact, now over, although the climber was some sixty or seventy feet from the ground.

"Which way mus go now, Massa Will?" he asked.

"Keep up the largest branch—the one on this side," said Legrand. The negro obeyed him promptly, and apparently with but little trouble, ascending higher and higher, until no glimpse of his squat figure could be obtained through the dense foliage which enveloped it. Presently his voice was heard in a sort of halloo.

"How much fudder is got for go?"

"How high up are you?" asked Legrand.

"Ebber so fur," replied the negro; "can see de sky fru de top ob de tree."

"Never mind the sky, but attend to what I say. Look down the trunk and count the limbs below you on this side. How many limbs have you passed?"

"One, two, tree, four, fibe—I done pass fibe big limb, massa, pon dis side."

"Then go one limb higher."

In a few minutes the voice was heard again, announcing that the seventh limb was attained.

"Now, Jup," cried Legrand, evidently much excited, "I want you to work your way out upon that limb as far as you can. If you see anything strange, let me know."

By this time what little doubt I might have entertained of my poor friend's insanity, was put finally at rest. I had no alternative but to conclude him stricken with lunacy, and I became seriously anxious about getting him home. While I was pondering upon what was best to be done, Jupiter's voice was again heard.

"Mos feerd for to ventur pon dis limb berry far—tis dead limb putty much all de way."

"Did you say it was a *dead* limb, Jupiter?" cried Legrand in a quavering voice.

"Yes, massa, him dead as de door-nail—done up for sartain—done departed dis here life."

"What in the name of heaven shall I do?" asked Legrand, seemingly in the greatest distress.

"Do!" said I, glad of an opportunity to interpose a word, "why come home and go to bed. Do—that's a fine fellow. It's getting late, and, besides, you remember your promise."

"Jupiter," cried he, without heeding me in the least, "do you hear me?"

"Yes, Massa Will, hear you ebber so plain."

"Try the wood well, then, with your knife, and see if you think it *very* rotten."

"Him rotten, massa, sure nuff," replied the negro in a few moments, "but not so berry rotten as mought be. Mought venture out leetle way pon de limb by myself, dat's true."

"By yourself!—what do you mean?"

"Why I mean de bug. 'Tis *berry* hebby bug. Spose I drop him down fuss, and den de limb won't break wid just de weight ob one nigger."

"You infernal scoundrel!" cried Legrand, apparently much relieved, "what do you mean by telling me such nonsense as that? As sure as you drop that beetle I'll break your neck. Look here, Jupiter, do you hear me?"

"Yes, massa, needn't hollo at poor nigger dat style."

"Well! now listen!—if you will venture out on the limb as far as you think safe, and not let go of the beetle, I'll make you a present of a silver dollar as soon as you get down."

"I'm gwine, Massa Will—deed I is," replied the negro very promptly—"mos out to de eend now."

"*Out to the end!*" here fairly screamed Legrand, "do you say you are out to the end of that limb?"

"Soon be to de eend, massa,—o-o-o-o-oh! Lor-gol-a-marcy! what *is* dis here pon de tree?"

"Well!" cried Legrand, highly delighted, "what is it?"

"Why taint noffin but a skull—somebody bin lef him head up de tree, and de crows done gobble ebery bit ob de meat off."

"A skull, you say!—very well!—how is it fastened to the limb?—what holds it on?"

"Sure nuff, massa; mus look. Why dis berry curious sarcumstance, pon my word—dare's a great big nail in de skull, what fastens ob it on to de tree."

"Well now, Jupiter, do exactly as I tell you—do you hear?"

"Yes, massa."

"Pay attention, then!—find the left eye of the skull."

"Hum! hoo! dat's good! why dare aint no eye lef at all."

"Curse your stupidity! do you know your right hand from your left?"

"Yes I nose dat—nose all bout dat—tis my lef hand what I chops de wood wid."

"To be sure! you are left-handed; and your left eye is on the same side as your left hand. Now, I suppose, you can find the left eye of the skull, or the place where the left eye has been. Have you found it?"

Here was a long pause. At length the negro asked,

"Is de lef eye of de skull pon de same side as de lef hand of de skull, too?—cause de skull aint got not a bit ob a hand at all—nebber mind! I got de lef eye now—here de lef eye! what mus do wid it?"

"Let the beetle drop through it, as far as the string will reach—but be careful and not let go your hold of the string."

"All dat done, Massa Will; mighty easy ting for to put de bug fru de hole—look out for him dar below!"

"Very well!—now just keep as you are for a few minutes."

During this colloquy no portion of Jupiter's person could be seen; but the beetle, which he had suffered to descend, was now visible at the end of the string, and glistened, like a globe of burnished gold, in the last rays of the setting sun, some of which still faintly illumined the eminence upon which we stood. The *scarabæus* hung quite clear of any branches, and, if allowed to fall, would have fallen at our feet. Legrand immediately took the scythe, and cleared with it a circular space, three or four yards in diameter, just beneath the insect, and, having accomplished this, ordered Jupiter to let go the string and come down from the tree.

Driving a peg, with great nicety, into the ground, at the precise spot where the beetle fell, my friend now produced from his pocket a tape-measure. Fastening one end of this at that point of the trunk of the tree which was nearest the peg, he unrolled it till it reached the peg, and thence farther unrolled it, in the direction already established by the two points of the tree and the peg, for the distance of fifty feet—Jupiter clearing away the brambles with the scythe. At the spot thus attained a second peg was driven; and about this, as a centre, a rude circle, about four feet in diameter, described. Taking now a spade himself, and giving one to Jupiter and one to me, Legrand begged us to set about digging as quickly as possible.

To speak the truth, I had no especial relish for such amusement at any time, and, at that particular moment, I would most willingly have declined it; for the night was coming on, and I felt much fatigued with the exercise already taken; but I saw no mode of escape, and was fearful of disturbing my poor friend's equanimity by a refusal. Could I have depended, indeed, upon Jupiter's aid, I would have had no hesitation in attempting to get the lunatic home by force; but I was too well assured of the old negro's disposition, to hope that he would assist me, under any circumstances, in a personal contest with his master. I made no doubt that the latter had been infected with some of the innumerable Southern superstitions about money buried, and that his phantasy had received confirmation by the finding of the *scarabæus*, or, perhaps, by Jupiter's obstinacy in maintaining it to be "a bug of real gold." A mind disposed to lunacy would readily be led away by such suggestions—especially if chiming in with favorite preconceived ideas—and then I called to mind the poor fellow's speech about the beetle's being "the index of his fortune." Upon the whole, I was sadly vexed and puzzled, but, at length, I concluded to make a virtue of necessity—to dig with a good will, and thus the sooner to convince the visionary, by ocular demonstration, of the fallacy of the opinions he entertained.

The lanterns having been lit, we all fell to work with a zeal worthy a more rational cause; and, as the glare fell upon our persons and implements, I could not help thinking how picturesque a group we composed, and how strange and suspicious our labors must have appeared to any interloper who, by chance, might have stumbled upon our whereabouts.

We dug very steadily for two hours. Little was said; and our chief embarrassment lay in the yelpings of the dog, who took exceeding interest in our proceedings. He, at length, became so obstreperous that we grew fearful of his giving the alarm to some stragglers in the vicinity;—or, rather, this was the apprehension of Legrand;—for myself, I should have rejoiced at any interruption which might have enabled me to get the wanderer home. The noise was, at length, very effectually silenced by Jupiter, who, getting out of the hole with a dogged air of deliberation, tied the brute's mouth up with one of his suspenders, and then returned, with a grave chuckle, to his task.

When the time mentioned had expired, we had reached a depth of five feet, and yet no signs of any treasure became manifest. A general pause ensued, and I began to hope that the farce was at an end. Legrand, however, although evidently much disconcerted, wiped his brow thoughtfully and recommenced. We had excavated the entire circle of four feet diameter, and now we slightly enlarged the limit, and went to the farther depth of two feet. Still nothing appeared. The gold-seeker, whom I sincerely pitied, at length clambered from the pit, with the bitterest disappointment imprinted upon every feature, and proceeded, slowly and reluctantly, to put on his coat, which he had thrown off at the beginning of his labor. In the mean time I made no remark. Jupiter, at a signal from his master, began to gather up his tools. This done, and the dog having been unmuzzled, we turned in a profound silence towards home.

We had taken, perhaps, a dozen steps in this direction, when, with a loud oath, Legrand strode up to Jupiter and seized him by the collar. The astonished negro opened his eyes and mouth to the fullest extent, let fall the spades, and fell upon his knees.

"You scoundrel!" said Legrand, hissing out the syllables from between his clenched teeth—"you infernal black villain!—speak, I tell you!—answer me this instant without prevarication!—which—which is your left eye?"

"Oh, my Golly, Massa Will! aint dis here my lef eye for sartain?" roared the terrified Jupiter, placing his hand upon his *right* organ of vision, and holding it there with a desperate pertinacity, as if in immediate dread of his master's attempt at a gouge.

"I thought so!—I knew it!—hurrah!" vociferated Legrand, letting the negro go, and executing a series of curvets and caracols, much to the astonishment of his valet, who, arising from his knees, looked, mutely, from his master to myself, and then from myself to his master.

"Come! we must go back," said the latter, "the game's not up yet;" and he again led the way to the tulip-tree.

"Jupiter," said he, when we reached its foot, "come here! was the skull nailed to the limb with the face outwards, or with the face to the limb?"

"De face was out, massa, so dat de crows could get at de eyes good, widout any trouble."

"Well, then, was it this eye or that through which you dropped the beetle?"—here Legrand touched each of Jupiter's eyes.

"'Twas dis eye, massa—de lef eye—jis as you tell me," and here it was his right eye that the negro indicated.

"That will do—we must try it again."

Here my friend, about whose madness I now saw, or fancied that I saw, certain indications of method, removed the peg which marked the spot where the beetle fell, to a spot about three inches to the westward of its former position. Taking, now, the tape-measure from the nearest point of the trunk to the peg, as before, and continuing the extension in a straight line to the distance of fifty feet, a spot was indicated, removed, by several yards, from the point at which we had been digging.

Around the new position a circle, somewhat larger than in the former instance, was now described, and we again set to work with the spades. I was dreadfully weary, but, scarcely understanding what had occasioned the change in my thoughts, I felt no longer any great aversion from the labor imposed. I had become most unaccountably interested—nay, even excited. Perhaps there was something, amid all the extravagant demeanor of Legrand—some air of forethought, or of deliberation, which impressed me. I dug eagerly, and now and then caught myself actually looking, with something that very much resembled expectation, for the fancied treasure, the vision of which had demented my unfortunate companion. At a period when such vagaries of thought most fully possessed me, and when we had been at work perhaps an hour and a half, we were again interrupted by the violent howlings of the dog. His uneasiness, in the first instance, had been, evidently, but the result of playfulness or caprice, but he now assumed a bitter and serious tone. Upon Jupiter's again attempting to muzzle him, he made furious resistance, and, leaping into the hole, tore up the mould frantically with his claws. In a few seconds he had uncovered a mass of human bones, forming two complete skeletons, and intermingled with several buttons of metal, and what appeared to be the dust of decayed woollen. One or two strokes of a spade upturned the blade of a large Spanish knife, and, as we dug farther, three or four loose pieces of gold and silver coin came to light.

At sight of these the joy of Jupiter could scarcely be restrained, but the countenance of his master wore an air of extreme disappointment. He urged us, however, to continue our exertions, and the words were hardly uttered when I stumbled and fell forward, having caught the toe of my boot in a large ring of iron that lay half buried in the loose earth.

We now worked in good earnest, and never did I pass ten minutes of more intense excitement. During this interval we had fairly unearthed an oblong chest of wood, which, from its perfect preservation and wonderful hardness, had plainly been subjected to some mineralizing process—perhaps that of the Bi-chloride of Mercury. This box was three feet and a half long, three feet broad, and two and a half feet deep. It was firmly secured by bands of wrought iron, riveted, and forming a kind of open trellis-work over the whole. On each side of the chest, near the top, were three rings of iron—six in all—by means of which a firm hold could be obtained by six persons. Our utmost united endeavors served only to disturb the coffer very slightly in its bed. We at once saw the impossibility of removing so great a weight. Luckily, the sole fastenings of the lid consisted of two sliding bolts. These we drew back—trembling and panting with anxiety. In an instant, a treasure of incalculable value lay gleaming before us. As the rays of the lanterns fell within the pit, there flashed upwards a glow and a glare, from a confused heap of gold and of jewels, that absolutely dazzled our eyes.

I shall not pretend to describe the feelings with which I gazed. Amazement was, of course, predominant. Legrand appeared exhausted with excitement, and spoke very few words. Jupiter's countenance wore, for some minutes, as deadly a pallor as it is possible, in the nature of things, for any negro's visage to assume. He seemed stupified—thunderstricken. Presently he fell upon his knees in the pit, and, burying his naked arms up to the elbows in gold,

let them there remain, as if enjoying the luxury of a bath. At length, with a deep sigh, he exclaimed, as if in a soliloquy,

"And dis all cum ob de goole-bug! de putty goole bug! de poor little goole-bug, what I boosed in dat sabage kind ob style! Aint you shamed ob yourself, nigger?—answer me dat!"

It became necessary, at last, that I should arouse both master and valet to the expediency of removing the treasure. It was growing late, and it behooved us to make exertion, that we might get every thing housed before daylight. It was difficult to say what should be done, and much time was spent in deliberation—so confused were the ideas of all. We, finally, lightened the box by removing two thirds of its contents, when we were enabled, with some trouble, to raise it from the hole. The articles taken out were deposited among the brambles, and the dog left to guard them, with strict orders from Jupiter neither, upon any pretence, to stir from the spot, nor to open his mouth until our return. We then hurriedly made for home with the chest; reaching the hut in safety, but after excessive toil, at one o'clock in the morning. Worn out as we were, it was not in human nature to do more immediately. We rested until two, and had supper; starting for the hills immediately afterwards, armed with three stout sacks, which, by good luck, were upon the premises. A little before four we arrived at the pit, divided the remainder of the booty, as equally as might be, among us, and, leaving the holes unfilled, again set out for the hut, at which, for the second time, we deposited our golden burthens, just as the first faint streaks of the dawn gleamed from over the tree-tops in the East.

We were now thoroughly broken down; but the intense excitement of the time denied us repose. After an unquiet slumber of some three or four hours' duration, we arose, as if by preconcert, to make examination of our treasure.

The chest had been full to the brim, and we spent the whole day, and the greater part of the next night, in a scrutiny of its contents. There had been nothing like order or arrangement. Every thing had been heaped in promiscuously. Having assorted all with care, we found ourselves possessed of even vaster wealth than we had at first supposed. In coin there was rather more than four hundred and fifty thousand dollars—estimating the value of the pieces, as accurately as we could, by the tables of the period. There was not a particle of silver. All was gold of antique date and of great variety—French, Spanish, and German money, with a few English guineas, and some counters of which we had never seen specimens before. There were several very large and heavy coins, so worn that we could make nothing of their inscriptions. There was no American money. The value of the jewels we found more difficulty in estimating. There were diamonds—some of them exceedingly large and fine—a hundred and ten in all, and not one of them small; eighteen rubies of remarkable brilliancy;—three hundred and ten emeralds, all very beautiful; and twenty-one sapphires, with an opal. These stones had all been broken from their settings and thrown loose in the chest. The settings themselves, which we picked out from among the other gold, appeared to have been beaten up with hammers, as if to prevent identification. Besides all this, there was a vast quantity of solid gold ornaments;—nearly two hundred massive finger and ear rings;—rich chains—thirty of these, if I remember;—eighty-three very large and heavy crucifixes;—five gold censers of great value;—a prodigious golden punch-bowl, ornamented with richly chased vine-leaves and Bacchanalian figures; with two sword-handles exquisitely embossed, and many other smaller articles which I cannot recollect. The weight of these valuables exceeded three hundred and fifty pounds avoirdupois; and in this estimate I have not included one hundred and ninety-seven superb gold watches; three of the number being worth each five hundred dollars, if one. Many of them were very old, and as time-keepers valueless; the works having suffered, more or less, from corrosion—but all were richly jewelled and in cases of great worth. We estimated the entire contents of the chest, that night, at a million and a half of dollars; and, upon the subsequent disposal of the trinkets and jewels (a few being retained for our own use) it was found that we had greatly undervalued the treasure.

When, at length, we had concluded our examination, and the intense excitement of the time had, in some measure, subsided, Legrand, who saw that I was dying with impatience, for a solution of this most extraordinary riddle, entered into a full detail of all the circumstances connected with it.

"You remember," said he, "the night when I

(Concluded on Fourth Page.)

extreme than Wilmer's observation had been, for his ex-friend's comment on 'the strangest of our literati' had been, 'poor fellow; he is not a teetotaller by any means, and I fear he is going to destruction morally, physically and intellectually'.

The decline his friends observed in Poe's condition paralleled Virginia's. Tuberculosis had now invalided her almost totally, and the pain of watching her slowly die stimulated Poe's self-destructiveness. A lady visitor to the house observed that 'he devoted himself to [Sis] with all the ardor of a lover', but the fact was he no longer had 'a lover'; indeed he was about to lose her for ever. Sis had been his frail but unique link with reality, a key subject of his most profound disturbances, the centre of his dreams and fantasies. She was truly the focus of his worlds both outward and inward, and he dreaded her imminent loss. Griswold described him rather theatrically at this time in a state of drunken or drugged misery:

> . . . He walked the streets, in madness or melancholy, with lips moving in indistinct curses, or with eyes upturned in passionate prayers, (never for himself, for he felt, or professed to feel, that he was already damned), but for their happiness who were at the moment the objects of his idolatry; or with his glance introverted to a heart gnawed with anguish, and with a face shrouded in gloom, he would brave the wildest storms; and at night, with drenched garments and arms wildly beating the wind and rain he would speak as if to spirits that at such times only could be evoked by him from that Aidenn close by [behind] whose portals his distributed soul sought to forget the ills to which his constitution subjected him....

Yet Poe still had moments of brilliance in which he could impress Philadelphians, though now such times were touched with fear that his charm might be suddenly dispelled by his daemon. Howard Paul, a nephew of Clarke's, described him as 'warm with wine and in genial, glowing mood', discoursing brilliantly during dinner:

> Poe was a slight, small-boned, delicate looking man, with a well-developed head, which at a glance, seemed out of proportion to his slender body. His features were regular, his complexion pale; and his nose was Grecian and well-moulded. He dressed with neatness, and there was a suggestion of hauteur in his manner towards strangers. He was impatient of restraint or contradiction, and when his Southern blood was up, as the saying goes, he could be cuttingly rude and bitterly sarcastic.

But after such a dinner Poe was capable, in company with a drunken friend, of meeting a Jewish stranger on the street and hanging him 'by his breeches on the pikes of a convenient area railing, where they left him kicking and howling while they pursued their tortuous way in gladsome mood'.

Often Poe's evenings were spent at the theatre, for he was attempting erratically and with little success to write drama, and theatrical images were much in his mind. In January 1843 he had published in *Graham's* a new poem which reflected these

*The Conqueror Worm*, illustrated by W. Heath Robinson.

interests together with his more fundamental preoccupations. The poem, *The Conqueror Worm*, is a melodramatic piece, but its final stanzas project very powerfully the image of the all-consuming worm or maggot. Puppets come and go on the stage of life at the 'bidding of vast formless things'. The motley drama continues with 'much of Madness, and more of Sin, and Horror the soul of the plot', until the final scene, when the horrible dénouement occurs:

But see, amid the mimic rout
   A crawling shape intrude!
A blood-red thing that writhes from out
   The scenic solitude!
It writhes! – it writhes! – with mortal pangs
   The mimes become its food,
And the angels sob at vermin fangs
   In human gore imbued.

Out – out are the lights – out all!
   And, over each quivering form,
The curtain, a funeral pall,
   Comes down with the rush of a storm,
And the angels, all pallid and wan,
   Uprising, unveiling, affirm
That the play is the tragedy, 'Man,'
   And its hero the Conquering Worm.

The theatrical excitement generated in Poe by contemplating the inevitability with which posturing man becomes food for maggots was a highly effective stimulant.

Yet perhaps the saddest aspect of Poe in decline was the disintegration of what had been a characteristically powerful will to pursue his objectives into paranoid fragments. Graham had begun, under pressure from Poe and in the light of the

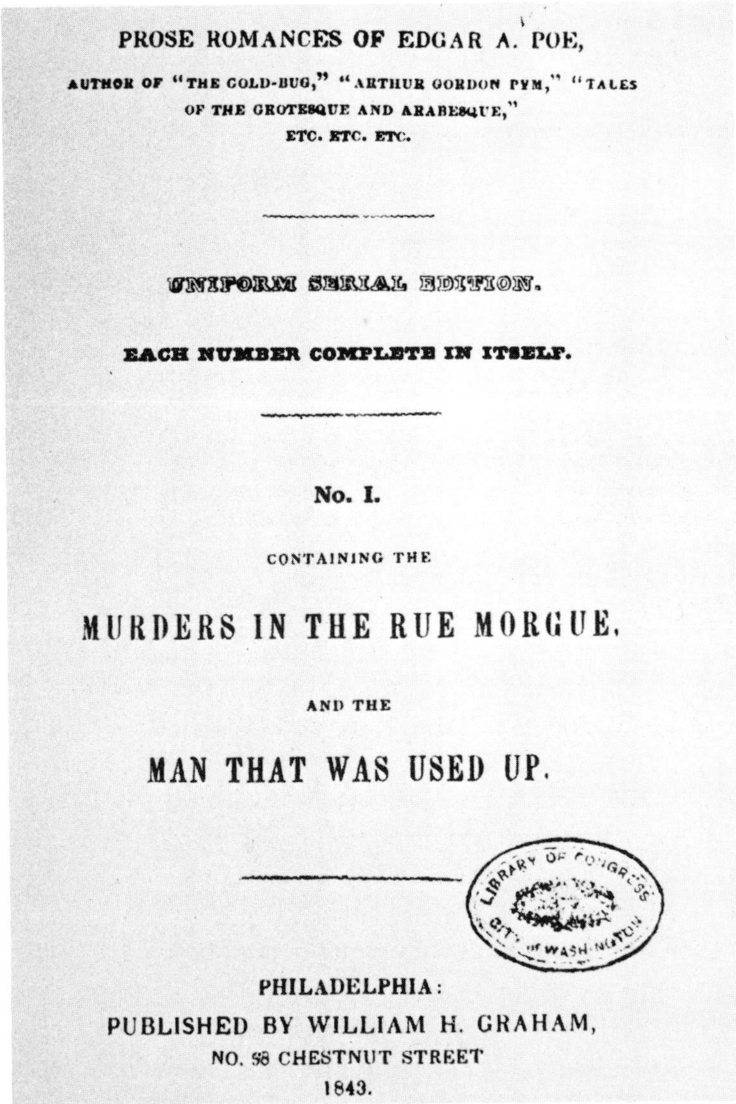
PROSE ROMANCES OF EDGAR A. POE,

AUTHOR OF "THE GOLD-BUG," "ARTHUR GORDON PYM," "TALES OF THE GROTESQUE AND ARABESQUE," ETC. ETC. ETC.

UNIFORM SERIAL EDITION.

EACH NUMBER COMPLETE IN ITSELF.

No. I.

CONTAINING THE

MURDERS IN THE RUE MORGUE,

AND THE

MAN THAT WAS USED UP.



PHILADELPHIA:
PUBLISHED BY WILLIAM H. GRAHAM,
NO. 98 CHESTNUT STREET
1843.

Title page of the first number of the serial edition of *The Prose Romances of Edgar A. Poe.*

success of *The Gold Bug*, the publication of *The Prose Romances of Edgar A. Poe* in a uniform serial edition. Number one appeared, comprising *The Murders in the Rue Morgue* and *The Man That Was Used Up*. Published at twelve-and-a-half cents, the first part of the paper-bound serial work quickly went out of print and is today one of the rarest of all published Poe items. But no further numbers appeared, for Poe was no longer capable of consistent effort. The public was still enormously interested in him and he lectured successfully that winter to fashionable Philadelphia audiences, drawn as much by the scandals associated with him as by his matter. Through the following spring he was away from home a good deal, his whereabouts not always being certain. He grew obsessed with *The Raven*, working on it and reciting it constantly. A local schoolteacher heard him do so and observed:

> His dissipation was too notorious to be denied; and for days, and even weeks at a time, he would be sharing the bachelor life and quarters of his associates, who were not aware that he was a married man. He would, on some evenings when sober, come to the rooms occupied by himself and some other writers for the press and, producing the manuscript of *The Raven* read to them the last additions to it, asking their opinions and suggestions. He seemed to be having difficulty with it, and to be very doubtful as to its merits as a poem. The general opinion of these critics was against it. . . .

This adverse general opinion was made mortifyingly clear one day when Poe arrived at the office of *Graham's* with a draft of *The Raven* for the editors to approve and buy for the magazine. If his poem were not enough in itself Edgar reminded them that Virginia and Mrs Clemm were hungry and that he was penniless. Yet he was confident that the poem, his greatest achievement, would move them without the appeal of his personal situation. He recited it to them, not only to Graham and his old enemy Charles Peterson, but to Godey, another magazine-owner, and all the clerks and printers too. Edgar read *The Raven* as he had never done before, with all the compelling theatricality dictated by the irresistible rhythms of the poem and his understanding of styles dramatic. After its immortal concluding lines, he lifted his eyes from the long roll of manuscript and scanned his audience. Their doubts were clear upon their faces. Charles Peterson brusquely turned the great work down. Graham, either from weakness or influenced by Peterson, also refused it. Godey made no separate offer for it. The clerks and printers' devils inevitably voted with their employers. *The Raven* was flying in the face of public opinion. But the workers were sorry for Edgar, and one of them suggested passing the hat around. Edgar had not the heart or spirit to walk out on the charitable impulse. The hat passed, all contributed a coin or two and $15 was collected, a poor price for the reading of a major work by a major innovative literary genius, but at least it was non-returnable. Poe's fierce, proud spirit had never sunk lower than in this moment of unbearable philanthropy. He took the money and left the office in silent despair.

## *The Raven Triumphant*

On the Sunday morning of 7 April 1844, Edgar Poe wrote a simple account of his feelings and situation, newly arrived with his sick wife in a New York boarding house. The letter, to Mrs Clemm, is one of the few of Poe's totally free of postures:

New York, Sunday Morning
April 7, (1844) just after
breakfast.

My Dear Muddy, – We have just this minute done breakfast, and I now sit down to write you about everything. I can't pay for the letter, because the P.O. won't be open to-day. In the first place we arrived safe at Walnut St wharf. The driver wanted to make me pay a dollar, but I wouldn't. Then I had to pay a boy a levy to put the trunks in the baggage car. In the meantime I took Sis in the Depot Hotel. It was only a quarter past six, and we had to wait till seven. We saw the Ledger and Times – nothing in either – a few words of no account in the Chronicle. We started in good spirits, but did not get here until nearly three o'clock. We went in the cars to Amboy, about forty miles from N. York. When we got to the wharf it was raining hard. I left her on board the boat, after putting the trunks in the Ladies' cabin, and set off to buy an umbrella and look for a boarding-house. I met a man selling umbrellas, and bought one for twenty-five cents. Then I went up Greenwich St and soon found a boarding-house. It is just before you get to Cedar St, on the west side going up – the left-hand side. It has brown stone steps, with a porch with brown pillars. 'Morrison' is the name on the door. I made a bargain in a few minutes and then got a hack and went for Sis. I was not gone more than half an hour, and she was quite astonished to see me back so soon. She didn't expect me for an hour. There were two other ladies waiting on board – so she wasn't very lonely. When we got to the house we had to wait about half an hour before the room was ready. The house is old and looks buggy . . . the cheapest board I ever knew, taking into consideration the central situation and the living. I wish Kate could see it – she would faint. Last night, for supper, we had the nicest tea you ever drank, strong and hot, – wheat bread and rye bread – cheese – tea-cakes (elegant), a great dish (two dishes) of elegant ham, and two of cold veal, piled up like a mountain and large slices – three dishes of the cakes and everything in the greatest profusion. No fear of starving here. The landlady seemed as if she couldn't press us enough, and we were at home directly. Her husband is living with her – a fat, good-natured old soul. There are eight or ten boarders – two or three of them ladies – two servants. For breakfast we had excellent-flavoured coffee, hot and strong – not very clear and no great deal of cream – veal cutlets, elegant ham and eggs and nice bread and butter. I never sat down to a more plentiful or a nicer breakfast. I wish you could have seen the eggs – and the great dishes of meat. I ate the first hearty breakfast I have eaten since I left our little home. Sis is delighted, and we are both in excellent spirits. She has coughed hardly any and had no night sweat. She is now busy mending my pants which I tore against a nail. I went out last night and bought a skein of silk, a skein of thread, two buttons, a pair of slippers, and a pan for the stove. The fire kept in all night. We have now got four dollars and a half left. Tomorrow I am going to try and borrow three dollars, so that I may have a fortnight to go upon. I feel in excellent spirits, and haven't drank a drop – so that I hope soon to get out of trouble. The very instant I scrape together enough money I will send it on. You can't imagine how much we both do miss you. Sissy had a hearty cry last night because you and Catterina weren't there. We are resolved to get two rooms the first moment we can. In the meantime it is impossible we could be more comfortable or more at home than we are. It looks as if it were going to clear up now. Be sure and go to the P.O. and have my letters forwarded. As soon as I write Lowell's article, I will send it to you, and get you to get the money from Graham. Give our best love to C.

(P.S.) Be sure and take home the Messenger to Hirst. We hope to send for you very soon.

The boarding house with the elegant and profuse meals was at 130 Greenwich Street, and Poe financed his stay there (at about $3 per week!) by completing and selling the story *The Balloon Hoax* to the *Sun* newspaper. The editor was amenable to Poe's ingenious notion of presenting a fiction as if it were a new item (a technique remembered years later by Orson Welles in his *War of the Worlds* radio production). On 13 April the following sensational announcement appeared in the *Sun:*

ASTOUNDING
NEWS!
BY EXPRESS VIA NORFOLK!
THE
ATLANTIC CROSSED
in
THREE DAYS!
Signal Triumph
of
Mr. Monck
Mason's
FLYING
MACHINE!!!!!
Arrival at Sullivan's Island near Charleston, S.C. of Mr Mason, Mr Robert Holland, Mr Henson, Mr Harrison Ainsworth, and four others, in the Steering Balloon 'Victoria' – After a passage of Seventy-Five Hours From Land to Land.

*The Balloon Hoax* was published in an 'extra' edition of the paper as if it were a scoop. Poe had the satisfaction not only of being paid well enough to cover the small costs of his board and lodging for several weeks, but also of beginning his New York career with a stylish hoax of the kind that delighted him. He took an extra room at the boarding house, Mrs Clemm and the cat were sent for, and it was discreetly 'leaked' that the new prosperity was due to Edgar's brilliant fooling of the readers of the *Sun*.

As always with Edgar, a sensational opening was followed up uncertainly. Though *The Balloon Hoax* instantly drew the attention of the literary world to his presence in New York, there were no editorships available, and so a return to the familiar, exhausting routine of freelance hacking was his only alternative. The story *The Oblong Box* was completed and sold to *Godey's Lady's Book;* his poem *Dreamland* was published in *Graham's*; but his fame and scandalous reputation had to be sustained with very little newly published material. He collected some sixty-six of his stories together and tried to find a publisher for them in four or five volumes, but, in spite of his now undenied status in American letters, no offer was forthcoming. By the summer he was still without regular employment or a publisher. *The Raven* was still unfinalized and unsold, though Edgar continued his practice of reading its latest version to whoever would listen among the bohemians with whom he spent much of his time, since he had now left Mrs Clemm and Virginia at the boarding house to share bachelor quarters with a friend. Doubtless the reduction in domesticity resulted in an increase in drinking, for the soliciting of freelance work involved endless discussions in taverns.

The summer in New York was very hot. Sis found it exhausting and Mrs Clemm insisted that she should be moved to the country. She was not unaware, too, that it was essential to get Edgar away from his destructive, bohemian way of life. A farm was found a few miles out of town on the Bloomingdale road, standing above the road on a rocky knoll a few hundred feet from what is now the north-east corner of 84th Street and Broadway. The house was a wooden-frame colonial building of some charm, with a small pond and two large trees in front of it. One of them, a weeping willow, was rumoured to have been grown from the seed of that shading Napoleon's tomb at St Helena. For miles around meadows and woods filled the landscape; and there were no public houses except for the nearby Stryker's Bay Tavern, so that if Edgar disappeared and was not on a walk, Mrs Clemm would know where to find him. The house belonged to Mr and Mrs Brennan, who with their six or seven children kept a farm of some 200 acres, producing fruit, vegetables and flowers for the city market. For a few coins a week they were happy to provide the Poes with rooms and board.

The Poes, regardless of the children and dogs, found the place 'a perfect heaven', and indeed the last happy times Poe was ever to know were to be spent here. Mrs Clemm's room was downstairs, while Edgar and Sis had a garret under the eaves. Poe's study below had a large open fireplace with a splendid carved mantel. Transformed, it became the setting for *The Raven*, for here, at last, the poem reached its finalized version. The study had a Gallic atmosphere which, together with the tree from St Helena, had been left behind by an exiled Napoleonic officer, the previous boarder. No one had claimed his Imperial souvenirs – some military prints, an impressive clock, heavy Empire drapes and a few pieces of furniture, a bookcase and a table-desk. Above the door stood the 'pallid bust of Pallas' memorialized in the poem; actually a small plaster cast. The house was much exposed to the wind,

*Long Island Farmhouses*, a painting by Sidney William Mount.

whose nocturnal wailings as it swept up the Hudson Valley are echoed in the rhythms of *The Raven*.

When Poe was not writing in his study he relaxed on a bench by the pond, joined there by Virginia when she was feeling strong. Sis would paste his manuscripts together into the long rolls which he preferred to separate sheets, and the admiration of his fine, clear writing and the extraordinary length of the rolls was perhaps the nearest the poor girl ever got to appreciating her husband's literary talent. But she and her mother listened to Poe's recitals with devotedly rapt attention, which was enough for his purposes. The rhythmical and euphonic effects in the poems and stories were of the utmost importance to Poe, so that recitation was an essential part of his method of composition; it was more important that his audience should be admiring and sympathetic than that they should presume to understand too well.

Few visitors came to the farm, and Edgar walked to New York, if he had to go there, to save the fare, for the family's board was always paid before anything else. Mrs Clemm, with her long experience, knew that they were blessed in their discovery of the kind Irish family who had taken them in, and she was determined not to lose the Brennans' good will. The situation was ideal from her point of view. There was the fresh, inexpensive produce from the farm, the good air, and a wonderful lack

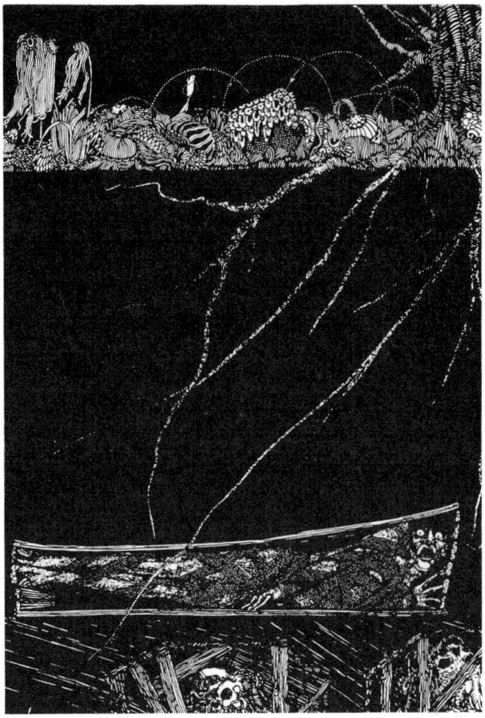

ABOVE LEFT Engraving by Doré for *The Raven*: 'And my soul from out that shadow . . . shall be lifted – nevermore!'

ABOVE RIGHT Illustration by Harry Clarke for *The Premature Burial.*

of visitors and temptations for Edgar. That summer was to be the best time of her life with her wayward but adored adoptive son. Expenses were covered by *Godey's*, *Graham's* and the *Columbian Magazine*'s acceptance of several minor stories and sketches. The most important of his tales published that summer in *The Dollar Newspaper* was *The Premature Burial*, as powerfully morbid a piece as Poe ever wrote. It, together with *Loss of Breath* and *The Tell-Tale Heart*, captures the physical quality of a heart attack – the rapid, loud beat, the sense of oppression, the overwhelming feeling of impending doom, the extreme fatigue, all the unforgettable consequences of his excesses. The weakened heart with its oppressive beat drove him out of rural bliss to contemplation of the grave and 'the shrouded bodies in their sad and solemn slumbers with the worm'. But though the occasional trips to New York to sell stories to the magazines were often followed by such painful reactions, the regimen of Mrs Clemm more normally held sway over Edgar, and his principal writing preoccupation was the completion and launching of *The Raven.*

Poe's unforgettable poem, so melodramatic and over-euphonic, so redolent of the contrived gothicity dear to mid-nineteenth-century taste, yet, in spite of the limitations of its period, so much embodying the sense of doom which may oppress any mortal at any time, a work which had engaged him for two years, was completed here at the Brennan farm. Poe had conceived the idea in Philadelphia some four years before while reviewing Dickens' *Barnaby Rudge*, in which a far less sinister raven, based upon Dickens' own pet birds, is to be found. Lowell recognized the source of Poe's bird:

> Here comes Poe with his Raven, like
>     Barnaby Rudge,
> Three fifths of him genius, and two fifths
>     sheer fudge....

Poe had tried at first to make an owl carry his symbolism, but the black bird had ousted it. As early as 1842 he had shown a draft of the poem to a writer for the *New York Mirror*. Work continued through the next year, and his Philadelphia acquaintance Rosenbach recorded reading a manuscript copy of it in the winter of 1843–4. He also remembered the unhappy occasion when the hat was passed around for Poe, and there are several other accounts of Poe reading it to groups through 1844. Hervey Allen carefully traced the genesis of the poem, demonstrating the long period of incubation Poe required for his poems, and his 'typically slow method of verse composition'. Poe himself wrote about the problems of writing poetry:

> Events not to be controlled have prevented me from making, at any time, any serious effort in what, under happier circumstances, would have been the field of my choice. With me, poetry has not been a purpose, but a passion; and the passions should be held in reverence; they must not – they cannot at will be excited, with an eye to the paltry commendations, of mankind.

In the Napoleonic study where he had added his signature to the carving on the fine mantelpiece, Poe finalized his highly theatrical poem. He might have fairly remarked of it what he had observed of Dickens' bird, that 'its croakings might have been prophetically heard in the course of the drama'. *The Raven* in the haunted gothic study, the wind without, the shadow of the bust of Pallas falling across the scene, is, of itself, mid-nineteenth-century theatricalia; yet it is totally authentic in its symbolism of despair and the profound melancholy of a depressive genius now no more than four years away from insanity. The unavoidable doom of the poet which is croaked out by the black bird of destiny, that chilling 'Nevermore', is, in a sense, a symbol of the oncoming blackness of the mental confusion which Poe knew lay ahead. The shadow of Pallas spreading over him owed something of its darkness to the deep brown-black tinge of laudanum. The addict in his chamber alone in eternity is only a stage away from being a total egomaniac, as Baudelaire (an addict himself) recognized:

> Finally, the drugged man admires himself, inordinately; he condemns himself, he glorifies himself; he realizes his condemnation; he becomes the centre of the universe,

certain of his virtue as of his genius. Then, in a stupendous irony, he cries: *Je suis devenu Dieu!* One instant after he projects himself out of himself, as if the will of an intoxicated man had an efficacious virtue, and cries, with a cry that might strike down the scattered angels from the ways of the sky: *Je suis un Dieu!*

Poe knew that he was damned, and that he was a genius. He knew also that opium was an integral part of both elements in his nature. He sensed them driving him towards the God-like delusions of his later work *Eureka*, in which he completed the process described by Baudelaire. There he becomes God, his superb intelligence having admitted him into the secrets of the universe, whereupon he cries, 'Eureka! I have found it!' He has the secret at last; he is the Deity and is finally insane. But for the moment, the great poem was completed and its author enjoyed, between times, the rural peace of the Brennan farm. Ironically, Mrs Clemm was responsible for the loss of this peace and the exposure once again of her vulnerable Eddy to the temptations of a journalist's life in the city.

Autumn was coming on and the Poe family income was once again inadequate to cope with even the small cash requirements of life with the Brennans. The great poem complete earned as little as ever, and Edgar had, for all practical purposes, withdrawn himself from any world in which money could be earned, and was enjoying it. Thus his creativity was supported by the relaxed reclusive life and his energies conserved by it for his work, and Mrs Clemm realized very well the advantages of life on the farm. But practical questions demanded practical answers, and before another winter froze them into penury yet again she was determined to take positive action. Some time in September she went to New York to search out regular work for Edgar. There she called upon Nathaniel Parker Willis, the editor and owner of the *New York Evening Mirror*. Willis was a popular, dashing, good-natured man of letters, who had risen from obscure poet to successful journalist. He prided himself upon his international range of contacts and experience, and valued Poe for his non-provincial qualities. Knowing that Edgar's literary credit was good with Willis, Mrs Clemm called at the *Mirror* office. Willis recorded the interview:

Our first knowledge of Mr Poe's removal to this city [New York] was by a call which we received from a lady who introduced herself to us as the mother of his wife. She was in search of employment for him, and she excused her errand by mentioning that he was ill, and that her daughter was a confirmed invalid, and that her circumstances were such as compelled her taking it upon herself. The countenance of this lady, made beautiful and saintly with an evidently complete giving up of her life to privation and sorrowful tenderness, her gentle and mournful voice, urging its plea, her long forgotten but habitual and unconsciously refined manners, and her appealing, and yet appreciative mention of the claims and abilities of her son, disclosing at once the presence of one of those angels upon earth that women in adversity can be....

Willis was about to extend and improve the *Mirror*, making it both a daily and a weekly. The weekly would be 'a journal of literature, news and the fine arts', and a writer of Poe's experience and talent would be a considerable asset to it. Christian charity (which Willis was not bohemian enough to sneer at) demanded that he aid his colleague, and Mrs Clemm made it clear that Eddy was not expensive. Willis thereupon engaged Poe as a 'mechanical paragraphist', a kind of columnist picking up unconsidered trifles, adding his own notes, and rewriting the mixed gallimaufry. Poe would have a desk in the office and would report daily at 9 am, working through till the paper went to press. It was a return to the grindmill for Edgar, but Muddy had decided that needs must. And it was simply unfortunate that Edgar could not commute such a distance daily, so that the job must bring their idyllic summer in the country to an end. Sadly and anxiously, the Poes moved back to New York, to a boarding house at 15 Amity Street in Greenwich Village. For Edgar it was a return to the tense and frustrating life of a hack; Sis had been better from time to time through the summer, but here she was at once ill again. Muddy knew the dangers to both her children in the contaminating city and she knew also that expenses would be higher, but in the country in the winter they would be penniless. Pursuing a journalist's life took Edgar away from the boarding house, back to the rackety bachelor existence which was so unsafe for him. He had drunk hardly at all while with the Brennans. Martha Brennan, daughter of the house, remembered that well: 'During the two years she knew him intimately and never saw him affected by liquor or do aught that evinced the wild impetuous nature with which he has been accredited. He was the gentlest of husbands and devoted to his invalid wife. Frequently when she was weaker than usual, he carried her tenderly from her room to the dinner-table and satisfied every whim.'

Now Edgar would roam the city at all hours of the day and night, sometimes in drink, often without food, invariably short of the few copper coins he needed to buy tobacco. A picture of this time in his life was sketched by Gabriel Harrison, an affable grocer with a store on the corner of Broadway and Princes Street. Harrison prided himself on looking like Napoleon III. He was president of a political club called the White Eagle, a cultivated literary gentleman who painted, was keen on elocution and oratory, and often entertained literary gentry on canned delicacies and port wine around the big stove in his shop. No doubt knowing that Harrison had an inclination towards the literary, Poe called on him one day to inquire the price of tobacco. Harrison later reported the occasion in his reminiscences in the *New York Times*: 'I had told him the price, he made no move to buy, and after a few general remarks started to leave. I was struck by a certain indefinite something in his manner, by his voice, and by his fine articulation.... So I offered the man a piece of tobacco. He accepted, thanked me and departed. Two or three weeks later he came in again. . . .' Harrison apparently still had no idea that the object of his generosity was Poe. They talked politics and Poe wrote a campaign song for the White Eagle, of which the first verse ran:

> See the White Eagle soaring aloft to the sky,
> Wakening the brood Welkin with his loud battle cry,
> Then here's the White Eagle, full daring is he,
> As he sails on his pinions o'er valley and sea.

Harrison was delighted. He offered to pay for the verses but Poe would accept only a bag of his best coffee. 'As he was going I said that I should like to know his name. "Certainly", he said, with a faint smile. "Thaddeus Perley, at your service".' Having established a base in Harrison's grocery Poe returned. On one occasion, finding the store apparently empty, he warmed himself at the stove. Suddenly Harrison entered with a Mr Halleck who knew Poe. Harrison was delighted to be able to introduce his lyric-writer:

> 'Why, good evening, Mr Perley', I began. Halleck interrupted me. 'Great heavens, Poe is this you!' he exclaimed. 'Poe? – this is Mr Perley', I broke in.
>
> Poe looked at me and then at Halleck and after an instant's hesitation said, 'The fact of the matter is, Halleck, I have made this gentleman's acquaintance under the name of Perley; no harm was intended and none done. I knew that the facts would develop themselves. I have walked several miles through the sleet and rain, and, seeing a light here, thought that perhaps Mr Harrison would let me warm up somewhat.'
>
> 'Why, of course', I answered; 'here is the stove behind the tea boxes almost red hot. Take off your coat and dry it. What will you have, some of this old port?' I spread out some crackers, an old English pineapple cheese, and we all nibbled and bent our elbows in homage to his majesty, the old port, and talked of pleasant things till my clock struck the hour of midnight. Poe left with Halleck and stopped at his house that night.

Harrison was delighted to know the true identity of his mysterious visitor, and they became good friends.

Poe supplemented the small income from being a paragraphist on the *Evening Mirror* with other chores. He returned to Philadelphia to supervise a third edition of *The Conchologist's First Book*, removing his name from the title page of that much contested work, and signing it only with his initials. The reissue of the book revived the charges of plagiarism against him, but he was now familiar with the slings and arrows of the hack's life and took little notice of them as he 'turned an honest penny or two'. In the course of the Philadelphia visit he also arranged for his *Marginalia* to be published, and placed a review in a local paper. With the *Marginalia* he had hoped to become the American Coleridge, but pedants, unable to appreciate the hoaxer aspect of his genius, attacked the work because

Poe had invented sources and used translations instead of original texts. As pedants usually do, they totally missed Poe's ironic intention.

In December, Poe's firm friend and supporter, Lowell, visited New York to stay with Charles F. Briggs who was about to start a new weekly, the *Broadway Journal*. Briggs was looking for an assistant and Lowell strongly recommended Poe, subsequently arranging for the two men to meet, and by the end of the year Poe had left the *Mirror*. Though Willis was unhappy about losing Poe, he was understanding. The *Mirror* had used very little of Poe's undoubted genius and Willis was philosophical about the necessary opportunism of the freelance. He was happy, furthermore, that before leaving Poe had arranged for him to scoop the publication of *The Raven*. Working from an advance proof of the poem from the *American Whig Review*, the *Evening Mirror* published it on 29 January 1845 under Poe's pen-name 'Quarles'. Poe's plan was that the poem which had taken him so long and such pains to complete should appear more or less simultaneously in as many places as possible. But Willis and New York had the honour of the first appearance. When *The Raven* appeared again in the *Mirror* on 8 February it was clearly attributed to Edgar Poe. Preceding it was an introductory paragraph almost certainly drafted by Poe himself:

> We are permitted to copy (in advance of publication from the 2d. No. of the American Review) the following remarkable poem by Edgar Poe. In our opinion, it is the most effective single example of 'fugitive poetry' ever published in this country, and unsurpassed in English poetry for subtle conception, masterly ingenuity of versification, and consistent sustaining of imaginative lift and 'pokerishness'. It is one of these 'dainties bred in a book' which we feed on. It will stick to the memory of everybody who reads it.

Within a few weeks it also appeared in the *New York Tribune*, *The Southern Literary Messenger*, the *Howard District Press*, and the *American Whig Review* to which it had been originally committed. The saturation technique was organized by Poe and is a superb example of his brilliance as an editorial promoter. The poem, so well 'puffed' and massively distributed, was an enormous and complete success, greater than any American poem had ever been. It was remarked that 'the raven threatened to displace the eagle as the national bird'. Mechanical paragraphists and magpie editors all over the country copied and reprinted it, and Poe's bird's appearances were seemingly endless and everywhere. In cases where the poem was unsigned, or attributed to 'Quarles', readers demanded the name of the author. When it appeared, a little later, over Poe's own name, it confirmed the American public's feeling that a great Romantic poet flew above them. Within a few weeks Edgar Poe, whose reputation had been waiting in the wings for so long, achieved his début on the national stage. He was a success in the adored and homely American

# New-York Mirror:

## A JOURNAL OF LITERATURE, NEWS AND THE FINE ARTS.

PUBLISHED EVERY SATURDAY MORNING.

THREE DOLLARS A YEAR.] OFFICE OF PUBLICATION, CORNER OF NASSAU AND ANN STREETS. [PAYABLE IN ADVANCE.

VOLUME I. NEW-YORK, SATURDAY, FEBRUARY 8, 1845. NUMBER XVIII.


We are permitted to copy (in advance of publication) from the 2d No. of the American Review, the following remarkable poem by EDGAR POE. In our opinion, it is the most effective single example of "fugitive poetry" ever published in this country; and unsurpassed in English poetry for subtle conception, masterly ingenuity of versification, and consistent, sustaining of imaginative lift and "pokerishness." It is one of these "dainties bred in a book" which we *feed* on. It will stick to the memory of everybody who reads it.

### The Raven.

Once upon a midnight dreary, while I pondered, weak and weary,
Over many a quaint and curious volume of forgotten lore,
While I nodded, nearly napping, suddenly there came a tapping,
As of some one gently rapping, rapping at my chamber door.
"'Tis some visiter," I muttered, "tapping at my chamber door—
Only this, and nothing more."

Ah, distinctly I remember it was in the bleak December,
And each separate dying ember wrought its ghost upon the floor.
Eagerly I wished the morrow;—vainly I had tried to borrow
From my books surcease of sorrow—sorrow for the lost Lenore—
For the rare and radiant maiden whom the angels name Lenore—
Nameless here for evermore.

And the silken sad uncertain rustling of each purple curtain
Thrilled me—filled me with fantastic terrors never felt before;
So that now, to still the beating of my heart, I stood repeating
"'Tis some visiter entreating entrance at my chamber door—
Some late visiter entreating entrance at my chamber door;—
This it is, and nothing more."

Presently my soul grew stronger; hesitating then no longer,
"Sir," said I, "or Madam, truly your forgiveness I implore;
But the fact is I was napping, and so gently you came rapping,
And so faintly you came tapping, tapping at my chamber door,
That I scarce was sure I heard you"—here I opened wide the door;—
Darkness there, and nothing more.

OPPOSITE *The Raven*, as it appeared in the *New York Mirror*.
ABOVE A lithograph by the French Impressionist painter Edouard Manet, illustrating *The Raven*

overnight tradition. His manuscripts and autographs were sought avidly, his letters searched out and sold. *Godey's* published his story *The 1002 Tale*; *Graham's* printed Lowell's highly flattering sketch of him, which was picked up by Willis and reprinted in the *Mirror*. On 28 February he lectured to the New York Historical Society before a distinguished audience, and was highly praised and admired. Willis reviewed him rapturously: 'He becomes a desk, – his beautiful head showing like a statuary embodiment of Discrimination; his accent drops like a knife through water, and his style is so much purer and clearer than the pulpit commonly gets or requires that the effect of what he says, besides other things, pampers the ear.' *The Raven* was flying high. Poe was famous – but still poor, for without copyright protection the endless reprints of *The Raven* brought him not one cent.

# *The Second Frances*

The *Broadway Journal* announced in March 1845, with considerable satisfaction and pride, that Edgar Poe had joined its editorial board and would, with Charles Briggs and John Bisco, be active in the conduct of the paper. For his editorial participation Poe was to receive a one-third interest in the *Journal*, for the author of *The Raven* could not be wholly purchased at the paper's basic rate of $1 per column. His involvement and famous expertise in the conduct of magazines would inevitably bring new subscribers, though Briggs wrote to their mutual friend Lowell that 'Poe is only an assistant to me, and will in no manner interfere with my own way of doing things.' Clearly this conclusion was reached before Mr Briggs had commenced working with Mr Poe. In the event Edgar was, almost from his first days with the *Journal*, its chief editor, bringing to it his very personal (and often dangerous) editorial foibles.

Poe had long been conducting a war against a sacred totem of the American *literati*, Mr Longfellow, and now, without the approval of his co-editors, transferred the battles to the columns of the *Journal*. His growing paranoia compelled him to challenge with charges of plagiarism not only Longfellow, but anyone of whom he momentarily disapproved, even his devoted penfriend and ally Lowell. The pursuit of plagiarists had become a monomaniac preoccupation, and Poe followed clues with the avidity of his own detective Dupin. Somehow, though, he maintained ostensibly good relations with the Rev. Dr Griswold, whose position as premier anthologer and encyclopedist of American literature made it necessary, Poe felt, for communications to be maintained, though he knew that, as Briggs wrote to Lowell, 'Mr. Griswold has told me shocking bad stories about Poe'. Griswold, generally regarded as a 'most irritable and vindictive man', resented Poe for both personal and professional reasons, but felt he was too significant to be treated as an overt enemy. Poe, therefore, was reasonably represented in the new edition of Griswold's poetry anthology and was included in his new volume, *Prose Writers of America.*

The success of *The Raven* brought Poe a popularity and a *réclame* difficult to imagine today. In the spring of 1845 he was the glamorous star of literate American society, sought after, written about, and pointed out as the satanic poet who had written America's most famous poem. Suddenly Edgar, who had always had a deal of fascination for certain women, found that ladies of all ages, besotted with his public image of the desperate diabolic poet, wanted (in their fantasies at least) to dive to the bottom of the maelström in his arms, or to save him and his great genius for respectable society. The excitement of so much success and the social rewards that accompanied it inevitably drew Poe away from the abstinence of that last summer in the country. Now he had to be brilliant day and night, and his fans

ABOVE LEFT Henry Wadsworth Longfellow, doyen of the American literary establishment and Poe's enemy.

ABOVE RIGHT The poet Lowell was a long-time penfriend of Poe's, but both men were disappointed when they met.

found the eccentricities and extremities of behaviour which accompanied his brilliance elegantly typical of their image of the artist possessed. By March he was drinking more heavily than ever, and Briggs was very concerned, for the chief editor of the *Journal* was becoming increasingly erratic and unreliable. But Briggs had fallen out with Bisco and was unable to muster the majority strength required to dispose of his violently gifted partner.

Poe was still undoubted boss of the *Broadway Journal*, even if he was often drunk and strange in his behaviour. He demonstrated the strength of his position with a somewhat theatrical scene which revenged him for the painfully unforgettable charity reading when the hat had been passed at *Graham's*. The occasion was recalled by Alexander T. Crane, who was an office boy on the *Journal* at the time. Poe, who was also drama critic, spent much of his time in theatrical circles. One day in the winter of 1845 he arrived at the office with a famous actor, James E. Murdock. Crane remembered that:

Mr Poe summoned the entire force, including myself, about him. There was less than a dozen of us and I the only boy.... When we were all together, Poe drew the manuscript of *The Raven* from his pocket and handed it to Murdock. He had called us to hear the great elocutionist read his newly written poem ... with the combined art of two masters I was entranced. It is the most cherished memory of my life that I heard the immortal poem read by one whose voice was like a chime of silver bells.

Thus Poe revenged the humiliating charity towards *The Raven* that had brought him a desperately needed $15 in the days of *Graham's Magazine.*

Edgar's fame brought invitations to repeat his lecture to the Historical Society. He accepted, but the weather was bad and young Crane, to whom he had given a complimentary ticket, reported that: 'There was scarcely a dozen persons present ... the lecture could not be given and badly as I was disappointed I could see upon his face that my master was much more so. It was a little thing, it is true, but he was a man easily upset by little things.' When Poe arrived at the office the following morning he was so drunk he had to be supported.

If Edgar had given that lecture he would certainly have repeated his former fulsome praise of a minor poetess whom he had met through Willis, Mrs Frances Osgood. He was deeply impressed by her, for she had many of the characteristics to which he had always been drawn in women:

> In character she is ardent, sensitive, impulsive – the very soul of truth and honor; a worshipper of the beautiful, with a heart so radically artless as to seem abundant in art; unusually admired, respected and beloved. In person she is about the medium height, slender, even to fragility; graceful whether in action or repose; complexion usually pale, hair black and glossy; eyes a clear, luminous grey, large, and with singular capacity for expression.

Frances Sargent Osgood was the wife of a minor painter, Samuel S. Osgood. She wrote sentimental verses which appealed to a wide public and had published volumes in both England and America. Poe praised her 'grace', overlooking her empty rhetoric and sickly sentimentality. 'She has occasional passages of true imagination,' the great critic observed. Mrs Osgood, for her part, had been profoundly impressed by Edgar when she met him after he had sent her, through Willis, a copy of *The Raven* with a request for her 'judgment' and an interview. How could she refuse? Mrs Osgood and Edgar Poe met, and she wrote of the occasion:

> I shall never forget the morning when I was summoned to the drawing-room by Mr Willis to receive him. With his proud beautiful head erect, his dark eyes flashing with the electric light of feeling and of thought, a peculiar, an inimitable blending of sweetness and hauteur in his expression and manner, he greeted me, calmly, gravely, almost coldly, yet with so marked an earnestness that I could not help being deeply impressed by it. From that moment until his death we were friends, although we met only during the first year of our acquaintance.

Mrs Osgood, ethereal as she appeared, was highly experienced in the handling of editors. She encouraged Poe immediately with a poem in the *Journal.* He picked up the poetic dialogue with verses dedicated *To F*, actually warmed-over lines written for another in *Messenger* days. But if Poe was an economical courtier so was the ardent *F*, for while encouraging Edgar she sent a valentine to Griswold. As always, Poe displaced the Reverend, pursuing the poetess passionately. He made no secret of his growing friendship with the lady and, surprisingly, Mrs Clemm and Virginia encouraged the 'affair'. Poor Sis was now declining rapidly, and anything which took off the burden of Edgar's dependence was welcome to both her and her mother. Inevitably the Poe–Osgood poetic dialogue brought scandal. Correspondence between them was hectic, and his contemporaries could hardly believe the passion would remain entirely platonic, for Poe was now at the high point of his fame, the cynosure of all eyes. One night at the Park Theatre an actor recognized him in the audience and introduced into his lines the words 'Nevermore, nevermore'. The ad lib produced a profound sensation and 'a thrill ran through the audience', while all heads turned to look at Poe and an awed whisper was heard.

Mr Briggs was very shocked by the scandal surrounding Poe, which was amplified by Griswold reminding the *literati* of Edgar's Saratoga Springs 'affair'. Poe, for his part, enjoyed his diabolic image and cultivated it. The atheism which was the sole idea he had ever shared with John Allan he now revived, dismissing the Bible as rigmarole, and expressing no faith at all in reformism. On the *Journal* he now associated himself with Bisco, making it clear that he was prepared to see Briggs out. The staff thought him a devil of a fellow and adored him, encouraging his mephistophelean arrogance. Even if they thought his attitude towards Briggs ungrateful and unfriendly, everyone knew that Poe was the heart and soul of the paper, writing endlessly on every subject under the sun. The *Journal* had a genius and they were proud that America knew it.

Edgar, stimulated by his successes, both professional and personal, took Virginia calling on important wives, and continued his courtship of Mrs Osgood while sitting to her husband for his portrait. His poems were being collected for publication by Wiley and Putnam and he was preparing a book (which he never finished) on *Literary America*. Throughout this time continued publication of *The Raven* maintained his reputation throughout the United States and in England and Europe too. Yet, extraordinary to relate, now at the very height of his fame, Poe was still so poor that he must move his family into a third-storey back room in a tenement on Broadway. Lowell called upon him there for the first time and was appalled at his poverty, though now not even his best friends could pretend that it was not connected with his uncontrolled drinking. On the occasion of the call by Mr and Mrs Lowell and their friends, Poe was found to be 'not tipsy – but as if he had been holding his head under a pump to cool it'. He was bad-tempered and ironic and Mrs Clemm remained in the room, presumably to intercede if Eddy's behaviour became any worse. She later wrote to Lowell, 'the day you saw him in New York *he was not himself*'. It was a sad and unfortunate first meeting between the two long-time penfriends. Lowell saw Poe as 'small with a chalky clammy complexion, fine dark eyes under broad temples and with a brow that receded sharply back from the eyes . . . very formal and pompous'. Poe was just as disappointed with Lowell and wrote, 'he was not half the noble looking person that I expected to see'. Drunkenness and its after-effects had something to do with the jaundiced atmosphere.

In the same period a librarian called Saunders met Poe on Broadway and found him 'effusive and maudlin'. Poe boasted that he had been invited to read *The Raven* to Queen Victoria and her family. Saunders observed that he had known Poe in drink before and that on such occasions he talked only of himself and his writing, expressing detestation of other writers:

> The next time I saw him he was very much depressed, and was suffering from a fit of melancholia to which he was subject. He spoke of a conspiracy among the other authors of America to belittle his genius and to smother his work. 'But posterity shall judge', he said, with a gleam of pride in his eyes. 'Future generations will be able to sift the gold from the dross, and then *The Raven* will be beheld, shining above them all, as a diamond of the purest water.'

In spite of the unremitting feud against him in particular, Longfellow generously observed that 'the harshness of Poe's criticisms I have never attributed to anything but the irritation of a sensitive nature, shaped by some indefinite sense of wrong'.

Poe's delusions of grandeur and persecution were growing and so was his dependence upon drink. In July a Dr Chivers came from Georgia to New York to arrange the publication of his poems, and to capitalize Poe's magazine project, *The Stylus*. Poe had cultivated Chivers in a long, flattering correspondence and he arrived in New York with profound admiration and respect for the genius of the great poet and critic. The miserable and difficult man he found was a sad surprise to him. On Nassau Street Chivers was supporting a drunken Poe when they ran into the editor of the *Knickerbocker*, Mr Clark. Poe, convinced that Clark was one of the 'conspirators' against him, threatened to attack the distinguished editor who, knowing Poe of old, quickly excused himself. That evening Poe was to give a reading to the literary societies at New York University, but he continued drinking and failed to arrive at the meeting. Chivers was unable to find him the next day, but Mrs Clemm apparently located him, for, when Chivers called the day after, she told him that Poe was ill. Dr Chivers found him in bed reading Macaulay. While he maintained friendly feelings for Poe it was clear to Chivers that, with the best will in the world, the poet was not one in whom to invest considerable capital.

The first number of the second volume of the *Broadway Journal*, published in July, describes Poe as the sole editor and one-third proprietor. Briggs had almost left the paper, and Poe was trying to buy out Bisco. But he was unable to scare his remaining partner off as he had the unfortunate Briggs, for not only did he finally cause the man who had given him his position and interest in the paper to leave but, on a drunken spree, he put it about that Briggs had insulted him and behaved unfairly and dishonestly. In fact it was Poe who owed his ex-partner money as well as gratitude. Now the attempt to raise the capital to buy out Bisco resulted in Poe floating notes all over town, most of which were due for payment on the first of the New Year. In the meantime Poe got through the money without moving any nearer to securing sole ownership of the *Journal*. Advertising in the paper was increasing, but subscriptions were falling off. Indeed from the time Briggs left the paper declined, revived sporadically by Poe's borrowings. Seeing it dying under his hand Poe drank more and more, and it was clear that the collapse of both the *Broadway Journal* and its editor were imminent. As the New York summer grew hotter and more unbearable day by day, Poe's behaviour deteriorated with it. A young poet, R.H. Stoddard, had sent the *Journal* a good Keatsian poem; Poe first mislaid it and then, in print, questioned its originality. Stoddard called on him after lunch one 'intolerably hot July afternoon'. Poe was in his sanctum, sleeping. He woke 'in a very stormy mood':

When summoned back to earth he was slumbering uneasily in a very easy chair. He was irascible, surly, and in his cups.

'Mr. Poe', I ventured to remark meekly, 'I saw you two or three weeks ago, and I read in your paper that you doubted my ability to write –'

'I know', he answered, staring up wildly. 'You never wrote the Ode to which I lately referred. You never –'

But the reader may imagine the rest of this unfortunate sentence. I was comminated, and threatened with condign personal chastisement. I left quickly, but was not, as I remember, downcast. On the contrary, I was complimented. The great American Critic had declared that I could not write what I had written. . . .

Poe's assumption was typical in this stage of his mental decline. If he thought a poem good, then he would lose it or cast aspersions upon the author. He would praise extravagantly the work of someone he thought could be of use, or a lovely lady like Mrs Osgood, but a colleague with ability he would threaten and attack. Yet his behaviour was only such under the deleterious effects of alcohol. When sober he could still be sensitive and considerate, as when the office boy Crane was 'overcome with heat and fainted dead away', coming round to find Poe bending over him 'bathing my wrists and temples in cold water'. Both aspects of Poe are equally well verified, so that as Professor Woodberry (who published a study of Poe's opium addiction in 1909), observed: 'I am unable to fall into the judgment which divides them [the witnesses for and against Poe] into the "goats" and the "sheep" – the "malignant" and the "amiable"; they all, divergent as they are, seem to me to have written, according to their knowledge and their conscience, sincerely.' Poe was now manifestly like William Wilson, his *doppelgänger* character, a man with two

Illustration by Harry Clarke to *William Wilson.*

conflicting personalities, the better of which was rapidly deteriorating, giving way under the weight of business, problems worsened by drinking and his characteristic inability to deal with money matters.

Worry about Virginia's health, which was fast declining, also contributed. Edgar flew to Mrs Osgood and, it was to the second Frances in his life that he was most drawn. Princess Bonaparte points out how Poe's excitement over Mrs Osgood relates to his basic preoccupation. His portrait of her, she observes:

> . . . reminds us of Elizabeth Arnold; the large 'expressive' eyes, the black hair, the pale complexion and the slender fragility. As if to confirm this likeness, Mrs Osgood, four years later, was to die of consumption and doubtless had borne marks of the disease when they met. She was four years older than Poe and was linked to him by another maternal attribute; her name, Frances.

The voluminous correspondence between Poe and Mrs Osgood was later destroyed as 'compromising', in itself an indication of the intensity of the 'mad' passion sustained (by letter at least), between the two. But Poe was unable to cope with sexual excitement, either that stimulated by Virginia as she approached death, or by

Frances, still far enough from it to be graceful and vibrant. He fled into dipsomania.

That summer the Poes again moved on. Seeking new neighbours with whom Edgar had not yet fought they took rooms at 85 Amity Street. Mrs Osgood found him working on *The Literati of New York*:

'See', said he, displaying in laughing triumph several little rolls of narrow paper (he always wrote thus for the press), 'I am going to show you by the difference of length in these, the different degrees of estimation in which I hold all you literary people. In each of these one of you is rolled up and fully discussed. Come, Virginia, help me!' And one by one they unfolded them. At last they came to one that seemed interminable. Virginia laughingly ran to one corner of the room with one end, and her husband to the opposite with the other. 'And whose lengthened sweetness long drawn out is that?' said I. 'Hear, hear!' he cried, 'just as if her little vain heart didn't tell her it's herself.'

But Edgar's ardour was beginning to frighten Frances, who could hardly know of his chronic difficulty in bringing an *amour* to a normal and ordinary conclusion. She fled New York and went to Albany. But he pursued her. She travelled on to Boston and Providence but Edgar, who was a travelling man by nature, continued to follow her, eventually catching up with her in Boston where he also lectured. The scandal worsened and Frances' family grew seriously alarmed. While Mrs Osgood enjoyed that hysterical excitement which often characterizes the last years of tuberculosis cases, and doubtless relished the chase, she was lady enough of her time to avoid

Sarah Helen Whitman, from an engraving made in 1838.

being caught. Edgar, too, preferred the chase to the capture, but was becoming too much of an embarrassment to Mrs Osgood when he caught up with her in Providence, Rhode Island. There she eventually managed to introduce him to a poetess friend, Mrs Helen Whitman, a widow, well-off, beautiful and a Transcendentalist. Poe had seen some of her poems which expressed moods he had thought peculiar to himself, but no doubt because of her sex, her beauty and her magic name he did not accuse Mrs Whitman of plagiarism, but hailed her instead as a 'spiritual sister'. Griswold, taking a line from a poem of Poe's literally, reported that their first meeting was in a garden of roses by moonlight, but Poe himself described the occasion more soberly in a letter to Mrs Whitman: 'You may remember that once when I passed through Providence with Mrs Osgood I positively refused to accompany her to your house, and even provoked her into a quarrel by obstinacy and the seeming unreasonableness of my refusal.' That very night however, Poe had left the hotel and walked to Mrs Whitman's house. There in the moonlight she stood by the door, taking the air, as she later irritably corrected Griswold (who had flirted with her in the past): 'I was not "wandering in a garden of roses" as Dr Griswold has seen fit to describe me but standing on the side-walk or in the open doorway of the house on that sultry "July evening" when the poet saw me and "dreamed a dream" about me which afterwards crystallized into immortal verse.' Thus by moonlight, but without roses, Edgar Poe passed from his second Frances to his last Helen.

## *The Wars of the Literati*

1845 in New York was the year of Edgar Poe, a year of great public triumphs and growing personal tragedy. It saw the publication of his eighth and ninth volumes, *Tales and The Raven and Other Poems*, both being published by Wiley and Putnam of 151 Broadway. The *Tales* comprised twelve of his most famous stories, well selected by an editor named Duyckinck, and included *The Gold Bug*, *The Black Cat*, *The Fall of the House of Usher*, *A Descent into the Maelström*, *Mesmeric Revelation* and the three Dupin stories. By this selection Duyckinck established the popular fiction image of Poe which has lasted till the present day. Poe himself received a royalty of eight cents per volume sold, and for once a book of his went well. But at $1 per dozen the success could scarcely touch his chronic financial difficulties, now compounded by being the principal owner of the *Broadway Journal*. By November he would be writing to Duyckinck, asking him to see if he could find funds for the paper, and confiding in his editor: 'I find myself entirely myself – dreadfully sick and depressed, but still myself. I seem to have just awakened from some horrible dream, in which all was confusion and suffering. . . . I really believe that I have been mad – but indeed I have had abundant reason to be so.'

Though his fame was at its height and America's public, always hungry for celebrities, would have been glad to find in him (and reward proportionately) its own Dickens, Poe was in no condition to take advantage of his opportunities. An invitation to lecture on the Boston Lyceum and read a new poem found him unable to produce one. Instead he recited *Al Aaraaf* and *The Raven* and, when attacked by the local critics for performing old work, defended himself by insisting that 'a poem composed, printed and published before we had fairly completed our tenth year' was quite good enough for the Bostonians. The incident raised an extraordinary amount of literary dust, and added to the scope of his reputation but hardly to its quality. The Bostonians, ponderous and powerful in the literary arena, rallied for the attack.

Poe now became sole owner of the *Broadway Journal*, buying Bisco out for a personal note for $50 endorsed by Horace Greeley. Other friends also held notes from him, the value of which consisted entirely in his autograph. Though the *Journal* needed a mere $140 to keep it going Poe's credit was now so strained that he was unable to raise the paltry sum. Knowing that his paper was dying he continued to use its columns to attack his enemies, consolidating their ranks against him. By the first week of December the *Journal*, unable to pay rents and other expenses, had become as peripatetic as its editor. Its last few issues were paid for by one of his last admirers, Thomas H. Lane. By 20 December Poe was ill himself and deeply depressed, for Virginia was now certainly dying. He called at Lane's lodgings, the last office of the *Journal*, with copy, and announced to Lane and his friend Thomas Dunn English that he intended to drown his troubles in a spree. Lane begged him not to, pointing out that the *Journal* needed him in full control of all his faculties in order to survive, but Poe would not be persuaded, and Lane decided he could no longer support the paper. The final number of the *Journal* appeared in the first days of the New Year. It contained the following notice:

VALEDICTORY

Unexpected engagements demanding my whole attention, and the objects being fulfilled so far as regards myself personally, for which the Broadway Journal was established, I now, as its editor, bid farewell – as cordially to foes as to friends.

Edgar A. Poe

Though the *Journal* had passed away, the literary ladies who dispensed hospitality in exchange for conversation, the so-called 'starry sisterhood', were still there, and Poe was more welcome than ever in their salons. Many of them called, as Mrs Osgood did, on the Poes in their lodgings on Amity Street. One such lady, in the same January that the paper failed, indicated clearly that Poe's business difficulties did not affect his social desirability:

I meet Mr Poe very often at the receptions. He is the observed of all observers. His stories are thought wonderful and to hear him repeat *The Raven*, which he does very quietly, is an event in one's life. People seem to think there is something uncanny about him, and the strangest stories are told, and, what is more, believed, about his mesmeric experiences, at the mention of which he always smiles. His smile is captivating.... Everybody wants to know him; but only a few people seem to get well acquainted with him.

Among these *literati* Poe, 'the observed of all observers', was the lion, and few of the guests who saw him arrogant, confident and electric in his magnetism could have believed that his personal circumstances were so appalling. His financial chaos he now attempted to resolve with a series of articles commissioned by *Godey's Lady's Book* and drawing upon his salon experience. It was to comprise thirty-eight profiles of New York writers under the title *The Literati*, and would add to Poe's public image as the great and fearsome critic and lion of lions. It would also provide him with the basis of his often discussed book 'on American Letters generally', entitled *Literary America*, with which he planned to displace Griswold as senior historian. The commission suited him well for he was unfit for intensive creative work and his present temperament inclined more towards literary punditry, skirmishing and politics. His pen always commanded attention when he turned his raven eye upon matters critical, and the series was a great success. Poe's candour regarding his subjects, his indiscretion and revelation of personal confidences were unheard of at the time. Indeed, his literary profiles anticipated that contemporary style of journalism which is guttering out nowadays in the sputtering paragraphs of faceless columnists and their armies of hired socialite stringers. New York's interest in Poe's pioneering pieces was feverishly high and there was endless speculation about whom he would next attack or praise.

Though most of his subjects are forgotten today, his judgments have, for the most part, been sustained. Nevertheless, Poe was intensely personal in many of his observations, paying off old scores and rewarding old friends. Briggs, who had first brought him into the *Broadway Journal*, had become a favourite target, as was Lewis Gaylord Clark, the editor of the *Knickerbocker*, a magazine which had never been friendly to Poe:

Mr Clark once did me the honor to review my poems – I forgive him.... As the editor has no precise character, the magazine, as a matter of course can have none. When I say 'no precise character,' I mean that Mr C., as a literary man, has about him no determinateness, no distinctiveness, no point -; – an apple, in fact, or a pumpkin has more angles. He is as smooth as oil or a sermon from Dr Hawkes; he is noticeable for nothing in the world except for the markedness by which he is noticeable for nothing.

Poe attacked others such as Thomas Dunn English much more personally, suggesting that the motto for his magazine should be 'I am just an ass.' He further observed that English had nothing remarkable about his personal appearance, except 'that he exists in a perpetual state of vacillation between mustachio and goatee'. Schoolboy enough, but it titillated the readers and added to the ranks of Poe's enemies.

While Edgar, her knight in black armour, was out there in the literary lists being foolhardy, brave and madly courageous, his 'dear heart' Virginia was at home in bed, or moved painfully about the dreary rooms coughing blood and asking Muddy when Eddy would be home with good news. One of the few letters Poe wrote to her is agonized and apologetic, redolent of anxious guilt:

To Virginia Poe

June 12th – 1846 (New York)

My Dear Heart, My dear Virginia! our Mother will explain to you why I stay away from you this night. I trust the interview I am promised, will result in some substantial good for me, for your dear sake, and hers – Keep up your heart in all hopefulness, and trust yet a little longer – In my last great disappointment, I should have lost my courage but for you – my little darling wife you are my greatest and only stimulus now, to battle with this uncongenial, unsatisfactory and ungrateful life – I shall be with you tomorrow P.M. and be assured until I see you, I will keep in loving remembrance your last words and your fervant prayer!

Sleep well and may God grant you a peaceful summer, with your devoted

Edgar

Details of the interview referred to are not known but doubtless it was one of many Edgar pursued in the hope of 'substantial good'.

The miserable little rooms in Amity Street were unbearable to Poe, the literary lion, and he detested visitors coming to see Virginia, for here his postures were absurd and too much was revealed. He arranged with the Brennans for Sis and Muddy to spend a few weeks at least at their farm in the spring. Though Mrs Clemm was a woman who became attached to any place she made her home, in the interests of Virginia's health the move was agreed, although it would make Poe's bachelor and bohemian pattern of life in New York even more inevitable.

Once Sis and Muddy were in the country Poe spent a good deal of time with Mrs Osgood and other 'starry sisters'. One of them, Mrs Shew, had been a nurse, and recognized that Edgar needed medical attention. She arranged for Dr John Francis to attend him and his wife. Francis was a friendly, charitable and sympathetic man, and he gave what help he could in the patently hopeless case of Virginia. He also advised Poe on some of the physical problems resulting from years of drink and opium, though he seems to have accepted Edgar's reasons for his addictions rather than reaching any psychological conclusions of his own.

Another 'starry sister' who competed for Poe's interest was Mrs Estelle Lewis of Brooklyn, who decorated her studio with a bust of Pallas and a stuffed raven,

Frances Osgood, the most senior of the 'starry sisters'.
Poe's attentions finally proved too embarrassing for her.

and liked to be called 'Stella'. Her lawyer husband was wealthy and indulgent and Poe found shelter, meals and drink in her salon until he produced an acrostic of 'Sarah Anne', her true name, which she detested. Mr Lewis paid him $100 to revise his wife's verses, and be positive about them when they were published. Mrs Clemm too 'borrowed' small sums from visiting 'starry sisters', committing Poe to further 'puffs' which he hated.

Inevitably, Poe's relations with the 'starry sisterhood' involved a good deal of emotional incest. Mrs Osgood remained the platonic bride of the Master, and the other 'sisters' were not too spiritual to be jealous. One of them, Mrs Ellet, persuaded dear Muddy to read her some of Mrs Osgood's letters. She dined out on the contents, much to the alarm of Mrs Osgood who had already cut down meetings with Poe because of the scandalous gossip. She sent Mrs Ellet and other 'sisters' to Poe to request the return of her letters. Poe was much put out, and made it clear while returning Mrs Osgood's letters that Mrs Ellet and other ladies might well be worried about their own unconsidered missives to him. The 'sisters' withdrew, furious and insulted, and though Poe subsequently left Mrs Ellet's letters on her doorstep, her brother, Mr Lummis, arrived demanding the letters and satisfaction. Mr Lummis was said to be an expert with pistols and Poe, highly excited, called on Thomas Dunn English, whom he had often insulted, argued with and borrowed money from, to be his second – yet another example of his compulsion to turn to known enemies. English was a contentious, not particularly admirable fellow, but his account of the scene has the ring of truth:

Mr Poe having been guilty of some most ungentlemanly conduct, while in a state of intoxication, I was obliged to treat him with discourtesy. Sometime after this, he came to my chambers, in my absence, in search of me. He found there, a nephew of one of our ex-presidents. To that gentleman he stated, that he desired to see me in order to apologize to me for his conduct. I entered shortly after, when he tendered me an apology and his hand. The former I accepted, the latter I refused. He told me that he came to beg my pardon, because he wished me to do him a favor. Amused at this novel reason for an apology, I replied that I would do the favor, with pleasure, if possible, but not on the score of friendship. He said that though his friendship was of little service his enmity might be dangerous. To this I rejoined that I shunned his friendship and despised his enmity. He beseeched a private conversation so abjectly, that, finally, moved by his humble entreaty, I accorded it. Then he told me that he had villified a certain well known and esteemed authoress, of the South (Mrs Ellet), then on a visit to New York, that he had accused her of having written letters to him which compromised her reputation; and that her brother (her husband being absent) had threatened his life unless he produced the letters named. He begged me for God's sake to stand his friend, as he expected to be challenged. I refused, because I was not willing to mix myself in his affairs, and because having once before done so, I found him at the critical moment, to be an abject poltroon. These reasons I told him. He then begged the loan of a pistol to defend himself against an attack. This request I refused, saying that his surest defence was a retraction of unfounded charges. He at last grew exasperated and using offensive language, was expelled from the room....

'Expelling' Poe from the room required a certain amount of violence which resulted in Edgar spending several days in bed in a state of collapse. Dr Francis attended him for nervous exhaustion, and also called upon Mr Lummis to explain that his sister had her letters back and that Poe was in no condition to fight a duel. The affair caused great publicity and much sniggering. Poe sued the *New York Mirror* over it and received $225 damages and costs a year or so later.

For many reasons then, Edgar decided to move out of New York again. Virginia could not bear the thought of another summer in the city, and he needed desperately to escape the attentions of his platonic sisters, their gossip and jealousies. On the old stage line northwards on the Kingsbridge road Poe had found the quiet village of Fordham where some of the New York families kept summer houses. A railway provided two trains daily to a station a mile and a half away, but there was little other communication with New York, not even a post office. In Fordham Poe found a cottage on an acre of ground, a wooden-frame workman's house built in the early years of the century, and owned by a friendly farmer. The cottage had a small porch which, in Edgar's romantic description, became 'the pillars of the piazza enwreathed in jasmine and sweet honeysuckle'. Here at Fordham in a pastoral, perfumed setting Edgar was to recover, very briefly, the peace of mind he had known during that idyllic summer on the Brennan farm. And here among the gorgeous flowers, under 'the vivid green of the tulip tree leaves', Sis would spend the last year of her short life.

# CHAPTER SEVEN
# 1846–1849

# *Appointment in Fordham*

Poe described his cottage at Fordham as flower-filled, with blooms on the parlour table, 'the fireplace nearly full with a vase of brilliant geraniums', flowers on the shelves and mantel, and violets on the window-sills of the ground-floor parlour where he wrote. There was little furniture: a round table, a few chairs, a rocking chair and sofa of painted maple. His bedroom was in the garret next to Virginia's: both rooms were low, with small windows. Mrs Clemm kept the place spotless, the lime-washed walls freshly gleaming, and the bare plank floors scoured to whiteness. Outside, the small yard was filled with lilac and dominated by an old cherry tree. Nearby were woods and orchards, and to the south wide views over the farms of the Bronx.

Here it was that the early spring came as a blessed relief to the Poes, the cherry blossom auguring a brighter year than they had known since the brief, happy time at the Brennans'. But by the time the cherries were ripe enough to be gathered the familiar scarlet phantom hung above Fordham. A Miss Cromwell who lived nearby was returning to her cottage when she was charmed by the sight of Poe picking cherries and tossing them into Virginia's lap. She had caught the couple in a rare light-hearted moment, Edgar feeling strong enough to climb the branches daringly and Virginia laughing, her white dress contrasting with the misleading glow of her cheeks. Then, reported Miss Cromwell, Virginia's laughter was choked by coughing and the blood spouted from her lips. Poe jumped down from the tree, picked her up in his arms, and carried her into the cottage. Virginia had suffered several such haemorrhages in the past two years and Edgar of course knew very well that neither prayers, nor medicine, nor the scented air of Fordham could cure her. He knew well that the Red Death was an irresistible and permanent guest in any house of his.

Poe's own health was poor almost from the first days in Fordham, and, though he answered many letters, he did little creative writing. By the year's end he was to find himself too disturbed and sick to write even many letters. One of them, to his friend Thomas Holley Chivers, notes:

For more than six months I have been ill – for the greater part of that time, dangerously so, and quite unable to write even an ordinary letter. My magazine papers appearing in

PREVIOUS PAGES The cottage at Fordham.

Elizabeth Barrett Browning wrote encouragingly to Poe.

this interval were all in the publishers hands before I was taken sick. Since getting better, I have been, as a matter of course, overwhelmed with the business accumulating during my illness.

That fateful year Chivers and other friends, including several of his 'starry sisters', encouraged and helped him either morally or practically. Mrs Shew sent Mrs Clemm a feather bed, bedclothes and 'other comforts'. She also started a subscription among friends to help the Poes, raising $60 which she sent to Mrs Clemm. Her activities humanized the feelings of the New York *literati* somewhat towards Poe, and would-be peacemakers visited Fordham. One of them was Mrs Gove Nichols, who subsequently published a detailed account in the *Sixpenny Magazine*, preserving an invaluable eye-witness experience of the cottage and its tragic tenants that summer:

The cottage had an air of gentility that must have been lent to it by the presence of its inmates. So neat, so poor, so unfurnished, and yet so charming a dwelling I never saw. The floor of the kitchen was white as wheaten flour. A table, a chair, and a little stove it contained seemed to furnish it completely. The sitting room was laid with check matting; four chairs, a light stand, and a hanging bookshelf completed its furniture. There were pretty presentation copies of books on the little shelves, and the Brownings had posts of honor on the stand. With quiet exultation Poe drew from his inside pocket a letter he had recently received from Elizabeth Barrett Browning. He read it to us. It was very flattering. . . . On the bookshelf there lay a volume of Poe's poems. He took it down, wrote my name in it and gave

Illustration by W. Heath Robinson to *Ulalume*.

it to me. I think he did this from a feeling of sympathy, for I could not be of advantage to him, as my two companions could.... He was at this time greatly depressed. Their extreme poverty, the sickness of his wife, and his own inability to write sufficiently accounted for this.

Mrs Nichols' party was joined by other visitors and the limited facilities of the small parlour were strained, so that Poe took the party out for a walk. In the woods his mood lightened and he challenged several of the gentlemen to a leaping contest. Mrs Nichols reported:

Poe still distanced them all. But alas! his gaiters, long worn and carefully kept, were both burst in the grand leap that made him victor.... I was certain he had no other shoes, boots, or gaiters. Who amongst us could offer him money to buy a new pair?.... When we reached the cottage, I think all felt we must not go in, to see the shoeless unfortunate sitting or standing in our midst. I had an errand, however – and I entered the house to get it. The poor old mother looked at his feet with a dismay that I shall never forget. 'Oh, Eddie!' said she, 'how did you burst your gaiters?' Poe seemed to have come into a semi-torpid state as soon as he saw his mother. 'Do answer Muddie', now said she coaxingly – I related the cause of the mishap, and she drew me into the kitchen.

'Will you speak to Mr –,' she said, 'about Eddie's last poem?' Mr – was the reviewer. 'If he will only take the poem, Eddie can have a pair of shoes. He has it – I carried it last week, and Eddie says it is his best. You will speak to him about it, won't you?'

We had already read the poem in conclave, and Heaven forgive us, we could not make head or tail of it. It might as well have been in any of the lost languages, for any meaning we could extract from its melodious numbers. I remember saying that I believed it was only a hoax that Poe was passing off for poetry, to see how far his name could go in imposing upon people. But there was a situation. The reviewer had been actively instrumental in the demolition of the gaiters.

'Of course, they will publish the poem', said I, 'and I will ask C – to be quick about it.'

The poem was paid for at once, and published soon after. I presume it is regarded as genuine poetry in the collected poems of its author, but then it bought the poet a pair of gaiters, and twelve shillings over.

The poem which puzzled the Nichols conclave was *Ulalume*, yet its preoccupations are no different from those which had characterized most of the works which had made Poe famous enough to be visited by literary ladies and gentlemen:

Thus I pacified Psyche and kissed her,
  And tempted her out of her gloom –
  And conquered her scruples and gloom;
And we passed to the end of the vista,
  But were stopped by the door of a tomb –
  By the door of a legended tomb;
And I said – 'What is written, sweet sister,

On the door of this legended tomb?'
She replied – 'Ulalume – Ulalume–
'Tis the vault of thy lost Ulalume!'

Poe's preoccupations at Fordham were still the tomb, and the 'sweet sister' he was about to lose to it.

Mrs Nichols visited Fordham again. On this occasion she felt confidential enough with Poe to question his suggestion that a reviewer might be bribed. 'Do reviewers sell their literary conscience thus unconscionably?' she asked. Poe flew at her, eyes flashing, 'If he were placed on the rack, or if one he loved better than his own life were writhing there, I can conceive of his forging a note against the Bank of Fame in favour of some would-be poetess, who is able and willing to buy his poems and opinions.... Would you blame a man for not allowing his sick wife to starve?' Mrs Nichols quickly changed the subject, for neither she nor the great man would have wished to become too particular about which 'would-be poetesses' had been able to pay a poor man with a sick, starving wife 'a hundred dollars to manufacture opinions of them'. But it was painfully clear that Poe had himself lodged notes against the Bank of Fame and that there was talk among the *literati* of the extremes to which poverty had driven his critical credibility.

Poe's poverty was also closely observed by his good neighbours, who noted that Mrs Clemm sometimes had to borrow small coins to pay for Edgar's mail, and several kind friends left unsolicited simple gifts of fruit and vegetables. Once the neighbourhood was roused by Poe to help him find his West Point greatcoat which he had left in a tavern. A warrant was issued by a local justice and the coat eventually recovered, but the fuss Poe made over an aging army overcoat seemed somewhat pitiful. Pitiful too were some of the devices to which he was reduced to raise money. Duyckinck was now acting as Poe's agent, and early in the year he had asked him to try and sell the copyright of a new collection of tales for as little as $50. When Poe was chosen by the literary societies of the University of Vermont as poet for an anniversary celebration that summer, he was unable to attend because of sickness and lack of funds. He wrote to Duyckinck asking him to publicize the invitation and to try to sell his correspondence, which contained many interesting autographs of statesmen and men of letters. So starved was Poe in pastoral Fordham that on Mrs Nichols' third visit he confessed to her vehemently: 'I love fame – I dote on it – I idolize it – I would drink to the very dregs the glorious intoxication. I would have incense ascend in my honour from every hill and hamlet, from every town and city on this earth. Fame! Glory! – they are life-giving breath, and living blood. No man lives, unless he is famous!'

Fame Poe had but, as always with him, not of the variety that produces a good fire and a full stomach. Through that summer and autumn Mrs Clemm managed tolerably, but the winter settled in early and as exceptionally cold as the summer had been hot. There was a small stove in the kitchen and an open fireplace in the parlour, and with the gifts of neighbours small fires were kept going in them. But it was impossible for the upstairs bedrooms to be kept warm and Virginia was moved down into a small boxroom next to the parlour. She was now unable to get up very often, but the room was near enough to Eddy for him to hear her breathing while he worked, and Mrs Clemm braved the snowdrifts to visit neighbours and beg the loan of a few poor comestibles. There, on a thin mattress, wrapped in Edgar's magic greatcoat and blankets given by friends, hugging Catarina, Virginia waited for death. Mrs Nichols braved the weather and made a surprise visit early in December:

I saw her in her bed-chamber. Everything here was so neat, so purely clean, so scant and poverty stricken, that I saw the poor sufferer with such a heartache as the poor feel for the poor.

There was no clothing on the bed, which was only straw, but a snow-white counterpane and sheets. The weather was cold, and the sick lady had the dreadful chills that accompany the hectic fever of consumption. She law in the straw bed, wrapped in her husband's great coat, with a large tortoiseshell cat in her bosom. The wonderful cat seemed conscious of her great usefulness. The coat and the cat were the sufferer's only means of warmth, except as her husband held her hands, and her mother her feet. Mrs Clemm was passionately fond of her daughter, and her distress on account of her illness and poverty was dreadful to see.

As soon as I was made aware of these painful facts, I came to New York and enlisted the sympathies and services of a lady, whose heart and hand were ever open to the poor and miserable. . . .

This was the harrowing situation which prompted Mrs Nichols to raise a subscription among her friends. Other ladies followed Mrs Osgood and her sister-in-law, Mrs Locke, who sent Poe some poems and a little money; Mrs Hewitt, who undertook to approach the press for help, though she feared 'it will hurt Poe's pride to have his affairs made so public'. Her activities produced a paragraph in the *New York Express*:

We regret to learn that Edgar A. Poe and his wife are both dangerously ill with the consumption, and that the hand of misfortune lies heavy upon their temporal affairs. We are sorry to mention the fact that they are so far reduced as to be barely able to obtain the necessaries of life. This is indeed a hard lot, and we hope the friends and admirers of Mr Poe will come promptly to his assistance in his bitterest hour of need.

When N. P. Willis saw the sad note he published in the *Home Journal* a moving appeal on Poe's behalf, coupled with the notion of a house of refuge for authors. Poe was shocked and dismayed at the publicity, and replied to Willis that he deprecated public charity. Yet as a result of Mrs Nichols' initiatory efforts conditions at Fordham were much alleviated, and late into December Poe worked as best he could on his continuing history *Literary America*. A thin Christmas came and went, enlivened by calls from the friendly ladies bearing small comforts and luxuries, the greatest of which for Edgar was the news that his work was being republished and attracting great interest in England, Scotland and France. Thus the year of bitter pastoral ended with a good fire in the parlour grate.

Throughout January Virginia barely moved from her mattress, and Eddy, Muddy and all their friends knew that the end was very near. On 29 January relatives and friends began to arrive, somehow aware of the imminent event. One of them was Poe's old Baltimore sweetheart Mary, to whom Virginia had borne his love letters when she was a little girl. She was amazed to find Virginia sitting up in bed, her mind quite clear and bright: 'The day before Virginia died I found her in the parlor. I said to her, "Do you feel any better today?" and sat down by the big armchair in which she was placed. Mr Poe sat on the other side of her. I had my hand in hers, and she took it and placed it in Mr Poe's, saying, "Mary, be a friend to Eddie, and don't forsake him; he always loved you – didn't you, Eddie?"'

The same day Poe wrote to Mrs Shew a note overflowing with gratitude:

> Kindest – Dearest Friend, – My poor Virginia still lives, although failing fast and now suffering much pain. May God grant her life until she sees you and thanks you once again! Her bosom is full to overflowing – like my own – with a boundless – inexpressible gratitude to you. Lest she may never see you more – she bids me say that she sends you her sweetest kiss of love and will die blessing you. But come – oh, come to-morrow! Yes, I will be calm - everything you so nobly wish to see me. My mother sends you, also, her 'warmest love and thanks'. She begs me to ask you, if possible, to make arrangements at home so that you may stay with us To-morrow night. I enclose the order to the Postmaster. Heaven bless you and farewell.
>
> Edgar A. Poe
> Fordham, January 29, '47.

Mrs Shew, arriving the next morning with dire expectations, found Virginia still rational. As she sat beside her, Virginia took from beneath her pillow a picture of Edgar, and the small chest which had belonged to his mother, and gave them to Mrs Shew. That night, in fulfilment of Poe's fearful obsession with death by suffocation, the poor girl coughed, choked and smothered herself to death.

After Virginia's death it was suddenly realized that no picture of her existed. She was propped up in bed and a poor watercolour sketch made by one of the ladies present. It showed her dead, with her eyes closed, but was later retouched when published to show the eyes open. Mrs Shew provided a linen dress for Virginia to be buried in, and she and Mrs Clemm worked together on the preparation of the body. On the day of the funeral the coffin lay on Poe's writing table. Neighbours came, and Willis with his partner Morris. Wearing the greatcoat which had not been magic enough to protect his sweet sister, Poe followed the coffin down an alley of trees to a burial vault in the graveyard of the Fordham Dutch Reformed Church. When they returned to the cottage he was in a state of collapse, almost as cataleptic as his character in *The Premature Burial*. He remained numb for several weeks. Hervey Allen reports an unbearably painful detail – Mrs Clemm trying to sell Virginia's gold thimble to Mary Devereaux, who had no money to buy the sad little memento.

The Poe-Lesque occasion had an aftermath worthy of the Master. In 1875, the cemetery in which Virginia was buried was destroyed, and the contents of the graves

Engraving by Birket Foster for *Annabel Lee*, a poem that synthesizes all Poe's relationships with women.

and vaults removed or scattered. Virginia's bones were rescued by Poe's biographer, Gill. He kept them in a box under his bed for a while, from where they continued their return to life as a travelling curiosity, 'the bones of Annabel Lee'. Finally they arrived in Baltimore and were buried beside Poe, and the prophecy of the poet was realized at last. The dust of the woman who epitomized all his women, she who had died all of their deaths, finally lay beside him.

For the moon never beams, without bringing me dreams
  Of the beautiful Annabel Lee:
And the stars never rise, but I feel the bright eyes
  Of the beautiful Annabel Lee:
And so, all the night-tide, I lie down by the side
Of my darling – my darling – my life and my bride,
  In the sepulchre there by the sea –
  In her tomb by the sounding sea.

## *The After-Dream*

Poe's stories and poems are consistent in their obsessed imagery. His preoccupations with the dying mother-sister, the red phantom of tuberculosis, the tomb, suffocation, premature burial, womb-like tunnels of darkness and light (as in Roderick Usher's painting), recur again and again in his writings; but in all of Poe's work there is no more complete statement than in the story *The Fall of the House of Usher*, first published in *Graham's Magazine* in 1839. Written eight years before her death, *Usher* expresses emblematically but quite clearly Virginia's part in Poe's inner life. When Roderick Usher's sister, the Lady Madeline, entombed by him while still alive, claws her way out of the vault to confront her guilt-maddened brother, Usher's cry, '*Madman! I tell you that she now stands without the door!*', is Poe's fear through those haunted nights at Fordham following the death of his sister-wife.

After Virginia's death, Poe was too ill to leave Fordham. It was whispered locally that he haunted the tomb in the churchyard, and his friend Charles C. Burr stated categorically: 'Many times, after the death of his beloved wife, was he found at the dead hour of a winter-night, sitting beside her tomb almost frozen in the snow, where he had wandered from his bed weeping and wailing.'

Mrs Clemm reported that he was unable to sleep, and that darkness and the wind at night made him frantically nervous, so that she had to sit with him for hours on end, her hand on his forehead. Often when she was about to leave him, thinking him asleep, he would beg her to stay, saying, 'Not yet, not yet'. Prostrate with grief, guilt and fear, Poe waited sleeplessly through those endless nights for the presence at the door, for 'the huge antique panels' to open 'their ponderous and ebony jaws' to reveal 'the lofty enshrouded figure' of the Lady of his own House standing there like Lady Madeline of Usher: 'There was blood upon her white robes, and the evidence of bitter struggle upon every portion of her emaciated frame. For a moment she remained trembling and reeling to and fro upon the threshold, then, with a low moaning cry, fell heavily inward upon the person of her brother, and in her violent and now final death-agonies, bore him to the floor a corpse, and a victim to the terrors he had anticipated.' The living-dead mother–sister wife would drag him down to her tomb as a punishment for his unfaithfulness and cruelty to all of them. In Poe's fantasy of the Ushers, Roderick ruthlessly thrusts his sister into the tomb, well aware that her 'mysterious malady' may merely be a simulation of death. Roderick's sadism is Poe's fantasy; such sadistic impulses, together with the intensely incestuous feelings of his relationship with Virginia, produced his horrifying sense of guilt. We must observe, too, that the teller of the story of the Ushers suffers 'an utter depression

Harry Clarke's interpretation of the shock appearance of Lady Madeline in *The Fall of the House of Usher*.

Illustration by Harry Clarke to *The Cask of Amontillado*, a tale of cold-blooded, paranoid revenge, published in 1846.

of soul which I can compare to no earthly sensation more properly than to the after-dream of the reveller upon opium'. *Usher* perfectly embodies Poe's opiate 'after-dream' of his entire life. It is, accordingly, one of the most perfect of his compositions, a pure embodiment of his complex and agonized genius.

But *Usher* was written years before that winter of 1847, when Edgar Poe shivered in the night, the hand of 'Muddy' upon his forehead. Since the move to Fordham he had published very little. The last of the *Literati* papers had appeared in *Godey's* in October 1846, and *The Cask of Amontillado*, also published that year, was written some time before. Income there was none, and the great-hearted ex-nurse Mrs Shew once again came to the rescue. She collected some $100 from well-wishers for the support of Edgar and Mrs Clemm, and arranged for Drs Mott and Francis to keep a close watch upon his degenerating condition. The libel suit which had been started in those now remote days of arrogance in New York came to trial that February, and the damages Poe received raised his spirits a little and further contributed to the household expenses. Mrs Clemm bought a new tea-set, carpets and a lamp, and occasionally a few carefully selected guests were invited to tea. One of them observed, rather shocked, that Mrs Clemm was very proud of her new china and that Eddy seemed over-fond of Mrs Shew – all so very soon after poor Virginia's death. But the only way in which Poe could live with the memory of Sis and the unspeakable emotions vested in it was by idealizing her. She became the lost Ulalume, the romantic, eternally sleeping Annabel Lee; from the fearful man-eater of his opium dreams she was transformed into the Romantic epitome of beauty and poetic suffering.

Poe's despair rebounded in other dimensions. As he poeticized and magnified his experiences, his disordered mind leapt into the infinite towards a confrontation with the Ultimate, the discovery of the final realities of God-in-Man and Man-become-God. During this time at Fordham he wrote his long prose-poem *Eureka*, apparently so calmly philosophical and actually so disordered. As Hervey Allen describes it:

It was a strange thing, this prose poem, a compound of many tides of thought at the time. It is the sophistry which Poe was forced to introduce into its pages in order to try to fuse its imponderable but antagonistic elements, by which the work finally falls. What was meant to be a chemical solution of ideas is found in reality upon analysis to be only an emulsion, but let us grant the fact, cleverly even subtly mixed. The unity is purely mechanical and literary, but *Eureka*, despite the bitter criticisms which it has received, remains a creditable piece of dialectic. Philosophically it is an Alexandrine concoction, but with this exception – it is animated by the imagination of an abnormally detached and exalted mind.

Mrs Clemm, his nurse, nanny, mother, his 'Muddy', described the recuperative period during which Poe wrestled with God:

He never liked to be alone, and I used to sit up with him, often until four o'clock in the morning, he at his desk, writing, and I dozing in my chair. When he was composing 'Eureka', we used to walk up and down the garden, his arm around me, mine around him, until I was so tired I could not walk. He would stop every few minutes and explain his ideas to me, and ask if I understood him. I always sat up with him when he was writing, and gave him a cup of hot coffee every hour or two. At home he was simple and affectionate as a child, and during all the years he lived with me I do not remember a single night that he failed to come and kiss his 'mother', as he called me, before going to bed.

At this time Willis, the editor of the *Home Journal*, showed deep friendship, kindness and the highest admiration for Edgar. In March he published Poe's lines *To M.L.S.*, an expression of deep gratitude to Mrs Shew with whom his relationship was becoming rather more than that of grateful genius to devoted patron. Lacking new material from Poe's pen, Willis announced the forthcoming book on the authors of America (the history which, so often projected, never materialized); he reprinted poems and published commendations and notices. Poe wrote to him of his plans and Mrs Clemm was a frequent caller, accompanied by her large basket and her ironclad determination to collect small sums whenever possible.

Poe spent the rest of the year like a hermit at Fordham. He had little alternative, for any excursion he made ended disastrously in a tavern, leaving him collapsed and disordered. Yet the excursions were few, and he passed the summer in gardening, walking and boating with the devoted Muddy. His familiars were his birds, a bobalink, a parrot, several canaries, and Catarina, Sis's dear companion. Mrs Shew visited, and so did writers, including a Mrs Weiss who was enchanted by Poe in his pastoral setting. 'The poet and his mother standing together on the green turf smilingly looking up and talking to their pets.... Most of his time was passed out of doors. He did not like the loneliness of the house, and would not remain alone in the room in which Virginia had died.'

In August, Poe visited Philadelphia with articles for *Graham's*. There he inevitably took drink and became 'exceeding ill – so much so that I had no hope except in getting home immediately'. He was saved by someone at *Graham's*, to whom he wrote that, 'without your aid ... I should not now be alive to write you this letter.' He returned with $10 from Mr Graham, for which he had left two articles. His condition was extremely disturbed, his weakening heart causing palpitations, and the effects of a lesion of the brain beginning to be apparent, so that the smallest quantity of alcohol was now extremely poisonous to him. Following his practice during periods of withdrawal Poe was using opiates (according to his sister), specifically morphine. Certainly the sublime opiate euphoria may be sensed in the soaring confidence of *Eureka*. Poe's afflatus was at times so great that 'my whole nature revolts at the idea that there is any Being in the Universe superior to Myself.' Borne up by such delusions of grandeur, he began to plan a great return to the world. With the assistance of Willis, he arranged to deliver a lecture on *The Cosmogony of the Universe* on 3 February 1848 at the Society Library in New York. The lecture, based upon *Eureka*, was intended to raise funds for the revived project of *The Stylus*. The grand revelation of his discoveries would follow a campaign similar to that which presented *The Raven* to a startled world. In December *Ulalume* appeared anonymously in the *American Whig*, Mrs Clemm's earlier arrangement with Mrs Nichols apparently having fallen through. Willis would reprint it the next month, and raise the question of the authorship of this new work of genius. In the new year a further instalment of *Marginalia* was published in *Graham's*; a biography of Poe by P.P. Cooke appeared in the Richmond *Messenger*; and the limited distribution of his collected *Tales* was publicized, establishing that 'a reader gathering his knowledge of Mr Poe from this Wiley and Putnam issue would perceive nothing of the diversity and variety for which his works are remarkable.' All the puffs were intended to revive interest in Poe and his work, moving towards the projection of a collected edition.

Shortly before giving his lecture, Poe distributed copies of *The Stylus* prospectus, his literary testament, and again announced his always impending definitive history of literary America. Willis advertised both the lecture and *The Stylus* in the *Home Journal*. When the great night came it was cold and stormy and the Society Library poorly heated. Even so, some sixty people attended and listened to Poe for two and a half hours. His performance of almost the entire text of *Eureka* was considered to be, theatrically, perhaps the best he ever gave. He was compared with the great Edwin Booth in manner and delivery; his voice was noted as well modulated, vital and thrilling. The theatrical talent inherited from his actor-parents had always imparted to him a quality described very aptly by Hervey Allen as that of 'a great tragedian off-stage'. The sense of dramatic placing so clearly apparent in his stories was a part, too, of the same theatrical tradition. The *Eureka* lecture presented Poe totally absorbed in the grand new part he had designed for himself – that of the Prophet of a new Revelation. His small audience, fascinated, forgot the cold and ignored the obscurities. But the newspaper reports annoyed him by their ineptitude, causing him to distribute 'a loose summary of my propositions and results' to his friends. But if the launching of *Eureka* was a success, its financial returns were hardly amazing. Poe may have made some $50 on the lecture, but the edition of 500 copies of the prose-poem published in March 1848 (his tenth volume and the last during his life) was hardly likely to earn him more than puzzled *réclame*. He prefaced the prose-poem with a superbly confident note suited to one who had achieved symbiosis with the Deity:

> To the few who love me and whom I love – to those who feel rather than to those who think – to the dreamers and those who put faith in dreams as in the only realities – I offer this Book of Truths, not in its character of Truth-Teller, but for the Beauty that abounds in its Truth; constituting it true. To these I present the composition as an Art-Product alone: – let us say as a Romance; or, if I be not urging too lofty a claim, as a Poem.
>
> What I here propound is true; – therefore, it cannot die: – or if by any means it be now trodden down so that it die, it will 'rise again to the Life Everlasting'. Nevertheless it is as a Poem only that I wish this work to be judged after I am dead.
>
> E. A. P.

Pre-eminent now among the few who loved Poe was Marie Louise Shew. Since the death of Virginia their friendship had developed on lines more practical and positive than those usually followed in Edgar's 'affairs' with the 'starry sisterhood'. Mrs Shew was a strong personality in her own right, the daughter of a doctor and a former nurse with a good deal of medical experience which precluded much of the mistaken sentimentality over Poe which confused more 'spiritual' women. She was less interested in his work than in himself, and she recognized and understood many of his psychological and physical problems. She also realized that material support was as essential for a poet as it is for other human beings, and both at Fordham and in her own home she was generous in her provision of it. Poe's initial gratitude bloomed typically into a wilder emotion, combined with

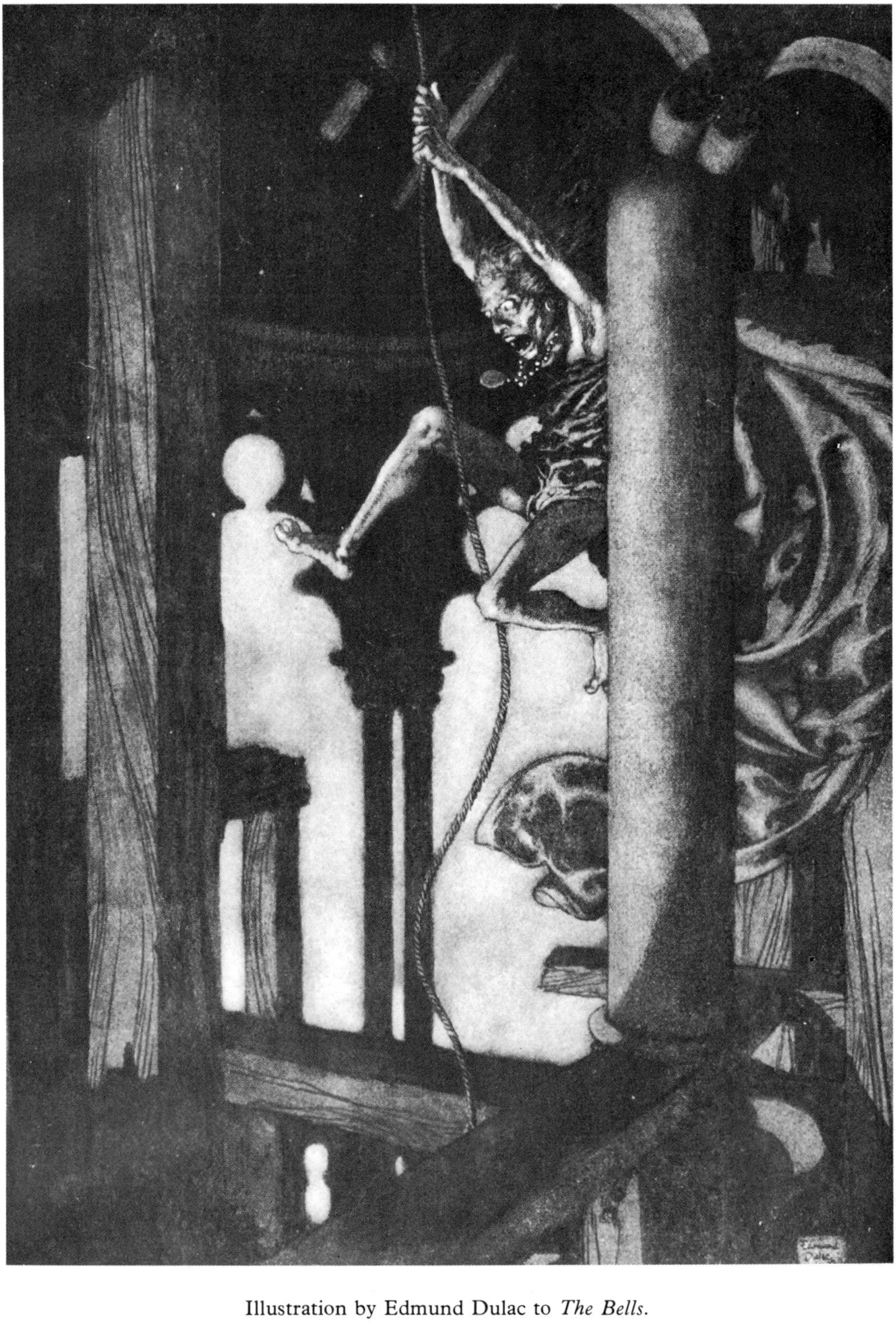

Illustration by Edmund Dulac to *The Bells*.

the worshipping, dependent love which it was his nature and necessity to offer to protective, motherly women. Early in 1848 Poe was often in the Shew house; indeed he was instrumental in its furnishing and the design of its décor, showing an amazed regard for Mrs Shew's taste – 'I wondered that a little country maiden like you had developed so classical a taste and atmosphere.' Together they attended church services, where Mrs Shew was impressed by Edgar's tenor and his knowledge (in spite of professed atheism) of the responses. For him, perhaps, it was a return to the happy days of his first discovery of a mother in Frances Allen, whom also he had accompanied to church.

Mrs Shew's diary contains a fascinating account of the writing of Poe's extraordinary and much criticized poem *The Bells*. Hervey Allen saw and summarized her account:

Poe and Mrs Shew retired to a little conservatory overlooking a garden, where they had tea. He complained to his hostess that he had to write a poem, but had no inspiration. Mrs Shew, to help him, brought pen, ink, and paper, and, while they sat there, the sound of church bells filled the air, and fell almost like a blow of pain on Poe's hypersensitive ears and jangled nerves. He pushed the paper away saying, 'I dislike the noise of bells to-night, I cannot write. I have no subject, I am exhausted.' Mrs. Shew then wrote on the paper, 'The bells, the little, silver bells' – and Poe finished a stanza, again almost relapsing into a state of coma. Mrs Shew then urged him again, beginning a second stanza with 'The heavy iron bells.' Poe finished two more stanzas, heading them 'by Mrs M. L. Shew,' after which he was completely unable to proceed. After supper he was taken upstairs and put to bed, where he appears to have lapsed into a coma. Mrs Shew called Dr Francis in. The doctor and Mrs Shew sat by the bedside and noted his symptoms. The pulse rate was very weak and irregular, and caused the doctor to say, 'He has heart disease, and will die early in life.' Mrs Shew had previously noted the symptoms also. Both of them felt that Poe was nearly dying, and that he was close to the verge of insanity. He remained for the night, but did not seem to realize his danger.

After this collapse Poe slept twelve hours and was then taken back to Fordham by Dr Francis who observed his condition of exhausted delirium. In such an 'afterdream' state he told Mrs Shew of a duel he had fought in Spain, where he had been nursed by a Scottish lady whose name was too well known for him to divulge, and he showed her a scar received in the duel. From Spain he said he went to Paris where he wrote a novel later published under Eugène Sue's name. The hand of opium upon such dreams is strong; but Mrs Shew understood, listened, and sympathized.

Yet for Mrs Shew the friendship with Poe, much as she desired to sustain it, grew alarming. His passionate dependence grew, and threatened her established social life. As other ladies had done in the past, she looked about for someone towards whom his intense attentions could be more profitably addressed, advising him to find a wife who could give him the continuous attention and total love which she, for all her friendship, could not. She prevailed upon Dr Francis to warn Edgar that stimulants would be the death of him. When he appeared to respond to the advice Mrs Shew, feeling her work done, withdrew determinedly. She had no intention of being driven out of society by the kind of scandal which dogged Poe wherever he went, and in June she wrote that her visits to Fordham and his visits to her house must cease. Edgar was not entirely surprised, but deeply hurt:

So I have had premonitions of this for months.... Are you to vanish like all I love, or desire, from my darkened and 'lost soul'?.... I felt my heart stop and was sure I was then to die before your eyes.... Such rare souls as yours so beautify this earth.... My heart never wronged you. I placed you in my esteem – in all solemnity – beside the friend of my boyhood, the mother of my schoolfellow, of whom I told you and as I have repeated in the poem [*To Helen*] as the truest, tenderest of this world's most womanly souls and an angel to my forlorn and darkened nature.

But Mrs Shew had already left the stage upon which Edgar's 'after-dream' was being played out. Another Helen was waiting in the wings.

## *Helen (and Annie) Revisited*

In 1848, a few weeks after his birthday, Poe received a late valentine:

Oh! thou grim and ancient Raven,
From the Night's plutonic shore,
Oft in dreams, thy ghastly pinions
Wave and flutter round my door –
Oft thy shadow dims the moonlight
Sleeping on my chamber floor.

Romeo talks of 'White doves trooping,
Amid crows athwart the night',
But to see thy dark wing swooping
Down the silvery path of light,
Amid swans and dovelets stooping,
Were, to me, a nobler sight....

Then, Oh! Grim and Ghastly Raven!
Wilt thou to my heart and ear
Be a Raven true as ever

Flapped his wings and croaked 'Despair'?
Not a bird that roams the forest
Shall our lofty eyrie share.

Providence, R.I. – Feb. 14, 1848

The valentine had been sent on by Miss Lynch from Mrs Osgood. Poe recognized the writing as that of Mrs Sarah Helen Whitman, 'the Seeress of Providence',

Harry Clarke's illustration of *Landor's Cottage*, an autobiographical piece written in Poe's last years.

whom he had met one night three years before outside her door, with or without roses.

The Providence referred to was the lesser one in Rhode Island. Mrs Whitman acquired her slightly absurd title as a result of being a well-known member of the Transcendentalists, whose preoccupation was with the transcendent life of the spirit and with occult, mesmeric, and spiritualistic investigations into its nature and whereabouts. Mrs Whitman herself simulated the 'spiritual dream of womanhood, gliding by upon dainty slippers, followed by undulating scarfs and a faint, deathly sweet odour of a handkerchief soaked in ether'. Her heart troubled her and she frequently wrote letters announcing a premonition of early death. She had a difficult family background, overpowered by a domineering mother, and neglected by a father who was absent from his family for nineteen years because of disagreements with his wife and the fortunes of war. She also had an 'eccentric' younger sister. After the death of her husband, 'a young lawyer with a sensitive arch-angelic face', a few years into their marriage, she returned to live with her difficult mother on Benefit Street where Poe first saw her by moonlight. She was, on that occasion, some forty-five years of age and unprepared by her poetic and spiritual studies for an assault by a passionate madman.

However, like other literary ladies, Mrs Whitman was an accomplished cultural coquette. She had flirted with the influential Jehu O'Cataract (Poe's early patron, John Neal), and she was visited in Providence by such fine conversationalists as John Hay, George W. Curtis, Ellery Channing, and the egregious Horace Greeley. All found her witty on European literature, music and painting, and among the versifying 'starry sisters' she was an authentic minor poetess whose status was generally accepted. When he received her valentine the 'Grim and Ghastly Raven' was ecstatically flattered, and he immediately read aloud his great poem *To Helen.* When the *Home Journal* published Mrs Whitman's valentine, Mrs Osgood, who, though dying, was still incurably addicted to scandal, wrote to her friend: 'I see by the Home Journal that your beautiful invocation has reached the 'Raven' in his eyrie [at Fordham] and I suppose, ere this, he has swooped upon your little dovecote in Providence. May Providence protect you if he has! for his croak is the most eloquent imaginable. He is in truth "A glorious devil, with large heart and brain...." ' By June Poe was well on the way to being in love with the second Helen, but other possible affairs would beset the path of passion.

In Poe's autobiographical piece, *Landor's Cottage*, there is an account of a meeting with 'a young woman about twenty-eight years of age – slender, or rather slight, and somewhat above the medium height'. She was Mrs Annie Richmond, whom Poe first met in July 1848 when in Lowell, Massachusetts, where he was to lecture on *The Poetic Principle*. Mrs Richmond exhibited very strongly the qualities always magnetic to Poe, and he instantly visualized her ensconced in Fordham.

So intense an expression of romance, perhaps I should call it, or of unworldliness, as that which gleamed from her deep-set eyes, had never so sunk into my heart of hearts before. I know not how it is, but this peculiar expression of the eye, wreathing itself occasionally into the lips, is the most powerful, if not absolutely the sole spell, which rivets my interest in woman. 'Romance', provided my readers fully comprehend what I would here imply by the word – 'romance' and 'womanliness' seem to me convertible terms: and, after all what man truly loves in woman, is, simply her womanhood. The eyes of Annie (I heard someone from the interior call her 'Annie, darling!') were 'spiritual grey'; her hair, a light chestnut; this is all I had time to observe of her.

Welcomed by Mrs Richmond, Poe established himself deeply in her family's bosom beside her husband and sister – with the inevitable results. Mrs Richmond soon discovered that their passionate new friend was an ardent verbal lover of great accomplishment and attack. She was thrilled and flattered, but frightened, and when Poe returned to New York a week or so after giving his lecture, his 'Annie darling' was in a state of considerable shock. So, indeed, must have been her entire family and no small section of the population of Lowell, Massachusetts.

Poe's plan was to use the proceeds of his successful lecture and various advances to finance a trip to the south where a subscription campaign for *The Stylus* would be launched. Divided in his passions between his second Helen and the newly discovered Annie, he arrived in Richmond on 19 July in a state of mental confusion, compounded with painful memories of his boyhood in that town. The pressures produced their inevitable result and he began to drink, disappearing for a fortnight into the lower depths of the city. From there he was rescued by John Thompson, editor of the *Southern Literary Messenger:* 'When I reached the purlieus of this abandoned quarter I learned that such a person had indeed been there, drunk, for two weeks, and that he had gone a few hours previous without coat or hat.... It was Poe.... I did all I could to restrain his excesses and to relieve the pressure of his immediate wants (for he was extremely indigent), but no influence was adequate to keep him from the damnable propensity to drink.' Edgar finally rested at the home of his good angels, the Mackenzies, where his sister Rosalie was still living. From there he ventured out when he could to bars and taverns, where he declaimed passages from *The Raven* and *Eureka* between drinks tossed back rapidly in his habitual manner. He was rarely lucid or in total possession of himself and, in short, became the town's principal side-show for some six weeks. *The Stylus* and other good intentions were entirely forgotten, but boyhood sweethearts were much remembered. He called on Robert Stanard, the son of his first Helen; visited, drunk, his first sweetheart, Catherine; and he checked on the tracks of his lost Elmira. But the most practical of the Richmond ladies he attended on this visit was a Mrs Clarke with whom he had boarded in 1835, and who was now a widow. She enjoyed, she reported, 'a good deal of his society', but understood that he

Duncan Lodge, in Richmond, home of Poe's relatives the Mackenzies, was the house in which he stayed during 1848. He spent his last happy times there.

was hoping to become engaged to Mrs Shelton, whom gossip had it he was trying to marry for her money. Altogether his pursuit of Mrs Clarke seems to have been a search for a good landlady rather than another sweet sister.

The short visits with the Mackenzies on this and subsequent occasions that year held many happy moments for Edgar in which he recaptured some of the rarer innocent joys of his boyhood. At Duncan Lodge, the Mackenzie house, he played leapfrog enthusiastically, and enjoyed much simple fun with the young Mackenzies. He also gave a reading at the music hall of the Exchange Hotel that mid-summer. Surprisingly only thirteen people, including the janitor, turned up. Poe shortened his address, delivered it mechanically, bowed and left. By now the funds he had raised for his Southern campaign were exhausted, and while the *Messenger* was prepared to take his writings, access to the *Examiner* was barred by disagreements with its editor, John M. Daniel. Daniel knew Mrs Whitman and had expressed doubts about Poe's motives regarding the revered 'Seeress of Providence'. His observations were reported to Poe, who instantly challenged Daniel to a duel, which his journalist friends failed to take seriously since Edgar was clearly drunk at the time. But Poe insisted upon pursuing the challenge, and eventually Daniel and he met at the *Examiner* office. There on Daniel's desk were two huge pistols, which the editor explained would enable them to settle their differences at once. Poe, thus challenged, sobered up rapidly, and after a brief discussion the differences between the two literary gentlemen were sorted out and the duel cancelled. The affair ended in considerable good humour, drinks all round, and a toast by Poe:

> I fill this cup to one made up of loveliness alone,
> A woman, of her gentle sex, the seeming paragon.

Honour was thus satisfied and the duellists retired with friends to the nearest bar.

That summer, soon after the 'duel', Poe, who had been sending signals through the intellectual sisterhood to Mrs Whitman earnestly requesting a meeting, received the following lines from the Seeress:

> A low bewildering melody
> Is murmuring in my ear –
> Tones such as in the twilight wood
> The aspen thrills to hear
> When Faunus slumbers on the hill
> And all entranced boughs are still.
>
> The jasmine twines her snowy stars
> Into a fairer wreath –
> The lily through my lattice bars
> Exhales a sweeter breath –
> And, gazing on night's starry cope,
> I dwell with 'Beauty which is Hope'.

Poe's response was instant and immense. He gave up other travelling projects in order to pursue 'sweet, sweet, Helen' and the 'divine dream of her love'. He left Richmond at once, returning to Fordham briefly and, without the blessing of Mrs

Clemm, set out for Providence having ascertained that Mrs Whitman was in residence. This he did with Dupin-like sublety, sending her a note in a disguised hand (signed 'Edward S.T.Gray'), asking for her autograph.

Receiving the assurance he required, he proceeded to Mrs Whitman's home town with a letter of introduction from a mutual friend. On 1 October he began the series of famous love letters to Helen. Never one to dally, Edgar took up, in that first letter, a powerful posture of attack: 'During a walk in the cemetery I said to you while the bitter, bitter, tears sprang to my eyes – "Helen I love now – now for the first and only time".' It was possibly a little strong and direct for Mrs Whitman's Transcendentalist taste, but quite irresistible. The correspondence proceeded, sustaining the same high temperature throughout. Around these letters there was to accumulate a massive posthumous squabble based upon jealousy, academic pettiness, and tedious arguments about whether Mrs Whitman or Virginia was the true Annabel Lee, and to what extent the Rev. Griswold interfered with the letters and such similar issues, all clouding the post-mortem evaluations of a great artist. The fact emerges that Edgar and Helen were both highly romantic writers responding intensely and theatrically to an archetypal literary situation. They were both familiar with the great verbal tradition of passionate exchanges, and doubtless were determined not to shame it. The question behind the endless curiosity of the *literati* was, of course, 'What actually happened?' But knowing what we do about the middle-aged Mrs Whitman and the rapidly disintegrating Poe there can be little doubt that the possibly disappointing answer is – nothing. The 'lovers' were perfectly approximated to one another's needs. Mrs Whitman was too spiritual ever to demand a physical proof of passion, and Poe far too deteriorated and depleted to be able to threaten it seriously. For Helen the 'affair' was to be a fount of inspiration and a source of fame for the rest of her days. Wearing the costume of Pallas and churning out second-rate verse, she worshipped her 'Raven' till she died.

But Helen dallied over Edgar's offer of marriage on the grounds that she was older than he, a widow and an invalid. Poe, deeply hurt by the hesitation, returned to Lowell and Annie. In her soothing presence, he awaited Mrs Whitman's final decision. By the time he received her still vacillating reply to his appeal he discovered that he was in love with Annie. Honour, however, required him to make one final trip to Providence, and when he left Annie he was in a near-insane state of confusion and despair. Three weeks later he wrote to her from Boston, confessing his attempt to resolve the impossible choice between the women in his life by committing suicide:

I remember nothing distinctly from that moment [the parting with 'Annie'] until I found myself in Providence. I went to bed and wept through a long, long hideous night of

Despair – When the day broke, I arose and endeavored to quiet my mind by a rapid walk in the cold, keen air – but all would not do – the Demon tormented me still. Finally I procured two ounces of laudanum, and without returning to my hotel, took the cars back to Boston.... When I arrived [in Boston] I wrote you [Annie] a letter in which I opened my whole heart to you – to you.... I told you how my struggles were more than I could bear. I then reminded you of that holy promise which was the last I exacted from you in parting – that promise that under all circumstances, you would come to me on my bed of death. I implored you to come then, mentioning the place where I should be found in Boston. Having written this letter, I swallowed about half the laudanum, and hurried to the Post Office, intending not to take the rest until I saw you – for I did not doubt for one moment, that Annie would keep her sacred promise. But I had not calculated on the strength of the laudanum, for before I reached the Post Office my reason was entirely gone, and the letter was never put in. Let me pass over – my darling sister – the awful hours that succeeded. A friend was at hand, who aided me.... It appears that, after the laudanum was rejected from my stomach, I became calm, and to a casual observer, sane – so that I was suffered to go back to Providence.

So Poe's desire to die in Mrs Richmond's arms was not to be fulfilled, and he continued to Providence, a distorted caricature of himself, more Roderick Usher than Edgar Poe.

Poe roamed Providence aimlessly, finally calling upon Mrs Whitman too early to be seen, but receiving a note from her suggesting a meeting-place. He replied explaining that he was extremely ill and ought to go home, but requesting a clear indication of her love and her commitment to him. While he waited, Poe was taken by a friend of the Whitmans, Mr Macfarlane, to the studio of Masury and Hartshorn for a daguerreotype to be made of him. Mrs Whitman called the sad result Poe's '*Ultima Thule* portrait', considering that it showed her unhinged lover 'immediately after being snatched back from the ultimate world's end of horror'. After leaving the unique record behind, Poe passed on to the Whitman house. The occasion was described by Mrs Whitman to her friend Miss Jacobs: '... in a state of wild and delirious excitement calling upon me to save him from some terrible impending doom. The tones of his voice were appalling and rang through the house. Never have I heard anything so awful, awful even to sublimity'. Not surprisingly Mrs Whitman was afraid to see him, but her mother persuaded her to do so and to promise him everything. After some two hours Helen appeared. Miss Jacobs described her friend's dramatic manner of entrance:

As she came flitting into the room and gave you her small, nervous hand, you saw a slight figure, a pale, eager face of fine spiritual expression and irregular features, the dreamy look of deep-set eyes that gazed over and beyond, but never at you. Her movements were very rapid, and she seemed to flutter like a bird, so that her friends asserted that she was always in the process of transformation either to or from the condition of a lapwing.

Poe's behaviour was extreme. He declared Helen an angel sent to save him from hell, and clung to her dress so violently that he tore the drapery off. Mrs Whitman's mother sent for hot coffee and Dr Okie, who quietly advised that the crazed poet and lover be removed.

Several other frantic interviews with Helen in Providence followed, during which Poe revealed his authorship of *Ulalume*, which they read together. At some stage in the passionate proceedings Mrs Whitman agreed to marry him, but only if he gave up stimulants entirely. Her promise rested upon the undertaking, and perhaps she was as aware as all his intimates that it was a condition now almost impossible for him to fulfil. But in his own estimation Poe left Providence on 14 November affianced. As soon as he left, the gossip-mongers got at it, with the effect of enraging Mrs Whitman's mother, while making Helen herself even more interested than she had previously been. While her relatives argued about the effect such a marriage would have upon her property, she walked in the garden looking up at Poe's favourite star, Arcturus, about which she wrote him a poem of passionate and whole-hearted commitment. But Edgar, en route to Fordham, was already torn with conflict again, feeling great guilt towards Helen and a growing need for Annie. He wrote to them determined to keep both possibilities (and his conflict) at white heat. To Mrs Richmond he wrote, 'Indeed, indeed, Annie, there is *nothing* in this world worth living for except love ... such as burns in my very soul for *you.*' And to Mrs Whitman, 'My sole hope now is in you, Helen.... As you are true to me or fail me, so do I live or die.' When Annie, understandably confused by this intense courtship from a man newly engaged, did not reply, Poe wrote to her sister, that 'her silence fills my whole soul with terror'. On the other hand Mrs Whitman's acceptance of his offer of marriage made him 'so terribly hopelessly ill in body and mind that I cannot leave unless I can feel your sweet gentle loving hand pressed upon my forehead, – oh, *my pure, virtuous, generous beautiful* sister Annie!' One must conclude that Annie was a protection against Helen, and Helen a defence against Annie, and that now that Virginia was dead the twin personalities of sister-bride and mother-wife were battling for the possession of Poe's confused and tortured soul. But neither Poe's painful confusion, nor Mrs Whitman's relatives, nor the distant siren call of sister Annie, were to prevent the destined match, for both Edgar and Helen saw in their marriage the fundamental element of a grand design – nothing less than a take-over of the leadership of America's intellectual life: 'Would it not be "glorious", darling, to establish, in America, the sole unquestionable aristocracy – that of intellect – to secure its supremacy – to lead and to control it? All this I can do, Helen, and will – if you bid me – and aid me.'

Poe returned to Providence in the second week of December to complete arrangements for his imminent marriage. He wrote to Dr Crocker, a local minister,

The *Ultima Thule* daguerreotype of Poe, taken in Providence, Rhode Island, in November 1848. Mrs Whitman disliked the picture, and thought it showed Poe 'immediately after being snatched back from the ultimate world's end of horror'.

asking for the banns to be published on the following Sunday and Monday, and arranged for him to perform the ceremony as soon as a day was set. Mrs Whitman found his attack irresistible, but her powerful and practical mother insisted that the family's assets should be protected. A marriage contract was drawn up in which Mrs Whitman's estate, valued at about $8,000, was transferred to her mother, Mrs Power, 'for her own use'. It was a very high price for Helen to pay, indicating her determination at this point to make the marriage. Poe returned to Fordham to tell Mrs Clemm of the arrangements and to prepare the place for his new bride. Muddy was not enthusiastic about receiving into their penniless family a newly penniless daughter-in-law.

When Edgar set out on the twentieth for Providence he seems to have had some doubts himself, for to a lady who asked him quite directly whether he was going there to be married, he replied, 'I'm going to deliver a lecture on Poetry.' He added after a moment, 'That marriage may never take place.'

The lecture certainly was a success. Nearly two thousand people heard it with enthusiasm, and in the blush of excitement Mrs Whitman named the following Monday as the day. The Friday before, yet another consent to the release of Mrs Whitman's property was presented to Poe and signed by him, and he wrote again to Dr Crocker regarding the banns. He also wrote to Mrs Clemm informing her that the marriage was set for Monday and that he and his bride would be 'at Fordham on Tuesday, in the first train'. That Saturday was immensely dramatic. With his uncanny capacity to select enemies to perform the duties of friends, Poe asked William Parbodie, at whose house he had stayed, to deliver his note to the minister. It was well known locally that Mr Parbodie was a long-time suitor of Mrs Whitman. Parbodie failed to deliver the note. Then, while Mrs Whitman was packing, a letter was delivered to her warning her against the marriage and telling her of Poe's involvement with Mrs Richmond, by now a scandalous subject of general discussion in Lowell. As Helen assimilated this shock, her suitor Mr Parbodie delivered the *coup de grâce*: Poe had been seen drinking wine that morning in the bar of the Earl House, thus breaking his promise to her, the agreed foundation of their understanding. She confronted Poe on both matters, observing that he showed no signs of drink. He denied all the charges against him, but Mrs Whitman was by now convinced that she must find a release from the insane life to which she had almost inescapably committed herself. Her sources could not be totally denied, and she felt that she would never be certain of her wayward and erratic lover. She suddenly knew that marriage, even with her, could not save Edgar Poe from his chosen destiny.

The engagement was terminated that very day in an almost ceremonial scene in the Whitman house, described in detail by Helen's sister. With Parbodie standing by, Mrs Power prepared letters and papers for return to Poe, and Helen hysterically sobbed into her handkerchief soaked in ether. Communication between the nearly-weds being effectively prevented, Mrs Power loudly and clearly reminded Mr Poe that the next train for New York was imminent. Poe fell to his knees begging Mrs Whitman to think again. She whispered, 'What can I say?' Urgently he begged her, 'Say that you love me, Helen.' The last words she ever spoke to him were, indeed, 'I love you', faint with hysteria and ether; after which Mr Parbodie firmly escorted Edgar to the New York train. Slowly, Providence, Rhode Island, reeling from shock, returned to its accustomed peaceful ways.

## *So Much to Say*

'Of one thing rest assured, from this day forth, I shun the pestilential society of literary women. They are a heartless, unnatural, venomous, dishonorable set, with no guiding principle but inordinate self-esteem.' Thus determined, Poe retired to Fordham, withdrawing from 'the pestilential society of literary women' and others, leaving them all to scandalize at their leisure and without contradiction. And of scandal there was to be no shortage. His associations with the Mrs Osgood, Shew, Richmond and Whitman, not to mention his passing flirtations with half a dozen minor members of the 'starry sisterhood', ensured a growing cacophony of jealous squabbling, for all the ladies had busy tongues and so did their friends; yet the advantage that emerges out of this clatter of women's talk, diary-keeping and letter-writing was an unusually close observation of Poe's movements, both physical and emotional, through the last two years of his life. But in the cottage at Fordham, under the stolid but determined protection of Mrs Clemm (much relieved at not having a daughter-in-law), Edgar could again involve himself totally in the writing and planning to which he habitually retreated when the complexities of life in the real world grew too great for him to control.

For the first half of the year 1849 Poe planned yet again the launching of *The Stylus*, always to be the power-base of his rule over the literary world. During this time he also finished *The Bells* and *Annabel Lee*, perhaps the most haunting and justly famed of his poems, celebratory of his ideal woman, according more closely to his heart's desire in poetry than ever she did in life. His plan of action was, as always in such periods of reconsolidation of his career, detailed and carefully constructed. By the end of January the plan of return to fame and fortune was well worked out:

... I am so busy, now, and feel so full of energy. Engagements to write are pouring in upon me every day. I had two proposals within the last week from Boston. I sent yesterday an article to the Am. Review, about Critics and Criticism. Not long ago I sent one to the Metropolitan called Landor's Cottage it has something about 'Annie' in it, and will appear, I suppose in the March number. To the S.L. Messenger I have sent fifty pages of Marginalia, five pages to appear each month of the current year. I have also made permanent engagements with another magazine, called The gentlemen's. So you see that I have only to keep up my spirits to get out of all my pecuniary troubles. The least price I get is \$5 per 'Graham page', and I can easily average $1\frac{1}{2}$ per day – that is \$$7\frac{1}{2}$. As soon as 'returns' come in I shall be out of difficulty.

Poe momentarily felt strong and well, capable of dealing with his own deepest problems and confident enough to give advice on what constituted a healthy life for the artist to his old friend F.W.Thomas:

... Right glad I am to find you once more in a true position – 'in the field of letters'. Depend upon it after all, Thomas, literature is the most noble of professions. In fact, it is about the only one fit for a man. For my own part there is no seducing me from the path. I shall be a litterateur at least, all my life; nor would I abandon the hopes which still lead me on for all the gold in California. Talking of gold and temptations at present held out to 'poor-devil authors' did it ever strike you that all that is really valuable to a man of letters – to a poet in especial – is absolutely unpurchasable? Love, fame, the dominion of intellect, the consciousness of power, the thrilling sense of beauty, the free air of Heaven, exercise of body and mind, with the physical and moral health which result – these and such as these are really all that a poet cares for: – then answer me this – why should he go to California?....

Everyone else, it seemed, had become a Forty-Niner, rushing after the gold in California, but Poe still believed that the true vein of the artist's wealth was within himself, and he was determined to mine it to the last. With gold on his mind he wrote his poem *Eldorado* and, in March, his hoax story of the alchemical production of gold from lead, *Von Kempelen and His Discovery*.

Mrs Clemm was well aware of the scandalous aftermath of Poe's 'misunderstood' relations with Mrs Richmond and Mrs Whitman, not to mention the rest. She knew too that Mrs Locke, sister-in-law to Mrs Osgood, having been 'insulted' by Poe's lack of attention on his visits to Lowell (where she regarded herself as a great patroness of the arts), was now writing to all and sundry determined to harm Eddy as much as possible. The Richmonds were holding out against this accomplished scandal-monger, but Mrs Clemm realized that Poe's attention needed to be turned in a new and more practical direction. When his mind turned even further back in his catalogue of ideal women to his boyhood sweetheart, Elmira Royster, Mrs Clemm was not averse to reminding him that the lost Elmira was now the widowed Mrs Shelton. Mrs Clemm was always as practical as she was devoted, and she could not fail to know that Mr Shelton had been a successful merchant, leaving a considerable income to his widow, now a charming middle-aged lady, self-possessed and pious, but available, like most widows, to the flattering attentions of an attractive, famous, and tragic man of genius. Fordham was once again feeling the pinch, for many of Edgar's plans had, through no fault of his own, but in accordance with his chronic bad luck, fallen through. He wrote to Annie:

... You know how cheerfully I wrote to you not long ago – about my prospects – hopes – how I anticipated being soon out of difficulty. Well! all seems to be frustrated – at least for the present. As usual, misfortunes never come single, and I have met one disappointment after another. The Columbian Magazine in the first place, failed – then Post's Union (taking with it my principal dependence); then the Whig Review was forced to stop paying for contributions – then the Democratic – then (on account of his oppression and insolence) I was obliged to quarrel, finally, with – ; and then, to crown all, the ' – – ' (from which I anticipated so much and with which I had made a regular engagement for $10 a week throughout the year) has written a circular to correspondents, pleading poverty and declining to receive any more articles. More than this, the S. L. Messenger which owed me a good deal, cannot pay just yet, and altogether, I am reduced to Sartain and Graham both very precarious. No doubt Annie, you attribute my 'gloom' to these events – but you would be wrong. It is not in the power of any mere worldly considerations, such as these, to depress me.... No, my sadness is unaccountable, and this makes me the more sad. I am full of dark forebodings. Nothing cheers or comforts me. My life seems wasted – the future looks a dreary blank; but I will struggle on and 'hope against hope'....

Poe was exhausted and depressed. All his planning and work seemed, once again, to be coming to nothing. His heartbeat was erratic, and he complained to Annie of a headache that had lasted for months. These symptoms, and the 'brain fever' from which he suffered from time to time, would seem to have been symptomatic of the lesion of the brain discovered after his death. For the present his problems, pressures and pains drew him back to opium. In June he called on John Sartain in Philadelphia demanding laudanum, of which his tolerance was now enormous. Relaxed into his dream-world, Poe passed the last creative months of his life. 'I have not suffered a day to pass without writing from a page to three pages. Yesterday, I wrote five, and the day before a poem considerably longer than *The Raven*.' Thus he wrote during this final brief period his satire on the future, *Mellonta Tauta*, a vision of the world in the year 2848, containing many prophetic observations. The strange allegory *Hop-Frog*, and the poems *To My Mother* and *Lenore*, were also composed or finished during this time. Yet, as always in Poe's life, the periods of intense literary activity were marked by a collapse of almost all sources of income. He must pull himself together, withdraw from his creative dream, and essay the world again. Richmond called with its still friendly newspapers, its pride in Edgar as a native son, and the possibility, in the person of the widow Shelton, of a solution to all his financial problems for ever. At this moment of decision the Imp of the Perverse entered once again into Poe's arrangements in the shape of a letter some five months delayed, from Oquawka, Illinois.

Oquawka, a small town on the Mississippi, possessed a weekly newspaper called the *Spectator*. The son of its late founder J.B. Patterson, young Edward, had just come of age and was determined to realize the literary ambitions he had inherited from his deceased father. He had written to Poe on 18 December 1848, but the letter was not received until April. Poe replied at once, stimulated by this unexpected gift of destiny; the offer of help from a wealthy admirer, for which every artist daily searches his mail, had finally arrived. It was nothing less than an offer to back *The Stylus*. Poe was very clear, after the long period of gestation, as to what was needed:

Experience, not less than the most mature reflection on this topic, assured me that no cheap magazine can ever again prosper in America. We must aim high – address the intellect – the higher classes – of the country (with reference, also to a certain amount of foreign circulation) and put the work at $5: – going about 112 pp (or perhaps 128) with occasional wood-engravings in the first style of the art, but only in obvious illustrations of the text. Such a Mag. would begin to pay after 1000 subscribers; and with 5000 would be a fortune worth talking about; – but there is no earthly reason why, under proper management, and with energy and talent, the work might not be made to circulate, at the end of a few years – (say 5) 20,000 copies in which case it would give a clear income of 70 or 80,000 dollars – even if conducted in the most expensive manner.... I need not add that such a Mag. would exercise a literary and other influence never yet exercised in America. I presume you know that during the second year of its existence, the S. L. Messenger rose from less than 1000 to 5000 subs., and that Graham's, in 8 months after my joining it, went up from 5000 to 52,000. I do not imagine that a $5 Mag. could even be forced into so great a circulation as this latter; but under certain circumstances, I would answer for 20,000. The whole income from Graham's 52,000 never went beyond $15,000: – the proportioned expenses of the $3 Mags. being so much greater than those of $5 ones.

My plan, in getting up such work as I propose, would be to take a tour through the principal States – especially west and south – visiting the small towns more particularly than the large ones – lecturing as I went, to pay expenses – and staying sufficiently long in each place to interest my personal friends (old college and West Point acquaintances scattered all over the land) in the success of the enterprise. By these means, I could guarantee in 3 months (or 4) to get 1000 subs. in advance, with their signatures – nearly all pledged to pay at the issue of the first number. Under such circumstances, success would be certain. I have now about 200 names pledged to support me whenever I venture on the undertaking – which perhaps you are aware I have long had in contemplation – only awaiting a secure opportunity....

I will endeavor to pay you a visit at Oquawka, or meet you at any place you suggest....

Patterson was too inexperienced in negotiating such projects to conceal his enthusiasm. He outlined an offer in detail by return of post:

I will furnish an office and take upon myself the sole charge and expense of Publishing a Magazine (name to be suggested by you) to be issued in monthly numbers at Oquawka, Illinois, containing in every number, 96 pages ... at the rate of $5 per annum. Of this magazine you are to have the entire editorial control, furnishing at your expense, matter for its pages, which can be transmitted to me by mail or as we may hereafter agree upon.... You can make your own bargains with authors and I am to publish upon the best terms I can ... and we are to share the receipts equally.... If my plan accords with your views, you will immediately select a title, write me to that effect, and we will both commence operations. We ought to put out the first number January next. Let me hear from you immediately.

Poe responded more slowly. He took a fortnight to reply, enclosing his design for the cover of the magazine, and requesting that Patterson's next letter be sent to him in Richmond. He also sought the inevitable advance: 'I fancy that I shall be able to meet the current expenses of the tour by lecturing as I proceed; but there is something required in the way of outfit; and as I am not overstocked with money (what poor devil author is?) I must ask you to advance half of the sum I need to begin with – about $100. Please, therefore, enclose $50 in your reply, which I will get at Richmond....' Now confident that his fortunes were restored, he went off to spend a week with Annie in Lowell. There he rested, relieved to find the Richmond family still accepted him warmly. He rewrote the third draft of *The Bells* and returned to Fordham. In June he was still waiting for the finance for his trip to Richmond to arrive, his nerves and heart again in poor condition, and his opium dreams no longer inspiring him to write. By the time the $50 arrived Poe had written the last of his works. Now, with June ending, he prepared to leave for Richmond; the cottage was closed up, and Mrs Clemm was sent to stay with Mrs Lewis, the friendly literary lady who kept a stuffed raven on her bust of Pallas.

Before leaving Fordham for the last time Poe seems to have had intimations of the tragic end of his final 'fugue'. He wrote to Griswold, asking him to overlook the publication of his collected works, and requested Willis to write a biographical sketch to preface the volumes. He bid goodbye to various friends and admirers, including Mrs Oakes Smith, who reported that he seemed extremely distressed, saying over and over: 'I am sorry I cannot talk with you, I had so much to say. So very much I wished to say.' Mrs Smith left in her carriage, looking back to note 'his look of pain, his unearthly eyes, his weird look of desolation'. He spent the night of 29 June at the Lewis house in Brooklyn, and the next morning was seen off bearing his carpet bag. Both Mrs Clemm and Edgar were in tears as they left. Mrs Lewis reported: 'He took my hand in his, and looking in my face, said, "Dear Stella, my much beloved friend. You truly understand and appreciate me – I have a presentiment that I shall never see you again.... If I never return, write my life. You can and will do me justice".' At the steamboat Eddy bade Muddy farewell: 'God bless you, my own darling mother. Do not fear for Eddy! See how good I will be while I am away from you, and will come back to love and comfort you.' In spite of his pitiful hopefulness there is a feeling of finality in his words. It was indeed to be their last farewell.

## *Lenore Found*

When Eddy left Muddy weeping at the wharf in New York he had in his flowered carpet bag a change of clothes and the manuscript of two lectures. In his wallet there was some $40. When he broke his journey at Philadelphia he was, then, in good order if somewhat depressed. Some days later, when he turned up at the office of John Sartain, his old friend and now the owner of *Sartain's Magazine*, he was totally disordered. In those few days Edgar had transformed himself into a paranoid wreck, dishevelled, penniless and filthy.

Sartain reported that Poe begged him for protection. He was a fugitive, he said, from an army of conspirators who pursued him like hounds through the streets of Philadelphia. Some of them, disguised as loungers, looked at him wickedly as he passed. He wept and trembled as he poured out his fears to Sartain, who, much distressed, took him home. There Poe asked for a razor to shave off his moustache to disguise himself from his enemies, but Sartain refused, fearing violence. He managed to get Edgar to go to bed and through the night sat beside him. The next day Poe talked continuously and feverishly, his images brilliantly irrational, his theme the vast conspiratorial plot against him. He insisted on getting up and the faithful Sartain accompanied him on an insane walk to the reservoir. There Poe insisted on climbing the steps to the highest point, where he felt he would find some sort of protection. Eventually Sartain persuaded him to return to the house; but Poe, with mad cunning, managed to escape, spending the next night roaming the fields, eventually falling asleep in a ditch. He dreamt of Virginia in a white robe and she begged him not to kill himself. When he awoke his fever had somewhat abated, he was more in possession of himself, and he returned to Sartain's. His erratic behaviour continued through the following days, with several periods of intoxication followed by amnesia. He was arrested for being drunk and spent a night in Moyamensing prison. There on the battlements he saw the same white-robed vision who whispered advice to him. He insisted later that if he had not attended to what she had said, 'It would have been the end of me.' The next morning he was brought up before Mayor Gilpin and, being identified as 'Poe, the poet', was dismissed without a fine. He told

Sartain that he had been imprisoned for forging a cheque and that he had contracted cholera; in fact he was now deeply distressed by stomach spasms and diarrhoea. He demanded laudanum constantly and the exhausted Sartain was much relieved when two other old associates, Charles Chauncey Burr and George Lippard, took over Edgar's care. Poe had constantly hallucinated Mrs Clemm's death, but by 7 July his delusions cleared sufficiently and he wrote to her:

My Dear, Dear Mother, – I have been so ill – have had the cholera, or spasms quite as bad, and can now hardly hold the pen.

The very instant you get this come to me. The joy of seeing you will almost compensate for my sorrows. We can but die together. It is of no use to reason with me now; I must die. I have no desire to live since I have done Eureka. I could accomplish nothing more. For your sake it would be sweet to live, but we must die together. You have been all – all to me, darling ever beloved mother, and dearest truest friend.

I was never really insane except upon occasions when my heart was touched.

I have been taken to prison once since I came here for getting drunk; but then I was not. It was about Virginia.

Burr and Lippard passed the hat around for Edgar, receiving contributions from Graham, Peterson and other old friends. As soon as there was sufficient money in the kitty and Poe in a more reasonable condition, Burr bought him a steamboat ticket to Baltimore. The carpet bag, having been lost for ten days, had now been found but the manuscripts of his lectures were gone; with $10 in his pocket Edgar was escorted to the dock by Burr. Two weeks after leaving New York he set sail from Philadelphia to Baltimore. It was Friday the thirteenth.

Poe managed to make the connection to Richmond that evening and, clearly in control of himself, he wrote a note to Mrs Clemm:

Near Richmond.

The weather is awfully hot, and besides all this, I am so homesick I don't know what to do. I never wanted to see any one half so bad as I want to see my own darling mother. It seems to me that I would make any sacrifice to hold you by the hand once more, and get you to cheer me up for I am terribly depressed. I do not think that any circumstances will ever tempt me to leave you again. When I am with you I can bear anything, but when I am away from you I am too miserable to live.

The next night he arrived in Richmond and went straight to the Mackenzie house, where he wrote an agonized note to Mrs Clemm:

... I got here with two dollars over – of which I enclose you one. Oh, God, my Mother, shall we ever meet again? If possible, oh COME! My clothes are so horrible and I am so ill. Oh, if you could come to me, my mother. Write instantly – Oh do not fail. God forever bless you.

Eddy

After a few days in the Mackenzie house Poe moved to the Old Swan Tavern. Dr George Rawlings, who lived next door, was called in to visit him and reported that Edgar was violent from time to time, and on one occasion drew a pistol and threatened to shoot him; but there is no record anywhere else of Poe carrying a pistol with him or, indeed, of his owning one. On the nineteenth he wrote to Mrs Clemm that he had not drunk anything since Friday morning, 'and then only a little Port Wine'. Knowing, however, the fatality of any kind of alcoholic drink to Edgar, his message would not have brought her much cheer. His depression was uplifted on receipt of a letter from her, to which he immediately replied:

Richmond, Thursday, July 19

My Own Beloved Mother – You will see at once by the handwriting of this letter, that I am better – much better in health and spirits. Oh! if you only knew how your dear letter comforted me! It acted like magic. Most of my sufferings arose from the terrible idea that I could not get rid of – the idea that you were dead. For more than ten days I was totally deranged, although I was not drinking one drop; and during this interval I imagined the most horrible calamities.

All was hallucination, arising from an attack which I had never before experienced –

The Old Swan Tavern, Richmond, scene of Poe's last days.

an attack of mania-a-potu. May heaven grant that it prove a warning to me for the rest of my days....

All is not lost yet, and the 'darkest hour is just before daylight'. Keep up courage, my own beloved mother – all may yet go well. I will put forth all my energies....

It had now become difficult for anyone to remember that the original objective of Edgar's seemingly aimless journeys was to meet Patterson at Oquawka and to complete arrangements for the publication of *The Stylus*. The preoccupation of the past twenty years was rapidly eroding, and now, as Poe settled into the comfortable atmosphere of the only city of which he ever considered himself to be a native, his dominant preoccupation was to be the wooing of the widow Shelton.

Mrs Barrett Shelton, Edgar's Elmira, was surprised when her butler informed her one Sunday morning, as she was about to leave for church, that she had a gentleman caller. She entered the parlour, first puzzled and then surprised, as Poe turned to her and with great emotion gasped, 'Oh Elmira, is it you!' She at once recognized her girlhood lover and was friendly, but insistent that she never allowed anything to interfere with her attendance at church. She invited Edgar to call again. He did so very soon, and after discussing nostalgic memories he reminded her that twenty-four years ago she had promised to marry him. Mrs Shelton remembered the promise very well of course, though she could hardly believe that Edgar was serious in his present proposal, but his desperate passion persuaded her. By the end of July she allowed it to be known that she and Edgar Poe had reached 'an understanding'. All these years later Elmira found herself living a dream of Edgar's, one that he had prophesied in his his boyhood poem *Tamerlane*:

> Her own Alexis, who should plight
> The love he plighted then – again,
> And raise his infancy's delight,
> The bride and queen of Tamerlane –

Suddenly, at the very edge of the abyss, one of Edgar's dream women was about to save him. If he married Elmira he would have a home in the only city which always, in spite of some unpleasant memories, welcomed him; he would be able to find work easily on the local newspapers; Mrs Shelton's fortune would be an even better basis upon which to build his kingdom of *The Stylus* than the business proposition offered by Patterson; and dear Muddy would have a home for the rest of her life. All these glories his 'Lost Lenore' (as he told Elmira she alone was), would provide. But Mrs Shelton was wiser now in the ways of the world than the little Elmira who had never realized that her young lover's passionate letters were being withheld from her. She had been the wife of a man of business, and practicality had rubbed off her wings some of the starry sequins left there by Edgar's early poems. She set about making arrangements which would protect her property, and by the beginning of August

Elmira, Poe's childhood sweetheart, in middle age.

a coolness between the parties threatened the engagement which was the talk of Richmond. Mrs Shelton asked Poe for her letters to be returned and was, thereafter, avoided by him. He totally ignored her after his successful lecture of 7 August at which she was present, and on the same day he renewed contact with Patterson, apologizing for delays in their meeting caused by cholera, calomel and congestion of the brain. He argued again for a more expensive magazine than Patterson favoured, and, while keeping the project alive, deferred publication to the summer of the next year. It was to be his last communication on the subject, the final deferment of a project which had obsessed him for half his life.

Now without 'starry sisters' to control him with promises of temperance, Edgar entered into a crowded programme of social commitments, informal readings, dinners and parties, with the fatal drinking that such activities inevitably involved. In August he was several times overcome, so that all of Richmond was convinced that he was hopelessly in the grip of alcohol. Doctors warned him that it could be fatal to him, and he wept and swore that he would give it up for ever. He even joined Shockoe Hill Division of the Sons of Temperance, where he took the oath to abstain totally, proudly administered by the president, Mr Glenn. Poe's conversion was noted in the local and Philadelphia papers and Mr Glenn swore that the great poet's abstinence was now a fact. Through the summer, elegant in a white suit with a black velvet waistcoat and a broad planter's hat, Poe was often at the offices of the

*Examiner*, surrounded by the literary figures and journalists of the city, by general consensus established once again as a literary editor. His controlled behaviour won him back his position in Mrs Shelton's affections, and early in September their engagement was announced. He wrote to Mrs Clemm who was, as always, uncomplaining but desperately short of funds in Fordham:

.... And now, my own precious Muddy, the very moment I get a definite answer about everything I will write again and tell you what to do. Elmira talks about visiting Fordham, but I do not know whether that would do. I think, perhaps, it would be best for you to give up everything there and come on here in the Packet. Write immediately and give me your advice about it, for you know best. Could we be happier in Richmond or Lowell? for I suppose we can never be happy at Fordham, and Muddy, I must be somewhere where I can see Annie....

With his new status as a citizen-to-be of Richmond and its most famous native son, Edgar entered now into a few brief weeks as an honoured and revered local hero. He met many old friends, read them his poetry, gave out autographs and interviews. On 15 September he lectured again with immense success, giving him cash in hand: 'I cleared enough to settle my bill at the Madison House with two dollars over.' And he had been given a wonderful commission: a Mr St Leon Loud had called on him at the *Examiner* office and offered $100 if he would come to Philadelphia to edit his wife's poems; 'Of course I accepted... the whole labor will not occupy me three days.' Euphorically Poe set about making his arrangements. He would go to Philadelphia, spend a day or so seeing to the poems, then, with money in his pocket, travel on to New York and before the end of that week send to Fordham for Mrs Clemm; then they would go to Richmond for his wedding. Dear Muddy's faith in him would be justified at last. Everything was going to be all right; they would all live happily ever after, in spite of the dreadful dreams. The marriage was set for 17 October, Poe gave Elmira a large cameo brooch, and that same day she wrote to Mrs Clemm a letter remarkable for the totality of her belief that all was to happen as planned:

Richmond, Sept. 22nd, 1849

My Dear Mrs. Clemm, – You will no doubt be much surprised to receive a letter from one whom you have never seen although I feel as if I were writing to one whom I love very devotedly, and whom to know is to love.... Mr Poe has been very solicitous that I should write to you, and I do assure you, it is with emotions of pleasure that I now do so. I am fully prepared to love you, and I do sincerely hope that our spirits may be congenial. There shall be nothing wanting on my part to make them so.

I have just spent a very happy evening with your dear Edgar, and I know it will be gratifying to you to know that he is all that you could desire him to be, sober, temperate, moral, and much beloved. He showed me a letter of yours, in which you spoke affectionately for me, and for which I feel very much gratified & complimented ... Edgar speaks frequently & very affectionately of your daughter & his Virginia, for which I love him but the more. I have a very dear friend (to whom I am much attached) by the name of Virginia Poe. She is a lovely girl in character, tho' not as beautiful in person as your beloved one.

I remember seeing Edgar, & his lovely wife, very soon after they were married.... It is needless (I know) for me to ask you to take good care of him when he is (as I trust he soon will be) again restored to your arms.

I trust a kind Providence will protect him and guide him in the way of truth, so that his feet slip not. I hope, my dear friend, that you will write to me, and as Edgar will perhaps reach you as soon as this does, he will direct your letter.

It has struck 12 o'clock, and I am encroaching on the Sabbath, and will therefore conclude. 'Good night, Dear friend', may Heaven bless you and shield you, and may your remaining days on earth be peaceful and happy....

Thus prays your attached tho' unknown friend.

Elmira.

On 24 September Poe lectured again on *The Poetic Principle* to an audience all of whom came knowing that he needed their 'pecuniary attendance in a delicate way'. 'A decent sum' was raised, and the next afternoon he spent with friends who noted that he had never seemed more cheerful and hopeful. He told them that this present trip to Richmond had been the happiest experience of many years, and that when he finally came back to live there he felt he would shake off the vexations of his past life for ever. He lingered on and was finally seen off by his hostess and her daughters, one of whom, Susan Talley (later Mrs Weiss), reported an extraordinary event: 'We were standing in the portico, and after going a few steps he paused, turned and again lifted his hat in a last adieu. At that moment a brilliant meteor appeared in the sky directly over his head, and vanished....'

Edgar spent the next night smoking and thoughtful at Duncan Lodge, the Mackenzie house, where he left his trunk, a small black leather one bound with iron hoops, containing manuscripts and his few other belongings, 'most of his estate'. The following day he passed through Richmond calling on friends, including Thompson of the *Messenger* who advanced him $5. As he left, Poe said, 'By the way, you have been very kind to me. Here is a little trifle that may be worth something to you.' The 'trifle' was a small roll of paper on which he had written, in his beautiful hand, the poem *Annabel Lee*.

The same day Poe sent Susan Talley a note enclosing his lines *For Annie*. In the afternoon he called upon Elmira, sad and feeling sick. She felt his pulse, thought him feverish and considered that he should not travel the next day. Edgar was comforted by her concern, and by the time he left her felt somewhat better. He called on Dr Carter where he read a newspaper; when he left he took the doctor's Malacca cane with him, leaving his own behind. He crossed the road to Sadler's Restaurant where he met several acquaintances with whom he spent the entire evening and part of the night, waiting for the boat to Baltimore which left at four in the morning.

J. M. Blakey, who was present that evening, reported that the party around Poe was a cheerful one, that the conversation continued into the late hours, and that they were joined by their host, Mr Sadler. Both Blakey and Sadler distinctly remembered that Poe was cheerful and did not appear to be drinking. He talked of his imminent journey to the north, and when they saw him shortly before he left they were still certain he was quite sober. It is the last observation of Poe made upon this, his final exit from the town which had adopted him. Escorted to the wharf by his cheerful acquaintances, Edgar Poe, Richmond's most famous foster-son, caught the steamer for his macabre appointment in Baltimore.

## *Appointment in Baltimore*

The trip from Richmond to Baltimore took about forty-eight hours and there were many stops. It was a tedious journey, but there was a bar in the forward part of the steamer where travellers might beguile the time in convivial conversation. Poe left Richmond unwell. Mrs Shelton had noted his fever; his departure at four in the morning had not been discussed with her and surprised her by its suddenness; he had been intensely active and was excited about his forthcoming marriage. All were factors of tension working upon his volatile temperament and weakened heart. As Hervey Allen pointed out: 'Poe was in that peculiar condition, a physical dilemma in fact, that few who have discussed his failings seem to realize, i.e., his failing heart required a stimulant which would be disastrous to his brain.' That Poe began to drink on the Baltimore boat seems certain; that he continued to do so after the landing at Baltimore on the morning of Saturday 29 September is sure. He had several hours to wait for his train for Philadelphia, where a day or so would do for Mrs Loud's poems. Feeling that he had time in hand, he could pleasantly and profitably look up old friends. He called upon one of them later that day, Dr Nathan C. Brooks, who observed that he was intoxicated. On leaving Brooks Poe simply disappeared for five days.

For someone as well known and as closely remarked as Edgar Poe to disappear totally for several days in a town with which he had long associations and where he had many acquaintances, is extraordinary enough, but the strangeness of the situation is made even more Poe-esque by the fact that through these days Baltimore was *en fête* with an election campaign for members of Congress and representatives to the State legislature. Now Baltimore was well known to be particularly corrupt politically. At election-time it was taken over by press-gangs financed by various candidates. There was no register of voters, the procedure being that a 'citizen' appeared before a judge of elections where he took an oath, risking being challenged.

The gangs rounded up derelicts and other helpless potential 'voters' during the days before the ballot and held them in virtual prisons called 'coops', keeping them happy with drink, drugs and a continuous lunch table. The election was on 3 October and the bullies were at their most active when Poe, drunk, left the home of Dr Brooks to join the Saturday-night crowds on the streets of Baltimore. Among those crowds the gangs worked, sorting out 'supporters' for their candidates, inveigling them with invitations to their parties or simply press-ganging them by force. Poe was in no condition to refuse or resist such invitations.

The Fourth Ward Club was a Whig 'coop' at the back of an old engine-house on High Street. There some 140 'voters' were enjoying a party which would put them into perfect condition to enjoy their democratic rights as citizens when they were wheeled out to vote under various false names in different sections of town. Poe reappeared on election day two blocks away from the Club at Cooth and Sergeant's Tavern on Lombard Street. He had been spotted there by a printer's compositor who recognized the name he gave, even if he was unsure of the identity of the man himself. Mr Walker wrote a note in pencil to Dr Snodgrass who lived nearby:

Baltimore City, 3rd, 1849

Dear Sir, – There is a gentleman, rather the worse for wear, at Ryan's 4th ward polls, who goes under the cognomen of Edgar A. Poe, and who appears in great distress, and he says he is acquainted with you, and I assure you he is in need of immediate assistance.

Yours in haste,
To Dr J.E. Snodgrass Jos. W. Walker

Dr Snodgrass hurried over to Cooth's where he found Poe in the bar, helpless in an armchair, surrounded by dubious 'voters'. He noted his appearance in great detail:

His face was haggard, not to say bloated, and unwashed, his hair unkempt and his whole physique repulsive. His expansive forehead . . . and those full-orbed and mellow, yet soulful eyes for which he was so noticeable when himself, now lusterless as shortly I could see, were shaded from view by a rusty, almost brimless, tattered and ribbonless palm leaf hat. His clothing consisted of a sack-coat of thin and sleezy black alpaca, ripped more or less at intervals of its seams, and faded and soiled, and pants of a steel-mixed pattern of cassinett, half worn and badly fitting, if they could be said to fit at all. He wore neither vest nor neck cloth, while the bosom of his shirt was both crumpled and badly soiled. . . .

Snodgrass arranged a room for Poe in the tavern, but while it was being prepared Poe's cousin Herring arrived. He and Snodgrass then decided that Edgar's condition

Illustration by Edmund Dulac to *Alone*, a poem which epitomizes Poe's life. 'From childhood's hour I have not been / As others were – I have not seen / As others saw – I could not bring / My passions from a common spring . . .'

required attention at the Washington Hospital. By now he was almost unconscious, muttering continuously and hanging on to Dr Carter's Malacca cane as if it were the life-saving spar of a wrecked ship. Thus he was taken by carriage to the hospital where he was received by the physician on duty, Dr J. J. Moran, at 5.00 pm on Wednesday, 3 October.

Poe was unconscious until 3.00 am the next morning when he revived, talking continuously to phantom figures that moved about his bed. Dr Moran questioned him but his answers were incoherent, except that he said his wife was in Richmond. Herring and other Poe relatives sent clean linen and other comforts, and arranged for Dr Moran to place Edgar in a private room near where he himself lived, and for Mrs Moran to give some nursing attention. But Dr Moran recognized the case as being advanced and hopeless. However, he sought to cheer the patient, telling him that 'in a few days he would be able to rejoin the society of his friends.' The news maddened Poe who 'broke out with much energy and said the best thing his best friend could do would be to blow out his miserable brains with a pistol – that when he beheld his miserable degradation he was ready to sink into the earth'. The degradation was to continue for a few days more without Mrs Clemm, nor Annie, nor Mrs Shelton knowing that the dregs of Eddy's life were rapidly evaporating in the despair, fear and agonizing remorse of *delirium tremens*. Eventually he was quiet and Mrs Moran came to him. He asked her if there was any hope and she replied that the doctor thought him very ill indeed. He said, 'I meant hope for a wretch like me beyond this life.' She tried to comfort him by reading the fourteenth chapter of St John: 'In my Father's house there are many mansions. Were it not so, I should have told you, because I go to prepare a place for you.' Mrs Moran wiped the sweat from Poe's forehead, and, certain that he was dying, made him as comfortable as possible, gave him 'a soothing draft' (doubtless containing laudanum), and left to make him a shroud. Poe persisted till Saturday night when he began to mutter and shout out troubled and fearsome dreams. As to what they were we can only apply ourselves, like Dupin, to the small shreds of evidence. Edgar Poe confronting death cried out again and again for 'Reynolds'. No one recognized the name as being that of the explorer whose project for venturing into the South Polar Seas had given Poe the idea for the horrifying journey of Arthur Gordon Pym. The last words of that narrative are: 'And now we rushed into the embraces of the cataract, where a chasm threw itself open to receive us. But there arose in our pathway a shrouded human figure, very far larger in its proportions than any dweller among men. And the hue of the skin of the figure was of the perfect whiteness of the snow.' The great white mother-wife from beyond the tomb had at last come to collect him. On the morning of Sunday, 7 October 1849, Edgar A. Poe ceased calling for Reynolds, his guide to the regions of eternal ice. He was quiet for a while and then, almost as if he were not personally involved, he whispered, 'Lord help my poor soul,' and died.

# Bibliography

An enormous number of books on Poe have appeared in many languages. The following are those which I have found most useful and stimulating in preparing this biography. Marie Bonaparte's book is particularly interesting for its psychological insights.

BIOGRAPHIES AND STUDIES

Allen, Hervey. *Israfel: The Life and Times of Edgar Allan Poe*, 2 vols, New York 1926.

Bonaparte, Marie. *The Life and Works of Edgar Allan Poe*, London 1949 and reprinted 1971.

Gill, William F., *The Life of Edgar Allan Poe*, New York 1877.

Ingram, John H., *Edgar Allan Poe: His Life, Letters and Opinions*, 2 vols, London 1880.

Mott, Frank Luther. *A History of American Magazines*, 3 vols, Cambridge, Mass. 1938–9.

Phillips, Mary E. *Edgar Allan Poe, the Man*, 2 vols, Philadelphia 1926.

Quinn, Arthur H. *Edgar Allan Poe: A Critical Biography*, New York 1941.

Robertson, John W. *Commentary on Edgar A. Poe*, 2 vols, San Francisco 1934.
*Edgar A. Poe, a Psychopathic Study*, New York 1923.

Woodberry, George E. *Edgar Allan Poe*, Boston 1885.
*The Life of Edgar Allan Poe*, 2 vols, Boston 1909.

SOURCES FOR LETTERS

Harrison, James A., ed. *Life and Letters of Edgar Allan Poe*, 2 vols, New York 1903.
ed. *The Complete Works of Edgar Allan Poe*, 17 vols, New York 1902.

Ingram, John H., ed. *Memoir to The Works of Edgar Allan Poe*, 4 vols, Edinburgh 1874.

'Notes on the Genealogy of the Poe Family' in *Gulf States Historical Magazine* I, January 1903.

Whitty, James H. 'Poe in England and Scotland' in *The Bookman* XLIV, September 1916.

POE'S WORKS

Selections of Poe's writings abound. Those listed below are the most complete collections.

Harrison, James A., ed. *The Complete Works of Edgar Allan Poe*, 17 vols, 1902.

Mabbott, Thomas O. *Collected Works of Edgar Allan Poe*: I. *Poems*, Cambridge, Mass. 1970. Further volumes will be published in due course.

Ostrom, John W. *The Letters of Edgar Allan Poe*, 2 vols, Cambridge, Mass. 1948 and revised edition 1966.

Stovall, Floyd. *The Poems of Edgar Allan Poe*, Charlottesville 1965.

Wilbur, Richard. Poe: *Complete Poems*, New York 1959.

# Acknowledgments

Numbers in *italics* refer to colour pages.

American History Picture Library: 67
Beevor Collection (© Hodder & Stoughton Ltd): 48, 92, 100, 108, 130, 142, 155, 176 right, 190, 209, 210, 217
© Bell & Hyman Ltd: 53, 72, 87, 169, 202, endpapers
British Museum: 22
Mary Evans Picture Library: 25 above, 31, 34, 42–3, 52, *57* (© Hodder & Stoughton Ltd), 82, 118, 162, 164, *160* (© Hodder & Stoughton Ltd), 214 (© Hodder & Stoughton Ltd)
Hackney Library Services: 26 above
Irvine Development Corporation: 25 below
Library of Congress: 79 (Orbis), 122, 138–9 (Orbis), 185 right (Orbis)
Mansell Collection: 11, 12–13, 16, 18–19, 21 left, 21 right, 33, 40 (© Hodder & Stoughton Ltd), 65, 86 (© Hodder & Stoughton Ltd), 96, 98, 136, *157* (© Hodder & Stoughton Ltd), 176 left, 191, 220, 234, 236, 241 (© Hodder & Stoughton Ltd)
Maryland Historical Society: frontispiece, 76–7, 125 (phot. Ed Whitman), 167
Metropolitan Museum of Art, New York (Gift of Louise F. Wickham in memory of her father): 175
Courtesy Museum of Fine Arts, Boston: 135 (Gift of Mrs Horatio A. Lamb in memory of Mr and Mrs Winthrop Sargent), *58–9* (M. and N. Karolik Collection)
National Maritime Museum (Orbis): 9
New York Public Library: 102–3 (Orbis), 161, *158–9* (Orbis)
Poe Foundation, Inc.: 28, 36, 56, *60 above left*, *60 above right* (phot. Sergei Troubetzkoy), *60 below*, 90 (phot. Sergei Troubetzkoy), 105, 112, 113, 225
Radio Times Hulton Picture Library: 80, 116, 185 left, 201
Collection Sirot-Angel: 141
The George Walter Vincent Smith Art Museum: 70–1
United States Naval Photographic Center, Washington (Orbis): 6–7
Victoria and Albert Museum, London: 10
Warner Books, Inc. (copyright): 93, 109
Weidenfeld and Nicolson Archive: 15, 26 below, 39, 56, 119, 123, 131, 143, 147, 152, 170, 182, 196, 198–9, 207
West Point Museums Collection: 67
Yale University Art Gallery, the Mabel Brady Garvan Collection: 44–5

The author and publisher have taken all possible care to trace and acknowledge the sources of illustrations in this book. If by chance we have made an incorrect attribution we will be happy to correct it in future reprints, provided that we receive notification.

Picture research by Darlene Bragg.

# Index


*Al Aaraaf*, 47, 52, 54, 61, 193
*Al Aaraaf, Tamerlane and Minor Poems*, 61–2, 63
Allan, Frances Kelling (foster-mother), 15, 17, 20, 21–3, 27, 29, 30, 33, 34–5, 38, 39, 46, 54, 56, 63, 64, 69, 215
Allan, John (foster-father), 15, 20–39, 43, 49, 61, 104, 106, 187; Edgar adopted by, 20–3; trip to England and Scotland, 24–8; bad relations with Edgar, 29, 32, 34, 35, 38–9, 49, 50–2, 54, 55–6, 63–4, 65, 66, 69; infidelities of, 30, 34; inherits $750,000, 32–3; Poe's letters to, 38–9, 52, 54, 56, 81, 91, 97; death of his wife, Frances, 50; illness of, 60, 88, 91, 96; marries Louisa Patterson, 66, 69; disowns Poe, 74–5; leaves him out of his will, 88–9; visits Virginia Hot Springs, 91; Poe's last visit to, 96–7; death of, 97
Allan, Louisa Gabriella (*née* Patterson), 66, 69, 75, 89, 91, 96, 104
Allen, Hervey, 29, 99, 114, 137, 165, 177, 207, 211, 215 239
*American Monthly Magazine*, 120
*American Whig Review*, 181, 212, 229
*Ancient Mariner* (Coleridge), 121
*Annabel Lee*, 208, 227, 238
Arnold, Benedict, 68, 73
*Atkinson's Casket*, 133
*The Balloon Hoax*, 173
Baltimore, 8, 14, 51–2, 54, 56, 61, 62, 65–6, 80–8 *passim*, 89, 91, 94–6, 97–8, 106, 119, 129, 133, 140, 166, 208, 233, 238, 239–40, 242
*Baltimore Book*, 120
*Baltimore Museum*, 124
*Baltimore Saturday Visitor*, 91, 94–5
*Barnaby Rudge* (Dickens), 177
Baudelaire, Charles, 99, 141–2, 177–8
*The Bells*, 215, 227, 231
*Berenice*, 99, 101, 107
*Biographia Literaria* (Coleridge), 78
Bisco, John, 184, 185, 187, 188–9, 193
Bittner, William, 37
*The Black Cat*, 143–4, 192
Blakey, J.M., 239
Bliss, Elam, 74, 78
Bolling, Thomas, 63
Bonaparte, ex-King Joseph, 137
Bonaparte, Marie, 24, 30, 32, 43, 115, 117, 165, 190
Boston, 14, 39, 41–3, 46, 129, 191, 193, 222, 223
Bransby, Rev. John, 27
Brennan farm, 174, 175, 176, 177, 178, 179, 195, 197
Brennan, Martha, 179
Briggs, Charles F., 181, 184, 185, 187, 188–9, 194
*Broadway Journal*, 181, 184, 185, 186, 187, 188–9, 192, 193, 194
Brooks, Dr Nathan C., 239, 240
Browning, Elizabeth Barrett, 201
'Buddie' (Poe's family nickname), 111–12
Burling, Ebenezer, 28, 39, 41
Burns, Robert, 84
Burr, Charles C., 208, 233
Burton, W.E., 124, 126–8, 133–4
Byron, Lord, 33, 68

Carey, Lea and Carey (publishers), 51, 54, 95, 97, 117
Carter, Dr John, 101, 238, 241
*The Cask of Amontillado*, 210
Channing, Ellery, 218
Charleston, 15, 47, 49
Charlottesville, Virginia, 35–8
Chivers, Thomas Holley, 188, 200–1
Clark, Lewis Gaylord, 188, 194
Clarke, Joseph J., 28, 29
Clarke, Mrs, 219–20
Clarke, Thomas C., 154, 156–61, 163, 165, 168
Clemm, Henry, 55, 80–1
Clemm, Maria Poe ('Muddy': aunt), 54–5, 66, 80, 89, 95–6, 106, 112, 115, 118, 148, 149, 150, 151, 163, 166, 171, 187, 188, 210, 211, 212, 226, 227, 228, 235, 242; Poe's attachment to, 62–3; witnesses Poe's marriage to Virginia, 111; moves to Richmond, 111; in New York, 119–20, 173, 174, 175–6, 178–9; in Philadelphia, 121, 127, 128, 136; Virginia's illness and, 140–1, 149; Edgar's letter from New York to, 171–3; at Fordham, 200, 201, 203, 204–5; and death of Virginia, 206, 207, 208; Edgar's last farewell to, 231–2; last letters to, 233, 234–5, 237; Elmira's letter to, 237–8
*Clinton Bradshaw* (Thomas), 133
Coleridge, Samuel Taylor, 68, 121, 165, 180
Collier, Edwin, 23
*The Colloquy of Monos and Una*, 137
*Columbian Magazine*, 176, 229
*The Conchologists' First Book*, 122, 124, 180
*Confessions of an Opium Eater* (de Quincey), 81–2
*The Conqueror Worm*, 169
*The Conversation of Eiros and Charmion*, 126
Cooke, P.P., 212
Cook's Olympic Circus, Philadelphia, 133
Cooper, Fenimore, 134
*The Cosmogony of the Universe* (lecture), 212–13
Crane, Alexander T., 185, 186, 189
Curtis, George W., 218

Dab (Allans' black servant), 39, 63, 88–9
Daniel, John P., 221
Darley, F.O.C., 154
*A Descent into the Maelstrom*, 91, 192
Devereaux, Mary, 83–5, 87–8, 101, 150, 206, 207
*The Devil in the Belfry*, 124
Dickens, Charles, 117, 137, 177
*The Dollar Newspaper*, 166, 176
*The Doomed City*, 73
Dow, J.E. ('Rowdy'), 154, 156–61, 163, 164

*Dreamland*, 174
Duyckinck, 192, 204

*Eldorado*, 228
*Eleonora*, 107, 114
Ellis, Charles, 20, 28, 29
Emerson, Ralph Waldo, 129
English, Thomas Dunn, 193, 194–5, 196–7
*Eureka*, 211, 212, 213, 219

*The Fall of the House of Usher*, 124, 126, 192, 208, 209–10
*Farmer's Cabinet*, 121
Fay, Theodore, 117
*For Annie*, 238
Fordham village, 101, 197, 200–2, 203–12, 215, 216, 218, 221, 224, 226, 227–9, 231, 237
Fortress Monroe, Virginia, 47, 49–50, 51, 64
Foster, Jane, 114
Francis, Dr John, 195, 197, 215, 216

'Gaffy' (Poe's nickname), 59
Galt, William, 32
*Gentleman's Magazine*, 124, 126–8, 133, 228
Gibson, Cadet, T.H., 72–3
Gill, William F., 208
*Godey's Lady's Book*, 95, 174, 176, 183, 194, 210
*The Gold Bug*, 47, 149, 166, 170, 192
Gowans, William, 120, 121
Graham, George R. and Mrs, 133–4, 136, 145–6, 166, 169–70, 173, 212, 223
*Graham's Magazine*, 133–6, 145–6, 166, 168–9, 171, 174, 183, 185, 186, 208, 212, 229, 230
Graves, Sergeant 'Bully', 64, 74–5
Greeley, Horace, 193, 218
'Grim and Ghastly Raven' (Helen Whitman's valentine), 217–18
Griswold, Rev. Rufus, 41, 145, 149, 166, 168, 184, 187, 192, 194, 222, 231

Harper Brothers (publishers), 117, 120–1
*Harper's New Monthly Magazine*, 72, 83, 87
Harrison, Gabriel, 179–80
Haswell, Barrington and Haswell (publishers), 122
Hatch and Dunning (publishers), 61
*The Haunted Palace*, 124, 145
Hay, John, 218
*Henry Eckford* (ship), 75
Herring family, 56, 88, 140, 149, 240, 242
Hirst, Henry Beck, 137, 144, 149, 154, 166, 173
*Home Journal*, 205, 211, 213, 218
*Hop-Frog*, 229
Hopkins, Charles, 8
House, Colonel, 50
Howard, Lieutenant J., 49, 51
*Howard District Press*, 181

*Irene*, 73
Irvine (Scotland), 24
Irving, Washington, 68
*Israfel*, 73

Jefferson, Joseph, 126
*The Journal of Julius Rodman*, 118

Kennedy, John P., 94, 97–9, 106–7, 110, 115, 118
*Knickerbocker*, 129, 132, 188, 194
'Knickerbocker' writers, 117, 120

*Ladies Magazine*, 62
Lafayette, Marquis de, 32, 79
*Landor's Cottage*, 218–19, 228
Lane, Thomas H., 193
Latrobe, J.H.B., 91, 94–5
Le Rennet, Henri (Poe's alias), 39, 41, 46
Lea and Blanchard (publishers), 127, 129
*Lenore*, 73, 106, 229
'Letter to Mr B.', 78
Lewis, Mrs Estelle, 195–6, 231–2
*Ligeia*, 99, 107
Lippard, George, 137, 144, 233
*Literary America* (unfinished), 187, 194, 206
*The Literati of New York*, 191, 194, 210
Locke, Lieutenant, 72, 74
London, 24, 27, 30
Longfellow, Henry Wadsworth, 134, 184
*Loss of Breath*, 176
*Love's Martyr* (Mrs Bacon), 81
Lowell, James Russell, 154, 165, 173, 177, 181, 183, 184, 187–8
Lowell (Massachusetts), 218–19, 222, 226, 231

Mackenzie, Mrs, 15, 17, 20, 35
Mackenzie family, 88, 89, 99, 104, 112, 219, 220, 233–4, 238
*Maelzel's Chess-Player*, 117
*The Man that was Used Up*, 126, 170
*Marginalia*, 180–1, 212, 228
*The Masque of the Red Death*, 146, 148
Mayo, John, 66
*Mellonta Tauta*, 229
*Memoir of the Author* (Griswold), 41
*Mesmeric Revelation*, 192
*Metzengerstein*, 81
Miller, James H., 94
*Minerva and Emerald*, 62, 64
Mitchell, Dr, 140, 149
Moran, Dr J.J., 242
Mordecai, Samuel, 15
*Morella*, 107, 126
*Ms Found in a Bottle*, 91
*The Murders in the Rue Morgue*, 170
Murdock, James E., 185
*The Mystery of Marie Rogêt*, 143

*The Narrative of Arthur Gordon Pym, of Nantucket*, 117, 120–1, 124, 128, 242
*Narrative of Four Voyages to the South Seas and the Pacific* (Morrell), 121
Neal, John (pseudonym: Jehu O'Cataract), 56, 61, 62, 218
New York, 66, 69, 75, 78–9, 119–21, 129, 150, 153, 171–97; *passim*, 212–13, 219, 231–2
*New York Evening Mirror*, 178–9, 180, 181, 183
*New York Express*, 205
New York Historical Society, 183, 186
*New York Mirror*, 177, 197
*New York Review*, 120
*New York Times*, 179–80
*New York Tribune*, 181
Newman, Mary, 83
Nichols, Mrs Gove, 201, 203, 204, 205, 212
*The North American*, 46
*North American Review*, 129, 133

*The Oblong Box*, 174
*The 1002 Tale*, 183
Oquawka (Illinois), 230–1, 235
Osgood, Mrs Frances, 186–7, 188, 190–2, 193, 195, 196, 205, 217, 218, 227
Osgood, Samuel, S., 186, 187

Parbodie, William, 226–7
Patterson, Edward, 230–1, 235, 236

Pease, Peter Pindar, 78–9
*The Penn Magazine*, 127, 129, 146, 149, 151; *Prospectus* of, 129, 131–3; *see also The Stylus*
Perry, Edgar A. (Poe's alias in Artillery), 46–7, 49–50, 51, 68
Peterson, Charles, 145, 166, 171, 223
Philadelphia, 52, 66, 101, 119, 121–8, 129, 133–54 *passim*, 156, 157, 164, 165–71, 180, 212, 229, 232–3, 237, 239
*Philadelphia Casket*, 68–9
Philadelphia Custom House, 151, 153–4
*Philadelphia Saturday Courier*, 81, 89
*The Philosophy of Composition*, 54
*Pioneer*, 154, 165–6
*The Pirate* (Henry Poe), 46
Placide, Mr (manager of Charleston Players), 15, 17, 49
Poe, David (father), 8–9, 14, 21, 32, 38, 55
Poe, 'General' David (grandfather), 8, 14, 32, 49, 51, 55
Poe, Mrs David (grandmother), 14, 51, 55, 80, 99
Poe, Edgar Allan: birth and early years, 14–17, 20–34; death of his mother, 17; adopted by Allans of Richmond, 20–3; bad relations with John Allan, 21, 23, 27, 29, 32–3, 34–5, 38–9, 49, 55–6, 60, 65, 68, 69, 88–9, 96–7; trip to England and Scotland, 24, 27; back in Richmond, 28; falls in love with Mrs Stanard, 29–30; elected lieutenant of Richmond Junior Volunteers, 32; love for 'Myra', 33–4, 35–6; attends University of Virginia, 35–8; debts, 35, 38, 60, 81; drinking habits, 37, 95, 101, 106, 110–11, 117–18, 126–7, 128, 134, 137, 140–2, 149–50, 153, 154, 156–7, 160, 165, 174, 185, 187, 195, 212, 219, 232–3, 236, 239–40, 242; returns to Richmond, 38; leaves home, 38–9; goes to Boston, 39, 41; first published poems, 41–3; enlists in US Army, 46–9; death of Frances Allan, 50; discharged from Army, 50–1; lives with Clemm family in Baltimore, 54–5, 62–3; returns to Richmond, 63–4; admitted to West Point, 65–6, 68–9, 72–4; his views on science, 68–9; night-writing, 73–4; discharged from Army, 75; goes to New York, 75, 78; returns to Clemm family, 80–1; begins writing horror fiction, 81, 89; opium-taking (laudanum), 81–2, 99, 101, 106, 115, 117, 124, 137, 149, 150, 159, 177, 178, 195, 223, 229, 231; 'love affair' with Mary Devereaux, 83–8; character and temperament, 83–4, 94–5, 148–9, 151, 153, 160, 165; sexuality, 85, 87–8, 101, 114–15, 117, 142–3, 190–1; appearance, 88, 94, 95, 124, 168, 240; abortive trip to Richmond, 88–9; wins *Baltimore Visitor*'s prose award, 91, 94–5; last abortive visit to Allan, 96–7; death of Allan, 97; Kennedy's help to, 97–9; secret marriage to Virginia, 101, 111; works for *Southern Literary Messenger*, 104, 106–7, 110, 111, 112, 115, 117; meets Elmira again, 104, 106; love for Virginia, 107, 110, 114–15, 136, 153; returns to Baltimore, 110–11; family life in Richmond, 111–12; second marriage to Virginia, 112, 114; attacks on fashionable writers, 115, 117; loses job on *Messenger*, 118–119; goes to New York, 119–20; moves to Philadelphia, 121–2; co-edits *Gentleman's Magazine*, 124, 126–8; interest in cryptograms, 127, 166; aims for *Penn Magazine* set out in *Prospectus*, 129, 131–3; friendship with Thomas, 133, 150–1, 153; works as editor for *Graham's Magazine*, 134, 136, 145; effect of Virginia's fatal illness on, 140–2, 149, 168; discharged from *Graham's*, 145; writes *The Masque of the Red Death*, 146, 148; trip to Saratoga Springs, 149; visits Mary Devereaux, 150; Thomas's plan to help, and visit to, 150–1, 153; job at Custom House falls through, 151, 153–4; gets backing for *The Stylus*, 154; disastrous trip to Washington, 154, 156–61, 165; wins *Dollar Newspaper* prize, 166; New York visit, 171–4; moves out to Brennans' farm, 174–6; gets job on *New York Evening Mirror*, 178–9, 180, 181; successful publication of *The Raven*, 181, 183, 184–6; joins *Broadway Journal*, 184, 187; romantic friendship with Frances Osgood, 186–7, 190–2; *Journal* closes down, 193; moves to Fordham, 197, 200; poor health, 200–1, 205, 212, 229, 233; poverty, 201, 203, 204–5; death of Virginia, 206–8; lecture at Society Library, 212–13; friendship with Mrs Shew, 211, 213, 215–16; receives valentine from Helen Whitman, 216–18; 'love affair' with Annie Richmond, 218–19, 222, 224, 226; revisits Richmond, 219–21; challenges Daniel to a duel, 221; 'love affair' with Helen Whitman, 221–2, 223–4, 226–7; Patterson's offer to back *The Stylus*, 230–1; bids 'Muddy' farewell for last time, 231–2; returns to Richmond, 233–5; wooing of Elmira, 235–6, 237–8; disappears for five days in Baltimore, 239–40; death, 240, 242
Poe, Eliza (aunt), 22–3, 56
Poe, Elizabeth (*née* Arnold: mother), 8–9, 14–15, 17, 23, 32, 43, 47, 49, 54, 68, 69, 74
Poe, Neilson (cousin), 62
Poe, Rosalie (sister), 14, 15, 20, 29, 32, 35, 88, 99, 101, 111–12, 219
Poe, Virginia Eliza

(*née* Clemm: 'Sis'), 55, 62–3, 65, 80, 83, 85, 89, 96, 97, 106, 117, 163, 222, 232; Edgar's secret marriage to, 101, 111; illness (tuberculosis), 107, 124, 136–7, 140–2, 145, 149, 150, 151, 156, 166, 168, 179, 187, 188, 191, 193, 195, 200, 205, 206; moves to Richmond, 111–12; second marriage to Edgar, 112, 114; his love for, 114–15, 136; in New York, 119–20, 171–2, 174, 175, 176, 179; in Philadelphia, 121, 128, 136–7, 148, 149; encourages Edgar's friendship with Frances Osgood, 187; moves to Fordham, 197, 200, 205; death of, 206–8
Poe, William Henry Leonard (brother), 14, 32, 35, 46, 55, 62, 80, 133
*Poems*, 74, 78
*The Poetic Principle* (lecture), 78, 218, 219, 238
*Poets and Poetry of America* (Griswold), 145
*Politian*, 91, 106
*The Premature Burial*, 176, 207
*The Prose Romances of Edgar A. Poe*, 170
*Prose Writers of America* (Griswold), 184
Providence (Rhode Island), 191, 192, 217, 218, 222, 223–4, 226–7

'Quarles' (Poe's pen-name), 181
de Quincey, Thomas, 81–2

*The Raven*, 43, 137, 144, 171, 174, 175, 176–7, 178, 181, 183, 184, 185–6, 187, 188, 193, 194, 212, 219, 229
Rawlins, Dr George, 234
Reynolds, J.N., 121, 242
Richmond (Virginia), 15, 17, 20, 23, 27–30, 32–5, 38–9, 49, 50, 51, 63–4, 65, 66, 69, 88–9, 96–7, 99, 104, 106–7, 110, 111–12, 114–15, 117–19, 219–20, 229, 231, 233–9
Richmond, Mrs Annie, 218–19, 222–3, 224, 226, 227, 228, 229, 231, 242
Richmond *Examiner*, 221, 236–7
Richmond Junior Volunteers, 32
Richmond Theatre fire (1811), 23, 50
Royster, Sarah Elmira ('Myra': later Mrs A. Barrett Shelton), 33–4, 35–6, 38, 43, 46, 54, 73, 104, 106, 219, 228–9, 235–6, 237–8, 239, 242

Saratoga Springs, 149, 166, 187
Sartain, John, 137, 229, 232–3
*Sartain's Magazine*, 229, 232
*Saturday Evening Chronicle*, 124
*Saturday Museum*, 154
Shelton, A. Barrett, 35, 104, 106, 228
Shelton, Mrs A. Barrett, *see* Royster, Sarah Elmira
Shew, Mrs Marie Louise, 201, 206, 210, 211, 212, 213, 215–16, 227
*Siope*, 120
*Sixpenny Magazine*, 201, 203
*The Sleeper*, 74
Snodgrass, Dr J.E., 240, 242
*Southern Literary Messenger*, 14, 98–9, 104, 106–7, 110, 111, 112, 114, 115, 117–19, 131–2, 181, 212, 219, 222, 228, 229, 230, 238
*Souvenir*, 97
*Spirit of the Times*, 154
Stanard, Mrs 'Helen', 29–30, 34, 43, 54, 69
Stanard, Robert, 29, 219
*The Stylus*, 151, 154, 161, 165, 166, 188, 212, 219, 227, 230–1, 235; *see also Penn Magazine*
*Sun* newspaper, 173

*Tales* (1845), 192, 212
*Tales of Mystery and Imagination*, 129
*The Tales of the Folio Club*, 81, 91, 95, 97, 99, 117
*Tales of the Grotesque and Arabesque* (1840), 122, 127, 129
*Tamerlane*, 41–2, 61, 62
*Tamerlane and Other Poems*, 41, 46, 52, 61, 235
*The Tell-Tale Heart*, 154, 176
Thayer, Colonel S. (Superintendent of West Point), 74, 79–80
Thomas, Calvin, 41
Thomas, F.W., 133, 137, 150–1, 153, 154, 156, 163–4, 165, 228
Thompson, John, 219, 238
*To Helen*, 30, 32, 33, 73, 216, 218
*To M.L.S.*, 211
*To My Mother*, 62–3, 229
*To Sarah*, 104, 106
*Travels in Arabia Petraea* (Stephen), 121
Tyler, President John, 150, 153, 156, 164
Tyler, Robert, 150–1, 153, 154, 156, 163

*Ulalume*, 203–4, 212, 224
University of Virginia (Charlottesville), 34, 35–8, 50, 51, 63, 68
US Army, 46–51; *see also* West Point

Valentine, Edward, 23–4
Valentine, Nancy (Aunt Nancy), 23, 38, 39, 63, 64, 88–9, 104
Van Cleef, Augustus, 83
*The Visionary*, 95
*Von Jung, the Mystific*, 120
*Von Kempelen and His Discovery*, 228
*A Voyage to the Moon*, 94

Walker, Joseph W., 240
Washington, 51, 54, 137, 150, 154, 156–61, 165
Washington Hospital (Baltimore), 242
*Weekly Messenger*, 127
Welles, Orson, 173
West Point Military Academy, 49, 50, 54, 55, 65–6, 68–9, 72–5
White, Eliza, 104, 114
White, Thomas Wylkes, 98–9, 104, 106, 107, 110–11, 114, 117, 118–19, 126, 134
White Eagle Club, 179, 180
Whitman, Mrs Sarah Helen, 192, 217–18, 219, 221–2, 223–4, 226–7, 228
Whitty, J.H., 151
Wiley and Putnam (publishers), 187, 212
*William Wilson*, 27, 126, 189–90
Willis, Nathaniel Parker, 178–9, 181, 183, 186, 205, 206, 211, 212–13, 231
Wilmer, L.A., 91, 95, 166, 168
Wordsworth, William, 68

*Yankee and Boston Literary Gazette*, 56–61
Yarrington, Mrs, 112, 114